NEOCLASSICAL INTERNATIONAL ECONOMICS

Also by Leonard Gomes

INTERNATIONAL ECONOMIC PROBLEMS
FOREIGN TRADE AND THE NATIONAL ECONOMY: Mercantilist and Classical Perspectives

Neoclassical International Economics

An Historical Survey

Leonard Gomes
Principal Lecturer in Economics
Middlesex Polytechnic, London

St. Martin's Press New York

First published in the United States of America in 1990

Printed in Hong Kong

ISBN 0–312–04000–8

Library of Congress Cataloging-in-Publication Data
Gomes, Leonard.
Neoclassical international economics: an historical survey/
Leonard Gomes.
p. cm.
Includes bibliographical references.
ISBN 0–312–04000–8
1. International economic relations —History—19th century.
2. International economic relations—History—20th century.
3. Commercial policy—History—19th century. 4. Commercial policy–
–History—20th century. I. Title.
HF1359.G66 1990
337—dc20 89–38690
CIP

Contents

Preface

This book is about the history of neoclassical international economics. It was conceived as a sequel to the author's well-received *Foreign Trade and the National Economy: Mercantilist and Classical Perspectives* (1987) which offered an historical perspective on the development of mercantilist and classical trade theory and policy.

It is generally recognised that the problems of international trade and finance have been amongst the earliest concerns of the subject of political economy. In the long history of economics the best minds in the discipline have been devoted to the analysis of such problems and until recently trade theory was the pacemaker for general economics. Given such a long and rich history of reflection, analysis and judgement it is not surprising that economists are at their best when they speak out on international trade. On such matters, not only do they speak with the almost unanimous backing of professional opinion, but what they do convey tends to command universal respect (if not always agreement or full comprehension) among the wider lay audience. Neoclassical trade theory, heir to the classical heritage, was forged under the anvil of often fierce but intellectually stimulating controversy and the theory still has its critics, hostile and friendly. On the monetary side, no single all-embracing theory has emerged. However, the centrality of the doctrine of comparative advantage and the international adjustment mechanism within the ambit of orthodox international economics imparts to its approach a coherence and unity of purpose unmatched by other branches of economics. This remarkable degree of professional consensus together with the general recognition of a unique intellectual competence in this field is often taken for granted by economists who nevertheless take great pride in the achievement.

This book tells the story of that achievement as it evolved from the beginning of the neoclassical period (1870–90), when economics became an academic discipline, to contemporary developments. It seems appropriate to have such a survey at a time when in so many of its areas economics is showing a tendency to go 'back to its roots'.

Chapter 1 provides a synopsis of the classical heritage. Chapter 2 discusses the important contributions of two forerunners of neoclassical trade theory – Cournot and Mangoldt. The development of the theory during the age of Marshall is the subject of Chapter 3, and

Chapter 4 reviews the role of the economists in the Tariff Reform debate initiated by Joseph Chamberlain in 1903. Two arguments for protection (including the famous Manoilescu argument) are briefly discussed in Chapter 5. Graham's constructive critique of the classical trade model, including his controversial argument for permanent protection, is the subject of Chapter 6. The Heckscher–Ohlin or general-equilibrium model of trade, comprising the four 'Core Propositions' of standard neoclassical trade theory, is treated in Chapter 7 which also reviews new developments. The final chapter is devoted to the evolution of balance-of-payments theory and policy right up to present-day models and issues.

No account is given of alternative paradigms such as the Sraffa-based neo-Ricardian critique of comparative advantage theory and the neo-Marxist 'unequal exchange' thesis. Any short doctrinal history of a field with a compass as vast as that of neoclassical international economics is bound to be selective, and hence there are no explicit treatments of the technical literature on the 'gains from trade' or matters relating to trade and development. However, the central lines of development are fully surveyed and policy episodes have not been neglected.

LEONARD GOMES

1 The Classical Legacy

INTRODUCTION

The early neoclassical economists were heirs to a rich legacy of classical writings: (1) The Ricardo–Torrens principle of comparative advantage; (2) John Stuart Mill's theory of international values in terms of reciprocal demand and supply analysis, i.e. the 'equilibrium' theory of trade. Complementing these essentially barter relationships, there was (3) a theory of balance-of-payments adjustment mechanism, i.e. Hume's price-specie flow mechanism and various statements of it by Ricardo, Thornton and Mill.[1] These three analytical building blocks constitute the core of present-day orthodox international economics. As recently as 1974, the late Joan Robinson lamented the fact that 'the development of the theory [of international trade] to this day runs in the narrow channel that was appropriate to Ricardo's demonstration of the principle of comparative advantage.'.[2]

Classical economists from Smith to Mill did not, of course, fill a vacuum – they did not work in a void. They inherited a mass of mercantilist writings concerned with international economic relations. They criticised much of it, but some valuable notions were retained: e.g. the law of one price, the purchasing-power parity theory of exchange rates, rudimentary versions of the international adjustment mechanism based on simple quantity theory of money reasoning, etc. Useful insights were gleaned from pre-classical writings: e.g. the doctrine which became known as the 'eighteenth-century rule' (the notion of absolute advantage), notions of macroeconomic magnitudes relating to international trade, such as 'balance of trade' and 'balance of payments', and crudely stated microeconomic concepts such as the elasticity of demand for exports and imports.

The discovery of the principle of comparative advantage was an outstanding achievement of the classical school. The formulation of the international adjustment mechanism was another; although here, much of the work was completed in the first half of the eighteenth century by Vanderlint, Gervaise, Cantillon, and Hume in particular. Both principles were devised with practical purposes in mind: the comparative cost principle was an intellectual answer to those who resisted free trade in grain as the solution to Britain's economic problems in the early 1800s; the theory of international monetary equilibrium was designed to shatter the intellectual credibility of mercantilist doctrine which pretended that a favourable balance of payments could be maintained indefinitely.

Both principles became valuable items in the stock-in-trade of later trade theorists who developed and refined them to unravel theoretical puzzles as well as to deal with other hotly disputed policy issues such as the debate on German reparations (1920s), the British tariff reform movement (1903) and the Australian tariff controversy (late 1920s). The classical economists' contributions to international economics may be summarised under three headings: (1) the statement and elaboration of the comparative cost doctrine; (2) the theory of commercial policy, and (3) contributions to balance-of-payments theory.

COMPARATIVE COST DOCTRINE

The whole point of the classical analysis of trade was to show the beneficiality of free trade. Adam Smith's case for free trade was merely an application of the principle of specialisation and division of labour on a global scale. It was firmly grounded on the 'eighteenth-century rule' concerning the mutual beneficiality of international exchange of goods when each country has an absolute advantage in the production of one or more commodities. Each country gains by specialising in commodities where (with the same quantity of productive resources) a larger output than that of any rival can be produced. This was a sound commonsense argument for the free movement of goods across national frontiers. But it offered no guidance for the extreme, though no less interesting and realistic, case of a relatively 'backward' country having no lines of production where it is manifestly efficient relative to the rest of the world. What happens when one country is more efficient in the production of *all* commodities, i.e. it can produce all goods in greater amounts with the same resources as compared with its trading partner?

The answer to this question was provided by Smith's early successors in the British classical school in terms of the principle of comparative advantage. David Ricardo, James Mill and Robert Torrens extended Smith's theorising and produced a more general and precise formulation of profitable international trade by showing that a country can gain from trade even if it has no absolute real cost advantage in the production of any commodity. A technologically backward country can engage in profitable trade with an advanced nation.

The demonstration runs in terms of a world of two countries, each being capable of producing two commodities using only one factor of production (labour), which is assumed to be completely immobile between the two countries but completely mobile within each country. Thus, in each country, the costs (and prices or exchange ratios) of both commodities are determined by their relative labour content, i.e. by the linear technology.

Ricardo's famous three-paragraph demonstration of the principle of comparative advantage in chapter 7 of his *Principles* – the arithmetical example of trade in wine and cloth between Portugal and England – can be found in all standard textbooks and need not be repeated here. In Ricardo's example, as long as the internal (opportunity) cost ratios differ between countries (i.e. whenever the *relative* ability to produce goods differs between countries), specialisation by each country in the commodity in which it has a comparative advantage can increase aggregate world output from the same quantum of labour resources. The statement of the principle has a clear hortatory or persuasive message: Free trade, like honesty, is the best policy. With international specialisation, free trade (a) allows each country to consume at least as much of each good as before specialisation, or (b) minimises the real cost (in terms of labour time) of obtaining a given income or quantum of consumption for the world as a whole; or, what amounts to the same thing, maximises the aggregate level of real income (in terms of a given price ratio) obtainable from a given (full employment) utilisation of labour resources.

As late as the 1920s the classical trade model continued to be used by writers like Edgeworth, Taussig and Viner. By that time the theory had evolved into a general model of production and trade capable of dealing with a wide range of problems, both theoretical and practical. For this development, credit must go to John Stuart Mill principally, but also to a succession of writers after Ricardo who developed the labour-cost basis of the theory into one grounded on real costs.

The theory of comparative costs as fashioned by Ricardo was incomplete, since without the introduction of demand (the preferences of consumers) the theory could not explain on what terms trade would take place – demand was necessary to close the model. The role of demand and its relevance in the determination of the terms of trade was appreciated by writers such as Torrens, Longfield and Pennington; but it was John Stuart Mill who first explicitly demonstrated how the gain from trade was determined by conditions of demand both at home and abroad.

The mechanism which determines the world price ratio (or terms of trade) is 'reciprocal demand', i.e. 'the amount and extensibility of demand' in each country for the other country's product. This ratio will be stable when 'the equation of international demand' is satisfied, i.e. when the value of each country's exports is just sufficient to pay for its imports.

Without the benefit of marginal utility analysis and relying mainly on verbal reasoning, Mill was able to develop a rigorous general-equilibrium model. Within this analytical framework, he shows how the reciprocal demand mechanism can be generalised to the case of more than two countries and two commodities. Marshall later refined Mill's analysis in terms of the geometrical technique of offer curves in which the excess supplies and demands of the two goods in each country were treated as functions of the terms of trade. Mill was bothered by the problem of multiple equilibria ('criss-crossing' of offer curves) which arises when either country has an inelastic demand for the other's product and the conditions prescribed in the equations of international demand are satisfied. Mill did however succeed in finding a *proof* of the existence of a unique equilibrium price ratio. He also established the conditions for complete specialisation by each country.

COMMERCIAL POLICY

The repeal of the English Corn Laws on 26 June 1846 was an epoch-making event in the history of international economic policy. The decision was significant, perhaps more because of its symbolic value than for any dramatic impact on international economic relationships. It was, however, preceded by a momentous and controversial debate in which most of the best minds in classical political economy participated.

The economists were on the side of free trade, of course – although Malthus was lukewarm. Surprisingly, however, arguments based on comparative-cost reasoning featured only marginally, if at all, in their attacks on agricultural protection. Ricardo, for instance, never made use of the comparative-cost idea in his criticisms of the Corn Laws, but relied instead on absolute cost differences between Great Britain (in manufactures) and the rest of the world (in agriculture). Ricardo clearly understood that there were two distinct benefits of foreign trade – the static gains in terms of a larger consumption bundle, and the dynamic effect on the growth rates of profits and the wages fund. Cheaper foreign food would cause rents to fall and thereby raise profits. Since capitalists were the ones who accumulated capital and invested (whereas landlords spent their income on luxury consumption), the shift in the distribution of income consequent upon the repeal of agricultural protection would raise the rate of economic growth. In his polemical campaign against the Corn Laws it was obviously more impressive to stress the dynamic argument based on absolute advantages. This is what he did in numerous correspondences, parliamentary speeches, two pamphlets and four chapters of his major work.

Robert Torrens called for free trade in corn as a means of securing power and prosperity. The cheapest means of obtaining food supplies for a growing population was to obtain them from abroad in exchange for manufactured goods. This would further extend Britain's undoubted industrial lead since it would widen the market for manufactures. On the basis of world industrial supremacy Great Britain could exercise an unchallenged political and military hegemony over all other nations.

Turning to commercial policy in general, two major exceptions to international *laissez-faire* were conceded: (1) the terms-of-trade argument and (2) the infant-industry argument for protection. The logic of these arguments had to be admitted, for they met the economists' own criteria of (a) buying in the cheapest market and selling in the dearest, and (b) long-run efficiency in the allocation of resources. Reservations relating to the practical application of these devices were made, of course; and, in addition, some cosmopolitan-minded economists objected to the narrow, national self-interest on which the first argument rested – just as, later, Edgeworth and Marshall did.

There was a logical flaw in early statements of the free-trade doctrine: when writers recommended free trade they often gave the impression that it was a choice between free trade and no trade, whereas in reality it was about free trade versus protection. Generally, these writers underestimated the adverse short-run effects likely to be caused by removal of restrictions. In particular, they implicitly might have assumed that the movement from protection to free trade would not alter a country's terms of trade. Of the leading writers, Malthus first faced this issue, and Torrens, J. S. Mill and others analysed the commercial policy implications of the terms of trade.

As far as Mill was concerned, the terms-of-trade argument arose naturally from his work on the market mechanism in international trade. Mill's analysis showed that tariffs affect the ratio of interchange between exports and imports, i.e. the reciprocal offers of the trading countries can be altered by exploiting monopolistic/monopsonistic advantages in foreign trade. Under certain circumstances, taxes on imports and exports can be paid entirely by the foreigner. Mill, however, clearly recognised the theoretical limitations and practical drawbacks of a policy of 'taxing the foreigner'. First, it only applies if the reciprocal demand of the outside world has a low elasticity and the tariff-imposing country's own reciprocal demand exhibits a high elasticity. Second, retaliation is likely; this tends to neutralise the initial advantage to the tariff-imposing country. Third, it is a desirable policy strictly from the national point of view. Better terms of trade for one country necessarily implies worse terms of trade for its trading partners. The misallocation of resources (i.e. the distortions in production and consumption) resulting from the pursuit of selfish national gains is a general loss for the world as a whole. If the losses of trading partners exceed the gain of the tariff-imposing country, then such an outcome is patently unjust as well as economically undesirable.

The other exception to the classical case for free trade – the infant-industry argument – was also legitimised by J. S. Mill. The argument in a crude form was of course of long standing, dating back to Elizabethan times when it was frequently invoked in pleas for the grant of monopolistic privileges, and it was reformulated with reference to young and developing countries by Alexander Hamilton, and later by the German national economist Friedrich List. The majority of English writers dismissed the writings of the national economists as being no more than naive reversions into a pre-scientific mercantilism; but Mill saw that the arguments of the national developmental economists did not contradict the main propositions of classical trade theory.

BALANCE OF PAYMENTS THEORY

At the time of the Cunliffe Report (1918) when official policy in Great Britain and several other European countries aimed at a restoration of the nineteenth-century international gold standard, contemporaries were in possession of a large body of monetary theory which provided a solid basis for this international monetary arrangement. The theory was virtually unquestioned, even by Keynes. But what was then regarded as standard orthodoxy was the subject of heated debate in England, first from 1797 to 1810 (known as the Bullionist controversy) and, second, the 1820–45 arguments of the Currency and Banking schools. As a result of these controversies, some of the best classical works on monetary theory and policy were written.

The issues dealt with in these writings included: (a) real and monetary aspects of balance-of-payments adjustment; (b) the distinction between real and nominal exchange rates; (c) attempts at resolving the 'transfer problem'; (d) the theory of a purely metallic currency, the theory of an inconvertible paper currency and the relevance of the quantity theory of money for each system; (e) the open-economy corollary of the quantity theory, i.e. the purchasing-power-parity theory of exchange-rate determination; (f) the need to distinguish between short-run and long-run adjustments to disequilibrium; and (g) the role of income and purchasing-power changes in balance of payments adjustment.

Writers shared a common framework of monetary analysis, but they disagreed on many technical details and proposed inconsistent solutions to international monetary problems.

Many of the theoretical differences among the writers can be traced to the use of different assumptions – e.g. whether gold coin still remains in circulation acceptable at par with notes or has been driven out of circulation, and whether the real exchange rate (the ratio of the mint prices of gold between two gold standard countries) is at or above the gold-export point.

More fundamental differences resulted when some writers applied the theory appropriate to an inconvertible paper currency to situations which called instead for the use of the model of a purely metallic currency, and vice versa. The point is that quantity-theory reasoning (the view that there is a strict proportionality between money and prices) is not relevant to the case of commodity money supplied endogenously through goldmining and international specie flows, i.e.

the case of a purely metallic currency such as the classical gold standard.

The leading figures in the debates were Ricardo, Malthus, Thornton and Tooke. Years later, J. S. Mill attempted to provide a synthesis of the various strands of classical monetary theory, and his account was taken as representative of the traditional approach by neoclassical economists.

DEVELOPMENT OF DOCTRINE

It was also from Mill with his theory of international values that later economists came to a full understanding and appreciation of the centrality of comparataive costs in international trade theory.

As is well known, Ricardian theory (including his doctrine of comparative costs based on the labour theory of value) never took root on the continent of Europe (except Italy) or the United States. The first serious challenge to his trade model and the free-trade ideas associated with it came from the American national economists (Daniel Raymond, Willard Phillips, Henry Charles Carey) and Friedrich List. The J.-B. Say tradition remained strong in France, while in Germany the 'romantic' economic and social philosophy of Fichte and Müller and later the Historical School could not accommodate the abstract, axiomatic theory of the Ricardians. On the other hand, most Italian economists accepted the theory of comparative costs. In Britain itself, Ricardo's economics came under attack shortly after his death and there ensued a gradual but continuous shift from the labour theory (costs of production) to a subjective theory of value, i.e. supply and demand (utility). Costs of production came to be treated not in absolute terms but in relative terms, i.e. as alternatives forgone; although until the 1930s some notion of 'real' costs determining production was retained in trade theory.

Compared with other branches of economics, trade theory has the longest history of continuous development. The classical trade model survived the 'marginal revolution' of the 1870s for three reasons: (1) Mill's incorporation of the demand side in his analysis of international values. (2) The transformation of Ricardo's labour theory into Marshallian 'real cost' theory. Even when the labour theory of value was retained, this was tolerated since it was simply illustrative of the gains from trade and did not clash with ideology and substantive matters – e.g. over distribution. (3) The concerns of trade theory with efficient allocations of given resources and the rational behaviour of economic agents who exchange commodities on world markets, fitted in nicely with the 'exchange paradigm' (catallactics) which came into vogue with the 'marginalists'.

The major influence on the early neoclassical writers on trade was of course J. S. Mill. But then they discovered the writings of Cournot, von Thünen, Mangoldt and other Continental economists. The fusion of the two streams of thought led eventually to new interpretations of the doctrine of comparative costs (and trade theory generally) which placed both firmly in the neoclassical mould. The neoclassical story begins, then, with the contributions of Cournot and Mangoldt.

2 Early Neoclassical Contributions

2.1 Cournot

Augustin Cournot (1801–77) was a major figure in the shaping of the basic structure of twentieth-century economics. He was among the first to model the actions of economic agents in terms of optimising behaviour which was therefore amenable to analysis as solutions to maximisation and minimisation problems. Cournot thought of economic concepts such as 'demand' and 'cost' as functional ones. He pioneered the treatment of economic phenomena as being in essence functional relationships (mutual interdependence) that could be expressed by behavioural equations between variables. Through him, relationships between economic variables came to be recognised as functional ones, e.g. a change in quantity demand with respect to a change in price or of cost as a function of price. As functional relationships, they could be expressed as equations and curves. He constructed a model determining the price and quantity demanded and considered how the equilibrium values would change as a result of changes in tax and transport costs, i.e. the method of comparative statics. Cournot started with a demand function (in fact, a sales function) without seeing the need to base it on utility; since as far as he was concerned, demand functions tell us all we need to know about market phenomena from the side of demand or consumption. As is well known, he developed quite modern-looking analyses of partial equilibrium, monopoly and oligopoly and elaborated the marginal principle in its application to the theory of the firm. He understood the concept of marginal revenue which was only rediscovered in the 1930s.

In trade theory, Cournot's signal contribution was the analysis of interspatial price equilibrium in the form of the 'back-to-back' diagram – the type of analysis used by Cunynghame, Pigou, Schüller, Barone and subsequently by many others to this day. Cournot's explorations in trade theory were in three areas: (1) the theory of interspatial price equilibrium, i.e. the effects of trade on markets previously isolated; (2) a welfare analysis of the effects of trade on real national income and (3) the theory of foreign exchange.

INTERSPATIAL PRICE EQUILIBRIUM

This is an extension to the case of two interconnected markets of the method of partial equilibrium Cournot used in the analysis of price determination in a single (closed-economy) market. The analysis is confined to a single commodity, *M*. Supply and demand functions are specified for the commodity in each of the two separate national markets. In each market the equilibrium price is determined by the condition that demand equals supply. Thus the equilibrium price equation is $S_A(P_A) = D_A(P_A)$ for country *A* and $S_B(P_B) = D_B(P_B)$ for country *B*; where *P* is the price of the commodity *S*(*P*) is the upward sloping supply function and *D*(*P*) the negatively inclined demand function, both assumed to be functions of price alone (the *ceteris paribus* assumption). If transport costs, *e*, are such that $P_B > P_A + e$ then the opening of trade between countries *A* and *B* under conditions of free competition suggests, in Cournot's words, that 'an article capable of transportation must flow from the market where its value is less to the market where its value is greater, until this difference in value, from one market to the other represents no more than the cost of transportation'.[1] The commodity *M* will be exported by *A*, since in that market its price is lower than in *B* (even after allowing for transport costs). The price of *M* will rise in *A* and fall in *B*. These price changes will result in: (a) an increase in production and fall in consumption in *A*, and (b) a contraction of production and expansion of consumption in *B*, with the difference accounted for by imports from *A*. Eventually, a uniform price (allowing for transport costs) will prevail in both markets signifying the equality of total demand and total supply for the commodity in the two markets taken together. The free-trade equilibrium equation is then

$$S_A(P'_A) + S_B(P'_A + e) = D_A(P'_A) + D_B(P'_A + e)$$

where P'_A and P'_B are the new commodity prices in *A* and *B* respectively. These prices are equalised when transport costs, *e*, are added. These results are illustrated in the famous 'back-to-back' diagram adopted by the Continental writers whose work on international trade lay mainly outside the Ricardo–Mill classical tradition. It was in fact first used by Cunynghame at the turn of the century when Cournot's work came to be better known and appreciated.

Free trade will normally result in a larger world output of commodity *M* compared with autarky; but Cournot's model, which is not based on the comparative-cost example suggests the possibility of an actual diminution of total output under free trade. Cournot regards this as 'improbable' but nevertheless gives an arithmetical example to illustrate the unusual case.[2] He then specifies the precise condition under which the normal result will obtain:

$$D'_B(P_B)S'_A(P_A) - D'_A(P_A)S'_B(P_B) < 0$$

where the functions D' and S' indicate the rates of change of quantities demanded and supplied in response to the price changes in the two countries. Cournot uses the model to analyse the effects on price of an export or import tax. Such a tax is equivalent to an increase in transport cost and Cournot shows as a consequence the price will fall in the exporting country by an amount greater or less than the absolute amount of the tariff; but in the importing country the price may either rise or fall. Cournot's solution is, of course, not only ambiguous but faulty. A proper analysis would have to consider supply and demand elasticities, not just gradients of curves; but even on Cournot's premises (increasing cost in both countries, perfect competition and no assumption about elasticities), as Edgeworth later showed, the tariff will always raise the price in the importing country and lower it in the exporting country by an amount less than the duty.[3]

EFFECTS OF TRADE ON INCOME

In chapter 12 of *Recherches*, Cournot presents an argument designed to show that the removal of trade restrictions leaves a country worse off than under protection. He investigates the effects of a move to free trade – i.e. the effects of the removal of a tariff on a single commodity – and got peculiar results. For Cournot, according to the principle of 'compensation of demands', only the impact effect matters, which is consistent with his treatment of price changes in a closed economy. Cournot shows that there will be a 'decrease in real income' of the importing country, because imports reduce a country's real income. He does not adequately take into account the effect of trade on the income of consumers but only the direct effects on the income of producers – so no reallocation of resources. He finds that in the exporting country the change in real income is always positive, but in the case of the importing country there is a 'decrease in real income'. Cournot concludes: imports diminish a country's real income.[4] He specifies several assumptions and qualifications to his peculiar procedure. Thus he does not include in his calculation of the 'real changes in social income' the advantages accruing to consumers in the importing country who are able to dispose of their income in a more satisfactory manner as a consequence of the price reduction on the imported good, i.e. the cash equivalent of the utility that consumers derive from their purchases of the imported good in preference to other domestically produced goods. He cannot do this, he says, because 'this advantage is incapable of valuation . . . and does not directly affect the national wealth in the commercial and mathematical sense of this term'.[5] What Cournot excludes from the calculation of the net benefits of trade is, of course, the increase in consumer surplus (the utility gain) – an omission which later economists reckoned a major weakness of his approach. Cournot recognises that in the case of non-competitive imports, what he called 'exotic' commodities, the national income of the importing country does not experience any change – the import of exotic commodities does not displace domestic production; hence no effect on the incomes of producers. He explicitly states that his analysis is confined to the instance of only one commodity, *M* being imported into the home country (the importing country), and that this must of necessity have as counterpart the export of a commodity of equal value from the home country; but he says that 'we have shown that this increase in exports from the home country . . . was more than offset by the impoverishment of the home producers of commodity *M* in consequence of importation . . . We have therefore accounted for all the data of the problem.'[6]

Cournot's results, much at variance with those derived by the use of comparative-cost reasoning, provoked a barrage of criticism from writers as early as 1844 down to Samuelson, including such acknowledged authorities as Edgeworth and Viner;[7] but as a piece of technical analysis it was path-breaking. Criticism was directed at several points of Cournot's premises, arguments and conclusion. (1) His single-commodity model was inadequate for the purpose in hand, in that it resulted in an unrealistic, static short-run view of the effects of trade on real income. (2) Because of this, the final effects of the removal of a restriction on import were obscured, since Cournot assumed that the prices of other goods (apart from the import commodity) and other incomes remained unchanged. This prevented him from dealing with the full reallocative effects on production and consumption. Thus, in the importing country, the lifting of trade restrictions and the consequent increase in imports would be matched by a corresponding increase in exports of equal value (given mobility of resources and the maintenance of full employment). Price changes affecting import and export commodities would induce changes in income and output such that export production expands as import-competing production contracts. Corresponding changes in income and output, but in the opposite direction, would take place in the exporting country. Since the movements in the composition of output, income and consumption are symmetrical (both countries considered) there is no reason to expect that one country would end up worse off than the other in terms of real income: or, what amounts to the same thing, no reason why there should not be an equal sharing of the benefits of trade. (3) Cournot fails to deal satisfactorily with the consumption effects because of his excessive concentration on the income-effect of production changes. The lack of a utility or other welfare criterion led Cournot to underestimate the consumption gains in the importing country. Later writers who adopted the idea of consumer surplus made this point, e.g. Edgeworth, Bertrand and Landry.[8] There were also some minor points of criticism, such as Cournot's use of money prices or values to estimate changes in real national income, and related to this, the inappropriateness of Cournot's calculation in terms of gross revenue or income instead of net income (gross income less costs).[9]

Cournot's analysis and results were savagely attacked by Viner in 1937. Viner declares that Cournot's argument 'scarcely deserves attention on its own account' but cannot wholly be ignored since it is often appealed to by protectionists as a refutation of the doctrine of comparative costs.[10] Viner summarises the criticisms made by previous writers of this piece of Cournot's work, and makes an additional critical comment on Cournot's claim that his procedure of dealing with trade changes wholly in terms of money values is unobjectionable since J. S. Mill had explicitly stated that the introduction of money would make no difference to the results obtained by barter analysis. Viner's comment is that this is an invalid inference from Mill's dictum which provides no warrant for an analysis wholly in money prices unsupported by comparative real costs. Viner implied that Cournot would have come to more sensible (orthodox) results if (a) he had started with comparative cost differences and had then translated these into money prices and (b) if he had included a satisfactory measure of consumer surplus. But Viner concludes, Cournot's analysis 'fails to deal intelligibly even with the pecuniary aspects of the problem'.[11]

J. W. Angell – 'the only writer who finds sense and significance in Cournot's thesis', according to Viner[12] – finds the clue to Cournot's peculiar results in an 'unstated premise as to the probable loss from a displacement of domestic industry',[13] i.e. lack of mobility of productive resources which remain unemployed when the import-competing industry contracts upon the removal of tariff protection. But in reply to an earlier critic, Carl Heinrich Hagen, who made essentially the same observation, Cournot maintained that on the contrary he had assumed a transfer of resources and had fully taken into account the generation of income caused by such transfer to more profitable employment.[14] However, Cournot was unable to persuade anyone that he had really done so since it is nowhere to be found in his actual calculations.

The confusion surrounding the reception of Cournot's analysis of this topic stems largely from the fact that no one was quite clear what Cournot's purpose really was in undertaking this analysis. Was he engaging in a purely positive exercise, the examination of 'a concrete economic phenomenon', i.e. the measurement of trade-related changes in income? Or was he outlining a technique for measuring the gains from trade? Many of Cournot's critics understood him to have been quite resolved on the second question, despite the declaration that his objective was to study the 'variations in the Social Income resulting from the communication of markets'. The majority of critics wedded to comparative-cost reasoning (and this includes notably Edgeworth, Bastable and Viner) interpreted Cournot as really having been involved in finding an argument for tariff protection through a dubious exercise in national-income accounting based on an obscure notion of 'the principle of compensation of demands'. In support of this understanding of Cournot's purpose they might have referred to his declaration that his analysis of the effects of trade on social income 'when considered in its theoretical aspect, can be reduced to very simple terms of which the mere statement, by overthrowing false systems, opens the way to the practical knowledge which essentially concerns the destiny of nations. It is on this account that the considerations which we are here examining appear to us something more than mere intellectual exercises or chimerical abstractions.'[15]

By 'false systems' does Cournot mean the classical theory of comparative costs and its corollaries? A balanced reappraisal of Cournot's contribution has recently been presented by Theocaris. He refers to the confusion among writers about the meaning and significance of Cournot's analysis. He traces the diversity of critical opinions, and the muddle, to Cournot's use of the term 'real changes in income'. For Cournot, he says, a 'real change in income' means a change in the quantity of goods that a given change in money income commands – it 'is therefore an index of changes in quantities over which one has command and has nothing to do with measuring benefits, which is an entirely different thing'.[16] Thus, in the importing country the fall in the income of producers, consequent upon the reduction of the price of the single commodity, all other prices and incomes remaining the same, means that command over goods is less compared with autarky. That was all Cournot wanted to prove – to arrive at conclusions about the effects of trade on incomes within his restrictive assumptions. Theocaris therefore feels that it is unfair to charge Cournot with putting forward a flawed procedure for measuring the gains from trade. That was not his intention. Nevertheless, Cournot did suggest that his analysis could offer guidance on important policy decisions, presumably protection versus free trade. On this score, though, there are certainly serious weaknesses with Cournot's procedure. His technique was unequal to the task, which was essentially one of estimating the effects on economic welfare of a change in trade policy. As Theocaris indicates, the source of the misunderstanding created in other writers' minds lay in Cournot's attempt to deduce these basically general-equilibrium effects from a partial-equilibrium model of income changes where all other prices and incomes are held constant.[17]

The classical and early neoclassical economists tackled Cournot's problem with a different technique – the simple general-equilibrium model of comparative cost. They looked at changes in prices, outputs and national product throughout an economy and compared these with changes in another country, and could not therefore understand Cournot's procedure of looking at a single market and deducing from this estimates of changes in national or social income. Cournot's failure to incorporate the two-way flow of commodities involved in trade, and the tracing of this back to systematic differences in structures of costs and prices, accounted for his ambiguous reasoning and spurious results. One gets the distinct impression that it was less Cournot's faulty computations and more his general protectionist conclusion which provoked the neoclassical writers' ire, as Viner's remarks suggest. The irony of it all, though, is that Cournot's method did not die a natural death. It was revived by economists at the turn of the century, and an amended version of it has been used ever since to show how changes in trade flows in a single commodity affect production and consumption in the domestic market. It can also be used to quantify the gains from trade and show the effects of a tariff in a single market, as all modern introductory texts do.

COURNOT ON PROTECTION

Cournot was, of course, a protectionist, apparently much influenced by Friedrich List;[18] although judging from his 1838 analysis of the profitability of import duties he was persuaded by the protectionist case at the level of pure theory before he encountered List's critique of free trade. Cournot's protectionist position is set out fully in the last section of his *Principes* written twenty-five years after the *Recherches* where he deals with questions of economic policy. He starts from the general classical position that consumption is the end of all economic activity, but adopts a wider perspective on consumption benefits, in that besides individual consumption he includes public (or collective) consumption and considers the intergenerational stream of consumption benefits. A *laissez-faire* policy aimed at 'wealth now' is contrasted with an optimal policy which maximises the power to create 'wealth in the future'. The provision of the flows of current and future consumption benefits cannot be left entirely to the free market. State intervention, apart from all the customary functions, is necessary for the creation of productive forces; for it is only through the development of the full productive potential of the economy that future consumption benefits can be satisfactorily ensured. On this premise, Cournot, like List, supports the infant-industry argument for the protection and encouragement of selected industries:

> When a new industry has just been born (even that which is destined to have the most vigorous growth) must it not at first be sheltered and get acclimatized and all those employed by it, must they not make their apprenticeship?[19]

Presumably recalling John Stuart Mill's endorsement of the argument, he says that 'nobody doubts any more, in principle, the utility of a temporary encouragement'.[20] No hard-and-fast rules can be laid down concerning the level and duration of the protective tariff; it depends on the circumstances. Cournot presents his case in cool, moderate language, in contrast to List's aggressive and polemical style, relying on the skilful use of rhetorical appeals for persuasive effect. Government intervention is necessary to stimulate the growth of productive forces – by reducing uncertainty over investment projects, undertaking infrastructural and other projects that are socially beneficial but privately unprofitable, encouraging savings, etc. But without restrictions on international trade such measures cannot realise their full potential; the nation will inevitably lag behind others more fully equipped with industrial capacity and skills. In addition, international commerce needs the protection of the state. Business interests 'need a flag to cover them, which will make them respected in the world; and this flag can only be that of a great nation'.[21] Industry needs the guiding hand of the State primarily to ensure that private and social interests converge towards the virtuous path of growth and development. He had no time for '*laissez-faire* dogmas' and was critical of what he called 'the dubious notion' of the natural harmony of economic interests espoused by native writers like Bastiat and Dunoyer. *Laissez-faire* free-trade propagandists had not shown to everyone's satisfaction that private and social interests would necessarily and always coincide under the influence of free market forces. Why then, asks Cournot, 'should government encouragement not be that additional force which might make the resultant of individual interests coincide in direction with that of the general interest?'[22]

Despite his general protectionist stance Cournot indicated that he was aware of the dangers of promiscuous protectionism. Protection once granted to a few deserving branches of industry tends in practice to be extended in an indiscriminate manner to all and sundry under the pressure of vested interests: 'The more the protective system becomes completed the more difficult it becomes to appreciate its consequences and measure its effect.' If the intended orderly protectionist policy threatens to become a jungle of trade barriers, and this is envisaged, then 'the maxim *laissez-faire*, even if it does not have (as some would like it) the value of an axiom or a theorem, must definitely be preferred in many cases as an adage of practical wisdom'.[23] Cournot's assault on orthodox opinion was therefore less an attack on the desirability of free trade and more in the nature of an indictment of domestic *laissez-faire*. However, Cournot hastens to add that his judgement derives solely from theoretical investigations, that he does not write in support of any social system, and that there is an immense gulf in passing from theory of governmental applications.

Two additional matters dealt with by Cournot are worth mentioning: his criticism of Mill's theory of international values and his mathematical treatment of the foreign exchanges.

COURNOT ON MILL'S THEORY

Cournot wrote his analysis of international trade before Mill's 1844 *Essays* and 1848 *Principes* made the classical theory of comparative costs more widely known. But even after he became familiar with Mill's work, Cournot stuck with his own analytical framework and felt that the classical theory as expounded by Mill was open to damaging criticism. In the *Principes* he criticised Mill's theory principally on two points: (1) Mill's gratuitous admission of the possibility that the equilibrium international exchange ratio might not be uniquely determined when the conditions of the equation of international demand were satisfied, and his clumsy attempt to look for further sufficient conditions, and (2) Mill's calculation of the gains from trade in his England–Germany example of trade in linen and cloth.[24]

On the first point, as is well known, Mill was bothered by the possibility of multiple equilibria in the determination of the international price ratio. Mill apparently took seriously the criticism of his general demand and supply theory of equilibrium by writers such as William Thornton and others, who illustrated the possibility of multiple equilibria and even the non-existence of equilibrium with hypothetical, though plausible examples, taken mainly from domestic trades. Cournot took Mill to task for conceding too readily to the notion of disequilibrium trading or the non-existence of equilibrium in the context of the determination of the international price ratio. Indeed, says Cournot, 'exceptional and singular cases' can be imagined of multiple equilibria, non-existence of equilibrium and disequilibrium trading not only in international trade but in all manner and variety of trades. However, general theories are not constructed for the purpose of explaining these exceptional phenomena but for shedding light on the normal functioning of the economic system. Hence, 'variations of the economic system, for the explanation of which theories are constructed, are usually contained within very strict limits so that there is no reason to admit the possibility of more maxima or of more than one situation of equilibrium in the interval of these limits'.[25] Leading neoclassical economists including Marshall, Edgeworth and Bastable also found fault with Mill's attempt to deal with questions of non-uniqueness of equilibrium, and referred to Mill's discussion as 'laborious', 'confusing' and 'unnecessary'. Recent writers, however, come to a more favourable assessment of Mill's work and find that he does actually arrive at a correct proof of the existence of equilibrium in international trade.[26]

On Mill's calculation of the gains from trade, Cournot detects an ambiguity in Mill's numerical results and holds that the underlying theory must be flawed. In his discussion of the law of International Value, Mill illustrated the analysis with an example of trade between England and Germany in cloth and linen: England could produce 10 yards of cloth or 15 yards of linen with a given amount of labour, and Germany 10 yards of cloth or 20 of linen. If a trading ratio of 10 cloth for 18 linen were established upon the opening of trade, then England would gain an advantage of 3 yards on every 15 and Germany would save 2 out of every 20. Thus England's gain would be 20 per cent and Germany would have an advantage of 10 per cent. Mill calculated the gain to each country in terms of linen; but Cournot shows there is another way of doing the sums. Cournot works out the benefits in terms of the cloth saved (in England) and gained (in Germany), and finds that Germany's advantage comes to 11.1 per cent and England's to 16.6 per cent. Hence, Cournot remarks, 'with this second method of calculation, as plausible as the other', England's gain is reduced and Germany's increased.[27] One may regard this as a minor arithmetical quibble of no consequence for the substantive matters considered by Mill in his 'great Chapter'; but Cournot thinks otherwise. He regarded the disparity in the reckoning of the gains as 'a proof of the imperfections of Mill's principles' and repeated the claim about the superiority of his own method.[28] He accused Mill and other writers on comparative costs of departing from the principle of logic which enjoins analysts to proceed from the simple to the complex. The theory of comparative costs was pitched at too aggregative a level and could not therefore deal adequately with the microeconomic repercussions of trade in both markets. But here again, as we saw earlier, Cournot misunderstood the nature of the theory of comparative costs. His criticism that the theory cannot deal adequately with the effects of trade on 'the whole of the economic system' is ill-founded, since the strength of the theory is that it is a simple general-equilibrium model designed to deal with precisely these total economic ramifications. Cournot's complaint would have had some substance if he had directed it at the unspecified assumptions or premises of the classical theory. His own preferred method of partial equilibrium was a useful adjunct to orthodox theory, but it was flawed by the ambiguous notion of 'compensation of demands'.

THE FOREIGN EXCHANGES

The last topic to consider is Cournot's theory of the foreign exchanges – the least contentious part of his writings on international economics. 'We may say with Jevons of this investigation,' remarked Edgeworth, 'that it is "highly ingenious, if not particularly useful"'.[29] The same could be said of some of Edgeworth's own investigations in pure theory; but Cournot's analysis is refreshingly modern and lucid. He deals solely with the principles of the subject and there are no applications to policy questions or suggestions for integrating exchange-rate matters with general macroeconomic relationships, e.g. inflation and exchange rates. He explains how exchange rates are defined under a silver standard, although the same principles apply under a gold standard. Each country defines its monetary unit as a specific quantity of silver and undertakes the free coinage of silver in this monetary unit. A mint parity for each country in terms of other silver standard currencies is thereby established. Given these fixed parities, exchange rates can vary only within narrow limits (the 'silver points') set by the cost of shipping silver from one centre to another. Cournot then deduces the condition that if there are n centres of exchange, there will be $n(n-1)/2$ bilateral exchange rates and $n(n-1)(n-2)/2$ triangular cross-rates. He correctly defines what became known in the 1960s as the 'Nth currency problem'. If there are N countries with N currencies, there can be no more than $N-1$ independently determined exchange rates or prices between these currencies. One of these countries must be passive with respect to the exchange rate of its currency.

According to Cournot's definition, the US dollar because of its international role as a key currency was the 'Nth' currency under the defunct Bretton Woods system. The exchange rate for the dollar was not under the unilateral control of the United States. The rate for the dollar was determined by each foreign government fixing the exchange rate for its national currency by intervening in its foreign exchange market with dollars. Cournot's definition was eventually of some practical use after all. Cournot states the proposition that the balance of payments of the world as a whole is identically zero, i.e. for all countries the identity

$$\sum_{i=1}^{n} B_i \equiv 0$$

must hold.[30] This identity is sometimes called 'Cournot's law' but is more generally known as 'Walras' law' – an open-economy extension of the widely used identity in general equilibrium analysis. Cournot deduces the proposition from a consideration, first, of the balance of payments equation setting out the multilateral balances of each of three countries and then of n countries. Then if two countries (or $n-1$) are in equilibrium, the remaining one must also be in equilibrium. Cournot derived his identity as the solution of a general equilibrium system of equations, an attempt which 'may well have provided the starting point of Walras' thoughts in this respect'.[31]

2.2 Mangoldt

Despite the dominance of the two phases of the German Historical School in the nineteenth century, some German economists (e.g. Hans Karl Emil von Mangoldt and Johann Heinrich von Thünen) made important contributions to neoclassical economic analysis. Von Thünen's *Der Isolierte Staat* contained a general statement of marginal productivity theory in terms of the principle of variable proportions and substitution.[32] Although the theory was applied to production, its relevance for distribution was firmly suggested. Von Mangoldt treated utility and cost of production in relation to value. He generalised the Ricardian rent concept to explain the determination of incomes other than those derived from the ownership of land – a procedure which resulted in the acquisition of an important neoclassical analytical tool. For Mangoldt, the economic value of factors of production are derived from their marginal productivities, and he formulates the rule that both wage rates and interest rates are equal to the last unit employed in production.[33]

MANGOLDT ON THE MULTI-COMMODITY CASE

In the field of trade theory Mangoldt extended the classical theory of comparative costs to a world of many commodities – a generalisation later outlined and developed by Edgeworth, Viner and Haberler.[34] In the Ricardo–Mill model, comparative cost schedules determine trade and reciprocal demand influences only the extent of trade and the barter terms of trade. But, as Mangoldt shows, the scale of comparative costs is not given, but is affected by the play of reciprocal demand. Information on comparative costs alone is not enough to determine which commodity will be exported and which imported.

The effect of trade is to alter the production pattern in each country. The range of commodities previously produced by the two countries will tend to fall into two broadly defined groups, with each country specialising on one of the groups according to the principle of comparative cost. Assuming constant costs and no transport costs, commodities within each country will exchange for each other in proportion to their costs of production; but in trade between the two countries – i.e. exchange of commodities from one group against those of another group – the terms of exchange will be the rate at which the produce of a unit of productive force in one country exchanges for that of the other. The international exchange ratio is therefore what later economists called the 'double factoral terms of trade'. Thus defined, this exchange ratio results from the play of reciprocal demand of the two countries for each other's export commodities upon the relative money rates of reward of the productive factors in the two countries. To determine the dividing line between export and import commodities in each country Mangoldt postulates the existence of a commodity that is produced in both countries.[35] Such a commodity, intermediate between the two groups, is one whose cost of production in each country adjusted for the difference in rates of remuneration is the same in both countries. Once this commodity is located, the pattern of specialisation, exports, imports and prices are all determined. Since the money price of each commodity must be equal to the cost in the low-cost country, then a commodity will be exported or imported by Country I, for instance, depending on whether the money price is lower or higher than that of the intermediate commodity – the commodity that is neither imported nor exported.

EDGEWORTH'S EXPOSITION OF MANGOLDT'S SOLUTION

Edgeworth was the first neoclassical economist to find merit and inspiration in Mangoldt's solution of the problem. Edgeworth gave an exposition of Mangoldt's method and devloped a variant of it.[36]

Mangoldt's solution depended critically on the assumption that there was some commodity produced in common and, moreover, that such a commodity could be identified *a priori* from the combined array of goods in the two groups. Edgeworth dispensed with this assumption by an ingenious sliding-scale construction of the logarithms of costs for both countries. To fix a point of reference on his scales, however, Edgeworth had to assume that the factoral terms of trade were given: i.e. 'the number of units of productive force in country No. II of which the produce is equivalent in the internal market to the produce of a unit of productive force in country No. I'.[37] The relative positions of the two scales (and the fixed cost of each country arrayed on them) were then determined by the assumed fixed difference in factor valuations. By means of his slide-rule method Edgeworth was able to read off what commodities each country would export and import and on what terms. For each of the commodities exported by country I, the ratio of the logarithm of costs in country I to country II (expressed in a common currency) will be lower than for any of the commodities imported by country I. The factoral terms of trade can alter, however, under the impact of shifts in reciprocal demand. Shifts in demand will be absorbed by compensating changes in the balance of payments adjustment mechanism. As a result of the monetary adjustment, a new equilibrium factoral terms of trade will be established, and hence a different set of goods imported and exported.

Edgeworth fully acknowledged an important limitation of his construction: it could not show how changes in the factoral terms of trade were determined. It incorporated no mechanism to show the play of reciprocal demand upon comparative factor rewards; and it was precisely these changes in factor valuations that caused alterations in the assignment of commodities from the import category to the export category and vice versa, i.e. by shifting the precise point where the chain of comparative advantage is broken. However, despite Edgeworth's inconclusive solution his argument (as well as that of Mangoldt) highlighted the fact that in the multi-commodity case, information on comparative costs alone was not enough to determine which commodities would be imported and which exported. As Edgeworth puts it: 'Comparative costs alone cannot be ascertained by simply comparing the costs of different articles in the two countries', since the crucial factoral terms of trade which determine the point where the chain is broken 'depends not only on the cost of production in each country, but also on the law of demand in each country for the different commodities.' Thus, 'in general no conclusion . . . can be drawn pending the determination of the relation on the international market between the productive powers of the two countries'.[38]

ELABORATION OF MANGOLDT'S MODEL

The basic method established by Mangoldt and Edgeworth was later elaborated upon by other writers, notably Viner and Haberler, still in the context of the classical model of comparative costs. The factoral terms of trade measure was replaced by relative money wage-rates, and the operation of reciprocal demand was analysed with the aid of the monetary mechanism of international adjustment. The procedure developed by Viner and Haberler is now the standard treatment of the matter and can be briefly summarised as follows: Let a_i/b_i denote the fixed factor (labour) input ratio in the ith commodity in countries A and B; then the comparative cost rankings for country A are as follows: $a_i/b_i < a_2/b_2 < \ldots < a_n/b_n$; i.e. country A is relatively most efficient in commodity 1, next most efficient in commodity 2 and so on, up to commodity n in which she is relatively least efficient. Each of a country's exports will rank lower in terms of relative labour costs than each of its imports. Let α and β stand for the money wage-rates in countries A and B on the assumption that the balance of payments is in equilibrium. Given a unique set of wage rates and an equilibrium exchange rate, whether commodity i is imported, exported or not traded depends on whether $a_i/b_i \gtreqless \beta/\alpha$ (where $i = 1, 2, \ldots n$). The break in the chain which separates import goods from export goods occurs when $a_1\alpha = b_1\beta$, i.e. where the money price is equal in both countries. There is no benefit or loss to either country in trading this commodity. The precise break in the chain will be determined by demand conditions operating through the balance of payments. Thus a disturbance to the balance of payments, by setting in motion equilibrating gold flows, will change prices and money wage-rates in both countries. There will be a new ratio and hence a new set of goods imported and exported by both countries. For the classical model, then, the conclusion for the multi-commodity case is that although the ranking of goods in terms of comparative production costs is independent of demand, the dividing line between export goods and import goods in each country is dependent on demand.

Viner's extension of the Edgeworth analysis to the case of many countries was quite straightforward. He simply superimposed the several Edgeworth logarithmic scales on each other (on the assumption that the wage rate for each country was given).[39] It was later shown by Whitin (1953) and McKenzie (1954) that Viner's technique was equivalent to the solution of the dual in a linear programming problem.[40] This seemed to vindicate the methods of Viner, Edgeworth and Mangoldt; but one problem remained – would the 'chain proposition' based on the bilateral comparison of labour-cost ratios (for all possible pairings of commodities and countries) be a sufficient condition (on efficiency grounds) for determining comparative advantage in a multi-country, multi-good world? It is tempting to use bilateral comparisons to infer the pattern of specialisation in a multi-country world; yet as Chipman noticed, the classical and early neoclassical economists never succumbed to the temptation.[41] Nevertheless, Jones considered this problem (also analysed by McKenzie) and found that the bilateral criterion (although correct) is not sufficient to exclude inefficient production patterns that would not be tolerated in a multilateral free-trade world.[42] In the analysis of such trade, using the bilateral criterion, it is not possible to distinguish efficient from inefficient specialisation with any given production assignment, i.e. for the class in which each country specialises in a different commodity. Jones proposed a general criterion for efficient specialisation which is really an appropriate generalisation of the two-by-two case: the efficient or optimal assignment is one (lying on the world efficiency locus) that minimises the product of labour requirements compared with all other possible assignments that involve no changes in the number of countries assigned to each commodity. Jones later remarked in connection with this minimum-product rule, 'the doctrine of comparative costs should, I think, be viewed as telling us not what will be produced (for that depends on demand as well) but what patterns cannot be produced in a world-wide competitive framework'.[43] What the Jones's demonstration indicates is how ruthlessly the force of free-trade competition eliminates inefficient production patterns (or assignments) – a process that cannot be abated by any imaginable pattern of demand.

The issues raised by Mangoldt continue to stimulate trade theorists. Dornbusch, Fischer and Samuelson (1977) have shown how, in a two-country Ricardian model with an infinite number of commodities, the competitive margin between imported and exported goods, the pattern of trade and the double-factoral terms of trade are all determined.[44]

3 Trade Theory in the Age of Marshall

3.1 Marshall

Marshall systematically developed and refined by means of geometrical and analytical methods the classical theory of international values, in particular the ideas originally expounded by John Stuart Mill. He combined Mill's analysis of demand (in terms of reciprocal demand) with the older emphasis on supply.[1] Marshall argues that the international exchange ratio (terms of trade) is influenced not only by demand, but also by the ability of a country to adjust supplies of its own products to the demands of foreign markets; although in practice the influence of cost factors is pushed into the background by the analytical assumption that each country specialises in one product. In addition to the presentation of Mill's reciprocal demand method in diagrammatic form, Marshall tries to improve upon labour time as a measure of costs (i.e. he includes capital and other production costs along with labour costs)[2] and to deal with the problem of aggregation over commodities. This he does by means of the concept of a 'representative bale' of a country's factors of production. In classical spirit, he wants to express the costs of production and gains from trade in real terms (effort, abstinence, etc.). Ricardo had measured the value of commodities in labour time; but, says Marshall, 'it seems better to suppose either country to make up her exports into representative "bales"; that is, bales each of which represents uniform aggregate investments of her labour (of various qualities) and of her capital'.[3] Each 'bale' corresponds to a fixed input of labour and capital (or factors of production in general). An increase in the efficiency of the factors or a reduction in costs will cause the size of the bale, reckoned in exportable goods, to expand. So although the costs of production were expressed in real terms, the value of commodities were not reckoned simply in terms of labour time. With the classical labour theory there was no means of comparing the costs of commodities produced with different capital structures or different qualities of labour – particularly when applied to more than two countries and two commodities. The representative bale was an effort to deal with the problem of aggregation and it appeared more realistic than the traditional two-good (linen and cloth) model.[4] These aggregates were then treated as the units in which national demand was expressed in world markets. But these aggregates were not clearly related to consumer tastes, e.g. the preferences of individuals; because of this limitation the bale concept was not widely used by other writers.

Marshall represented reciprocal demand schedules as curves. The curves are complex; they attempt to represent general equilibrium in trade. Each point on the curve is a point of potential equilibrium, and a movement along it presupposes that the economy has rearranged its internal trade to conform to the new equilibrium conditions. The commodity composition of Marshall's bales changes (1) when the curves shift (e.g. through technological change) and (2) as a result of balance-of-payments adjustments to disturbances where commodities can shift from the export side to the import list. Marshall was able to construct reciprocal demand (or offer curves) for the two-country case even when the number of commodities in each country is large (provided they are produced at constant cost) through the representative bale idea. As indicated above, the bale is not a typical assortment of exports or imports but the units of 'productive power' embodied in each country's exports; hence the terms of trade are not measured by the ratio of commodity prices, but the rate at which the units of productive power of one country exchange for those of another – the factoral terms of trade. Marshall used these curves to examine the stability of world markets, the influence of elasticity on trade flows and effects on the terms of trade of shifts in the curves, e.g. in relation to import duties.

SHIFTS OF INTERNATIONAL DEMAND AND THE TERMS OF TRADE

In *Money, Credit and Commerce* Marshall discussed the effects of changes in international demand on the terms of trade and gave a solution in appendix J.[5] Suppose demand for imports increases in one country, England for example, how will the terms of trade and volume of trade change? Marshall shows that the deterioration of England's terms of trade will vary directly with England's elasticity of demand for imports and inversely with the other country's (Germany's) elasticity of demand for imports. The increase in the volume of trade will vary directly with both of the elasticities:

> The more elastic the demand of either country, the elasticity of the other being given, the larger will be the volumes of both her exports and of her imports; but the more also will her exports be enlarged relative to her imports; or, in other words, the less favourable to her will be the terms of trade. Thus both sides of the trade will be very greatly enlarged; if both elasticities are great. But if both are small *G*'s exports will be increased by the original amount and a very little more in addition.[6]

His solution aroused controversy because of an ambiguity in the term 'increase in demand' and Marshall's practice of dealing only with curves of the 'normal' type, i.e. where the elasticity of both offer curves exceeds unity. The type of demand shift Marshall had in mind was one where there was an increase in uniform proportion, of the amount of one commodity (exports) offered in exchange for a given amount of the other (imports) – in his example, a uniform increase in the amount of *E*-goods offered per unit of *G*-goods shown by a uniform shift to the right of *E*'s offer curve. The fact is, however, that there are at least three distinct types of demand shifts, all consistent with Marshall's definition of the problem, each of which can lead to a different result – for instance, Graham defined a demand shift as an increase in imports demanded for a given amount of exports.

There was nothing wrong with Marshall's solution. His conclusion was reaffirmed by several writers who later examined the issues involved in the controversy, involving Graham and Viner among others.[7] The matter will be taken up later in the section dealing with Graham's critique of the conventional exposition of classical theory.

GAINS FROM TRADE AND THE TERMS OF TRADE

Mill had claimed that rich countries gain less from trade than poor countries:

> The richest countries, *ceteris paribus*, gain the least by a given amount of foreign commerce: since, having a greater demand for commodities generally, they are likely to have a greater demand for foreign commodities, and thus modify the terms of interchange to their own disadvantage.[8]

There are two aspects to this: (1) a general increase in productivity or neutral technological change may lead to a worsening of the country's terms of trade, since the increased output could only be sold on world markets at less favourable terms, and (2) because the demand for foreign commodities is greater, the terms of trade are turned against her.

Marshall referred to the role of supply factors in modifying this conclusion. He agreed that small countries tend to gain more from trade; but Marshall nevertheless pointed out that the rich country can develop (invent) new products, has extensive and highly organised transport and commercial relations with many markets and 'need not push any one variety of any product on a market which shows signs of being glutted with that variety', and 'has better opportunities for adapting her output to the receptivity of various markets than the poor one is likely to have'.[9] The relevance of supply conditions to the terms of trade in the case of an advanced industrial country was also emphasised in another passage; Marshall's reasoning was: 'the elasticity of her effective demand for foreign goods is governed not only by her wealth and the elasticity of the desires of her population for them; but also by her ability to adjust the supplies of her own goods of various kinds to the demands of foreign markets'.[10] He was convinced that the demand for imports by an industrial country was generally elastic and that the world's demand for its goods was also relatively elastic; but there were exceptions – e.g. the British demand for foreign wheat was probably inelastic and the foreign demand for British coal was also inelastic.

THE NET BENEFIT FROM FOREIGN TRADE

In *Money, Credit and Commerce* Marshall suggested as a measure of a country's 'net benefit' from its foreign trade the excess of the number of 'representative bales' that it would be willing to give up for the quantity of bales it imports, over the amount it actually trades at the equilibrium 'rate of interchange' or terms of trade.[11] It was an application of his concept of consumer surplus to the problem – the maximum amount of money a consumer would be willing to pay for a commodity and the amount he actually pays, the gain being conceived as the area between the two prices bounded by the demand curve. Applied to the gains from trade expressed in terms of specific product prices, the 'net benefit' measure is simply the sum of the excesses of the unit prices at which a country would have purchased successive amounts of imports over the equilibrium terms of trade. Marshall developed an ingenious graphical construction incorporating the country's offer curve to show the total surplus or net benefit, reckoned in terms of representative bales of export goods, as a triangular area (under the import demand curve) representing the sum of the series of unit surpluses.[12] Viner finds fault with Marshall's procedure; in fact, he says, the results are 'invalid'.[13] Marshall's measure exaggerates the country's net benefit from trade because he implicitly assumed that the importing country's offer curve remained the same whether the country paid the equilibrium price or the maximum price it was willing to pay for the intra-marginal units of imports – i.e. Marshall assumed constancy of the marginal utility of exportables. This is an unwarranted assumption, argues Viner; for since a given number of imported bales costs more if the maximum price were paid, the marginal utility of exportables must be greater. This being the case, the country will offer fewer export bales in return for a marginal import bale if previous bales were paid for at the maximum price rather than the equilibrium price. Hence Marshall's measure produces an overestimate of the gain.

Viner proposed to correct Marshall by going directly to the country's utility function and deriving from it an offer curve showing the maximum price it was willing to pay (in terms of exports) for each successive unit of imports. An accurate measure can then be found by aggregating the excesses of the prices so estimated over the equilibrium price. Viner's amended version shows a smaller surplus or net benefit compared with Marshall's defective procedure, and is in fact more consistent with the traditional interpretation of consumer surplus. Marshall's measure was an attempt to find an objective counterpart to the idea of total utility which could be applied to the gains from trade; but he mistakenly believed that the offer curve could be identified with a total utility curve, and this was responsible for his dubious results, as Viner showed.[14] Consequently, few economists followed Marshall's attempt to apply consumer surplus analysis when working in a general-equilibrium framework. However, in partial-equilibrium work (e.g. to show the economic effects of the imposition of a tariff on the product of a single industry), Marshallian surplus analysis found a place and is now a standard tool of analysis in such partial-equilibrium treatments.

In Marshall's time, a more promising search for some index of the net benefit from the total trade of a country was undertaken by Edgeworth. He derived a 'no gain from trade' curve (indifference curve) based on a general utility function and related it to the country's offer curve. The gain from trade, he measured as the distance between this curve and the indifference curve.[15] Edgeworth's device, however, was not a quantitative indicator; it showed only the direction of the change in the amount of gain. Subsequent developments in demand theory led to the abandonment of measurable utility in favour of ratios of marginal utilities, and this factor reinforced the neglect of Marshallian surplus analysis. It was only after Hicks's rehabilitation of consumer surplus theory in 1941 that the concept came to be seen as a theoretically valid one. Bhagwati and Johnson (1960) discussed the various ways in which this could be done in the light of Hicks's reconstruction.[16] They identified six alternative measures for a single country (Marshallian surplus, compensating variation or equivalent variation, each measured in terms of either exportables or importables) and illustrated the cases with the aid of 'no trade' indifference curves in a general-equilibrium framework. What Bhagwati and Johnson did was to show precisely how theoretically meaningful measures of a country's gain from trade could be devised. However, as Currie, Murphy and Schmitz rightly note, 'any attempt to estimate the actual gain of a country from foreign trade would lead to highly dubious results'.[17] Marshall's vision of a simple, objective (quantifiable) measure of a country's trading gains proved elusive, and the quest taken up by later neoclassical economists ran into a dread-end. Ironically, Marshall's concept of economic surplus retained its place in international trade theory not in the form he proposed, but as he used it in his analyses of domestic trade problems, i.e. partial-equilibrium welfare analysis.

The idea of consumer surplus figures prominently in modern debates about protection vs. free trade. For the free trader, national economic welfare is measured by command over goods and services; and since all citizens, capitalists and workers alike, are necessarily consumers, everyone is better off when given the opportunity to buy from the cheapest source. Free trade, which provides that opportunity, therefore maximises the sum of consumer surplus from trade. Interfere with the free international flow of goods and services, and you reduce the total of national income that can be spent on the consumption of various goods and services, i.e. you diminish the nation's consumer surplus from international trade.

MARSHALL ON THE STABILITY OF WORLD MARKETS

Marshall's discussion of the stability of world markets in terms of stable and unstable equilibria is still held in high regard. Murray Kemp says it 'must rank among the most remarkable contributions ever made to theoretical economics'.[18]

Many neoclassical trade theorems are based on comparative statics. If the equilibria being compared in the comparative-static analyses are not stable, then such analyses may be of little interest. In addition, for some policy purposes – e.g. exchange-rate policy – the stability question is highly relevant – would a devaluation restore equilibrium to a country's balance of payments? The stability of theoretical models needs to be demonstrated for the basic reason that we cannot compare one state of affairs with another – e.g. free trade compared with autarky – unless stability is demonstrated. If the existence of a free-trade equilibrium point is established, one has to ask the question: Is that point stable? Stability conditions have to be derived to deal with disturbances to equilibrium (e.g. the imposition of tariffs, a domestic excise tax on the imported good, a unilateral transfer, technological change, etc.) – that is to say, situations where market and equilibrium values differ. In such treatments, the analyst needs to show how the introduction of disturbances which change the existing equilibrium allows the system to converge to a new equilibrium, i.e. to show that there is a tendency for the differences between market and equilibrium values to disappear with the passage of time. If the economic system is stable, then one can narrow down the range within which the response to a disturbance must lie.

Chipman observes: 'Few subjects have been so controversial as the question of stability of equilibrium in international trade.'[19] It is therefore of interest to review Marshall's treatment of the matter. In his theory of international values, Mill solved equations numerically to show the existence of equilibrium and attempted to deal with the possibility of multiple equilibria; but Marshall said, 'His treatment of the matter is certainly inadequate; for he has failed to discover the laws which determine whether any particular position of equilibrium is stable or unstable.'[20] After giving what he regarded as a solution of Mill's problem of indeterminancy of equilibrium, Marshall asserted: 'Mill's example therefore does not afford any aid towards the solution of the class of problems which are suggested by the intersections of the curves in Figure 4', i.e. in the offer-curve diagram showing multiple equilibria.[21]

Marshall then analyses stable and unstable equilibria, and starts by supposing trade is not in equilibrium because of some shock, e.g. 'a war or a bad harvest has jerked the exchange-index to some position such that the trade corresponding to it is not in equilibrium',[22] and sets out to investigate the forces which govern its motion, i.e. the dynamic adjustment mechanism. He makes the point that when the terms on which trade are conducted are such that the rate of profit in the export industry is abnormally high, then competition of traders to obtain high profits will lead to an expansion of production and an increase in the exportation of goods. This situation will occur at points between the country's offer curve and the axis measuring its imports where, for a given level of import volume, there is an excess of exports offered over current exports. So adjustment comes about through changes in exports of cloth and linen in the two countries. Marshall gives an analogy in terms of the attraction of particles to a rigid wire to illustrate the movement of the exchange index or trading point in relation to the offer curve: 'if we chose to assign to these horizontal and vertical forces any particular laws, we should obtain a differential equation for the motion of the exchange index. This equation when integrated would give us the path which on this particular supposition the particle would describe.'[23]

Marshall provided only this brief description of the economic processes at work in the derivation of his stability conditions, and did not translate his dynamic adjustment process into mathematics. What is clear, however, is that his analysis of stable and unstable equilibria is in terms of the dynamic movement of the exchange index, i.e. the point in his phase diagram which corresponds to the actual position of the trade between two countries at any time; that is to say, he was looking at the properties of a system of first-order differential equations. The only prices mentioned are 'rate of interchange' and 'terms of trade', which are the same. Prices are the dependent variables, and quantities (imports and exports) are the independent variables. Marshall's adjustment process is therefore a non-*tâtonnement* type which Samuelson analysed.[24] According to the Walrasian *tâtonnement* (or 'groping') interpretation of the adjustment process, no actual exchange takes place before equilibrium prices are reached, i.e. there is a recontracting process at work. It is based on the notion that in a competitive trading world, the price of a commodity must increase or decrease according as the demand for it is greater than or less than the supply. By contrast, Marshall's discussion is in terms of output adjustments, and trading at 'false' prices is allowed, i.e. at points off the offer curves, not necessarily at the intersection points of the two curves.

One way to read Marshall in this context is to say that he was outlining a 'buffer stock' interpretation of the stability of equilibrium. Each country is portrayed as increasing or decreasing its offer according to whether the demand price in the international market (the terms of trade) for the quantity of exports currently being supplied is greater or less than the price required to bring forth this supply. Offers are in equilibrium when stock levels are stable; and these will be constant when, at the prevailing price ratio, the amount country A is willing to offer in exchange for country B's good is equal to the amount country B is willing to offer in exchange for country A's good. In other words, equilibrium is stable when A's excess demand plus B's excess demand for each of the two commodities is zero. This is a plausible description of Marshall's adjustment mechanism, but it is clear that Marshall does not envisage a situation where inconsistent trades are brought into equilibrium through changes in inventories (stocks).

Marshall's assumption is that each country's offer adjusts gradually at a determinable rate per unit of time to match the current volume of imports in the long run (i.e. assuming unlimited time for the adjustment). So exports adjust, as we have already indicated. This implies, of course, adjustments in production, i.e. in the level of output of export goods (with imports and the domestic consumption of exportables held constant). How is this accomplished? Marshall was not explicit on the precise process which determined the behaviour of each country's exports, given the assumption of complete specialisation and therefore no scope for adjustment in an import-competing sector. Chipman finds a puzzling question about all this that calls for explanation.[25] If adjustment takes place only via the production of export goods, then this is impossible unless a domestic sector is assumed. Chipman finds confirmation of this in a passage where Marshall criticises Mill for overlooking the possibility of a movement of resources out of domestic industry which produces goods that do not enter into international trade (i.e. non-traded goods). Marshall himself noted that 'every movement of the exchange-index entails some alteration in the shapes of the curves, and therefore in the forces which determine its succeeding movements'.[26] Corresponding to each level of trade volume as indicated by the exchange index or trading point, there will be a different pattern of domestic consumption and production. If the output mix changes then the shape of the offer curves will alter. Chipman refers to this suggestion of Marshall's as indicating the 'extreme subtlety of the Marshallian conception', and believes that modern interpreters of Marshall, by neglecting the role of domestic (non-traded) production in the adjustment process may have oversimplified Marshall's conception.[27] Nevertheless, Marshall's static offer curves are clearly meant to reflect long-run equilibrium in the conditions of domestic demand and supply. 'At all events, the general character of the curves will seldom be changed', he writes;[28] and therefore the assumption that the curves remain rigid and unchanged in the course of adjustment continues to hold. Is there then an inconsistency in Marshall's system? Akihiro Amano thinks not. He admits that the interpretation of Marshall which excludes the domestic sector is indeed an oversimplification, but says that he is 'yet unconvinced that Marshall's system contains a logical inconsistency as it stands'.[29] Amano derives stability conditions for a Marshallian model (one where the production of exportables adjust sluggishly to the state of profitability) based on dynamic behavioural assumptions of consumers and producers in a competitive trading economy. Amano's analysis of the stability of long-run equilibrium in Marshall's model extends to the output behaviour of the import-competing industry in each country, as well as to cases where specialisation is complete in one or both countries. Answering the question posed by Chipman, he concludes that 'no difficulty appears in Marshall's system even without the domestic sector. Probably Marshall did not intend to exclude the adjustment on the import side, but considered it only necessary to specify the behaviour of each country's exports (or rather the level of output of export goods).'[30]

Marshall is perhaps deliberately vague about his dynamic adjustment mechanism because he realises that in practice trading takes place out of equilibrium; as such, no precise analysis can be given of the process of adjustment which is rather complex. This point has recently been emphasised by Harvey Gram, who writes: 'efforts to formalize Marshall's "dynamics" [by Samuelson, Kemp and Amano] are but valiant attempts to come to terms with an approach to equilibrium which itself moves in an unspecified manner as a consequence of not being attained initially'.[31]

THE ANALYSIS OF TARIFFS

Marshall used his curves to analyse the effects of the imposition of duties, and dealt with cases of both elastic and inelastic reciprocal demand (or offer) curves. His results were in line with classical economists like Mill, Torrens and Senior – but shown graphically within an analytical framework. The imposition of a tariff can improve the terms of trade of a country large enough to influence world prices. The size of the improvement may be large if the government spends the tariff proceeds on the country's export good. Such gains are however likely to be offset by losses from resource misallocation and the distortion of consumers' choice. Moreover, in practice, Marshall thought that the possibility of rigging the terms of trade was extremely limited. The reciprocal demand of the foreign country must have a low elasticity and the country's own reciprocal demand a high elasticity. Retaliation by the foreign country can nullify the gain; and furthermore, the foreign country can divert its exports to third-country free-trade markets (in the realistic multi-country case). Marshall's position was therefore quite classical – the belief that in the long run the scope for nationally profitable gains at the expense of trading partners was severely restricted.[32]

Marshall discusses the case where tariffs are imposed across-the-board, i.e. the effects of general tariffs. Having done the analysis in real terms, i.e. in terms of 'representative bales', he shows that the conclusion can be stated in terms of gold prices. Gold flows and consequent changes in price levels (including money-wage levels) will adjust to the new terms of trade in equilibrium. The purchasing power of money in the tariff-imposing country will be affected (i.e. lowered) by its tariff policy – tariffs will alter the general level of prices. Hence the real increase in price consequent upon the tariff may be less when redistribution of gold is considered: 'the real values that her people give in return for the foreign goods . . . are a little lower than is suggested by the high prices which they pay'.[33] Mill had previously discussed this in the context of the monetary adjustment process, and said that the tariff-imposing country would obtain imports relatively cheaper consequent upon the reduction in the relative price of its import good in the outside world. The domestic price of imports would exceed what it previously was by less than the full amount of the duty, while consumers' means of purchasing them would be increased by the rise in their money incomes. Thus, in real terms, the foreigner pays a part of the duty. In general, however,

Marshall shows the real effects are independent of money in the long run. The shift in the terms of trade will cause welfare changes. In the case of an adverse movement in the terms of trade, it means an increase in the quantity of the produce of her labour and capital that the country has to give in return for a given quantity of the other. Both the terms of trade and the incidence of the duties would be determined by the relative elasticities of reciprocal demands in the two countries.

FREE TRADE, TARIFFS AND PROTECTION

(1) *'Taxing the Foreigner'*: On the possibility of taxing the foreigner through a favourable terms of trade shift induced by tariffs.

Marshall's writings contain many variations on the above theme, summarised in this passage from his *Memorandum on the Fiscal Policy of International Trade*:

> There has, indeed, never been a country, the whole of whose exports were in such urgent demand, that she could compel foreigners to pay any large part of any taxes which she imposed on her imports.[34]

A country is not likely to be able to throw the burden of its import duties upon foreign countries 'unless, either all the exports consist of things of which she has at least a partial monopoly; or she is the only important consumer of most of the commodities which she imports from those countries'.[35]

Britain was able to tax the foreigner in the first half of the nineteenth century, he says, but not now: because (1) British technology has become the common property of all countries in the West, and some countries have even surpassed Britain, and (2) the growth of population in Britain has made her demand more urgent for some of her imports. However, in his early writings on trade, he felt that Britain could 'throw upon her neighbours some of the burden of an export duty on coal', and he produced current statistical evidence to show the possibility of so doing. He also suggested that the Americans could do the same with their cotton exports. 'England in selling her coal to foreign nations, is in some measure selling to strangers the birthright of her children that are to come.'[36] There was therefore a strong case for the imposition of a duty on the export of steam coal from Britain, despite the fact that such a duty would appear niggardly and illiberal. Several years later, when the British government introduced an export duty on coal payable from 1901, Marshall strongly objected to the measure in a letter to *The Times*. The tax presented many technical difficulties, he wrote; it was not worth the disturbance it was bound to cause, and moreover, it was 'a breach of international comity . . . while we are in a specially defenceless position against some export duties that certain other countries might conceivably levy'.[37]

(2) *The infant-industry argument*: Marshall recognised the validity of the infant-industry argument for protection, and criticised the older British economists for ignoring the fact that 'protection to immature industries is a national good' and that 'it would have been foolish for nations with immature industries to adopt England's system pure and simple'. However, his American experience convinced him that the infant-industry argument could be misapplied, since it afforded excessive protection to 'industries which were already strong enough to do without it' in the United States.[38] Marshall was against the imposition of retaliatory tariffs against countries which levied discriminatory duties on British goods as (a) a method of forcing them to reduce their tariffs, and (b) as a cure for unemployment. Experience did not afford any ground for believing it would achieve either of those ends, and, moreover, 'It is easier to begin than to end a war of hostile tariffs.'[39] Earlier, before the lurch to general protectionism in Europe, he thought an additional argument against the British use of such taxes was that other countries might delay going over to free trade if they saw that Great Britain could easily be persuaded to levy discriminatory duties.

(3) *On protection*: Marshall had been a firm supporter of free-trade policies ever since 1875 when he visited the United States to study protection on the spot. As a result of that experience, he came away quite settled in his mind that, 'if an American, I should unhesitatingly vote for Free Trade', mainly on account of the political corruption involved in tariff lobbying in a democratic society and consideration of the interests of the agricultural classes.[40] He contested the arguments of the American protectionists that high wages meant they could not compete with European manufacturers except with the aid of protective tariffs, and also disputed the claim that protection tended to diminish fluctuations in prices, wages and employment. Marshall's role in the British tariff controversy of 1903 will be discussed in Chapter 4.

Some writers notice a curious disjunction between theory and practice in Marshall's thought on the subject of protection. He disapproves of protectionism when he sees it in operation, yet as Jha notes, 'his theoretical writings had a contrary effect'.[41] After all, Marshall was the first neoclassical economist to treat external economies and increasing returns in a fairly rigorous manner.[42] Adam Smith had pointed out the benefits to be derived from large-scale production, and Marshall himself observed that in the century following Smith's work, 'England's export trade has exerted a quiet but constant influence in developing broad inventions and economies of manufacture' and that 'such economies when they have once been obtained are not readily lost'.[43] It appeared to Jha, therefore, that 'Marshall's concept of external economies and his emphasis on the desirability of promoting increasing returns industries reinforced the case for the protection of manufactures in the underdeveloped countries, brought forward by Hamilton and List.'[44] Why, then, did Marshall believe that for a country like Britain 'a Protective policy . . . would be an unmixed and grievous evil',[45] and disapproved of American protectionism? It is clear that what bothered Marshall was the *practice* of protectionism, even when a theoretically valid case could be made out for it in special circumstances. He did not credit politicians with having the skill, judgement and integrity in the degree necessary for the implementation of a rational protective policy. A protective system, like any measure of government intervention in a democracy, was open to political abuse under the clamour of vested interests. The great virtue of free trade (and its irresistible attraction) for Marshall is that 'it is not a device, but the absence of any device'. As such it is immune to political mismanagement and therefore the advantage of free trade 'may continue to outweigh the series of small gains which could be obtained by any manipulation of tariffs, however scientific and astute'.[46]

Marshall's attitude to protection and free trade was thus classical in spirit, close to the 'rent-seeking' view of Adam Smith, in fact. He himself believed that free trade could not be defended solely on 'absolute a priori reasoning'; that changing circumstances might, after careful consideration, signal new departures from established commercial policies – in particular, limited protection may be necessary at certain stages of development; and perhaps such intervention could not do much harm in the case of certain countries. Thus, he claimed, that on account of its vast natural resources and large domestic market, 'foreign trade is not necessary to the United

States'; consequently protection 'could not do her very much harm'[47] and that the expansion of the protected industries compensated for the economic loss. He praised the *Zollverein* as 'one of the most important movements towards free trade that the world has ever seen'[48] – presumably on the ground that its trade-creating gains outweighed the trade-diverting effects.

TRADE, TECHNOLOGY AND ECONOMIC DEVELOPMENT

In his classic history of production and distribution theories, George Stigler commented on an important characteristic of Marshall's work – that 'Marshall was so concerned with historical economic developments that he had relatively small patience with the theoretical economics of a stationary state'.[49] Everyone knows the famous baffling quotation from Marshall, that 'the causes which determine the economic progress of nations belong to the study of international trade.'[50]

In his theory of international trade and even more so in his trade-policy analyses (e.g. in *Memorandum on the Fiscal Policy of International Trade*) Marshall placed much emphasis upon the roles of increasing returns to scale, technological innovation and the transfer of technology in determining the pattern of trade and changes in that pattern over time. He sees the pattern of trade in manufactures as being determined by a continuing process of innovation and technology transfer. Technical progress leads to monopoly gains which are soon wiped out by a rapid international diffusion of knowledge. As a matter of practical policy, therefore, his defence of free trade is couched ultimately not so much in terms of the conventional mode of reasoning based on static allocative efficiency as on the need to keep an industrial country abreast of 'progress in the arts and resources of manufacture', i.e. changes in the 'state of the arts' or technological advances abroad.

Like Mill, Marshall therefore has some interesting things to say about trade, technology and economic development. Foreign competition through trade (1) increases the efficiency of domestic industry; (2) provides opportunities for the migration of capital and labour; (3) exerts an influence on the steadiness of employment; and (4) assists in the development of large-scale industry. The chief benefit of foreign trade for Britain was that it enabled the country to obtain ample supplies of raw materials and foodstuffs at stable prices;

another benefit was, through the finance of foreign trade, the development of the English money market.

On technology, Marshall feared that Britain's superiority in the production and export of manufactures would be weakened in the course of time, owing to the international diffusion of technology:

> Every improvement in the manufacturing arts increased England's power of meeting the various wants of backward countries . . . the progress of invention opened a wider field for the sale of her special products . . . But this good fortune has been short-lived. Her improvements have been followed, and latterly often anticipated, by America and Germany and other countries; and her special products have lost nearly all their monopoly value.[51]

But Marshall realised that a technological leader could keep ahead of imitations abroad by developing new products. In 1903, he referred to the example of France:

> New Parisian goods are sold at high prices in London and Berlin for a short time, and then imitations of them are made in large quantities and sold at relatively low prices. But by that time, Paris . . . is already at work on other things which will soon be imitated in like way.[52]

The French have been pioneers in a number of notable inventions, but thanks to native ingenuity, skill and organisation British entrepreneurs have developed and standardised them into new, mass-produced products. Thus:

> the same faculties is shown in such manufactures as those of the bicycle, motor-car, submarine, and aeroplane: where French inventors have led, and a few French operative mechanics displayed a skill, a judgment and a resource which are nowhere surpassed. As these new delicate industries have reached the stage of massive production, the faculty of disciplined steadfast work becomes more important: the motor-car, the submarine and the aeroplane tend to find their chief homes in other countries, as the bicycle did long ago.[53]

Marshall was quite certain that the international diffusion process had accelerated in the new environment of intense international competition

> broad ideas and knowledge, which when once acquired pass speedily into common ownership; and become part of the collective wealth, in the first instance of the countries to which the industries specially affected belong, and ultimately to the whole world.[54]

Germany, Marshall says, now enjoys a competitive advantage 'in industries in which academic training and laboratory work can be turned to good account'; but this was the culmination of a prior process of successful imitation and absorption of foreign technology:

> In the early stages of modern manufacture, scientific training was of relatively small importance. The Germans accordingly, recognising their own weakness in practical instinct and organising faculty, took the part of pupils, whose purpose it was to outrun their teachers. They began by the direct copying of English machinery and methods . . . And all the while Germany has been quick to grasp the practical significance of any master discovery that is made in other countries and to turn it to account.[55]

Arthur Bloomfield said that Marshall was 'the only earlier writer of whom I am aware who explicitly distinguished between . . . two kinds of improvements that were later to be called "export-biased" and "import-biased"'. Marshall made the distinction in a passage where he contrasted the trade effects of technological change affecting export industries ('leading industries') and import-competing industries ('lagging industries'):

> Other things being equal, an increase in the efficiency of those industries in which a country is already leading will increase her foreign trade more than in proportion. But an increase in the efficiency of those in which she is behind will diminish her foreign trade.[56]

Finally, Marshall noted that improvements in international transport expanded the volume of trade; they reduced the costs of imported foodstuffs and raw materials, enlarged markets for finished exports and steadied demand.

3.2 Edgeworth

TOOLS AND TECHNIQUES

Marshall's reciprocal demand or offer curves summarised the ultimate data for the analysis of exchange between two countries in terms of demand and supply. What was not clear, however, was: How were these curves related to underlying utilities? An answer that suggested itself was to treat each country as a single individual. Demand functions for each country could then be derived from its preferences or 'tastes' as described by indifference curves. Modern expositions of neoclassical trade theory do likewise: i.e. it is assumed that consumer preferences can be aggregated, so that community indifference curves are radial expansions of individual indifference curves. The offer curve is defined as the locus of points of tangency of different price lines (parametrically given for each country considered in isolation) and the country's community welfare indifference curves.

This important development of Marshall's construction was initiated by Edgeworth long before Marshall's diagrams were published.[57] In *Mathematical Psychics* (1881) Edgeworth derived the offer curve from indifference curves in the context of individual exchange or barter in a manner analogous to that now used in contemporary trade theory. Thus Edgeworth defines the offer curve as 'the locus of the point where lines from the origin touch curves of indifference'.[58] The lines from the origin being different price ratios, the offer curve thus summarises the conditions for constrained utility maximisation; for at all points on the offer curve, the price ratio equals the ratio of marginal utilities of the two individuals. Applied to international equilibrium, the offer curve analysis can then be used to show (as Marshall did) how the terms of trade are determined by the interplay of demand and supply.

Edgeworth also introduced into economics another important theoretical construct, the contract curve. As used in trade theory, the contract curve is the locus of points at which one country's indifference curve is tangent to the other country's indifference curve. In other words, it is the locus of points at which one country cannot increase its welfare without decreasing the welfare of the other, given the total world output of both goods. By bringing together the two countries offer curves it can be shown how international equilibrium occurs at the intersection of the offer curves. But, moreover, this point of intersection lies on the contract curve; and by virtue of this, welfare significance can be read into the equilibrium terms of trade.

Edgeworth first illustrated this result again in the context of individual competitive barter. He showed that the competitive solution must lie on the contract curve on the assumption that individuals maximise their utilities in terms of their own consumption; and this competitive equilibrium coincides precisely at the point of intersection of the two traders' offer curves.[59] Edgeworth – 'the toolmaker', as Pigou called him – added quite significantly to the common toolbox of neoclassical economists. Edgeworth's analysis was, however, conveyed in mathematical language, and when he extended it to trade problems the geometrical counterparts were not fully explained or developed.

Edgeworth's techniques were subsequently refashioned for use in trade analysis by Leontief (1933), Lerner (1934) and Meade (1952), among others.[60] Meade's innovation of the 'international trade butterfly', described as 'one of the most compact and also prettiest graph in economics',[61] was particularly noteworthy in that it presented for the first time an integrated treatment of production, consumption and trade. Edgeworth's tools (e.g. trade indifference curve, his box diagram, etc.) were developed for use in the analysis of exchange where individuals held fixed quantities of goods. They therefore had to be adapted for general equilibrium use (production, consumption, trade flows and relative prices), i.e. freed from the limiting assumption of fixed production levels.

OPTIMUM TARIFF AND PROTECTION

Edgeworth had a hand in formulating the terms of trade argument for protection and orthodox optimal tariff theory – the analysis of which goes back to Torrens and Mill and revived by Bickerdike. The optimum tariff is one where the gain due to improved terms of trade exceeds the loss from reduced volume of trade by the greatest possible margin. A 'large' country concerned solely (i.e. myopically) with its national economic interest can take advantage of less than infinitely elastic foreign reciprocal demand curve and thereby exploit its potential monopoly or monopsony power by restricting trade to its advantage.

Edgeworth used his apparatus of offer curves and trade indifference curve to show the geometrical basis of the optimum tariff argument. The geometrical basis was present in the work of Auspitz and Lieben who used the total demand curves similar to Marshallian reciprocal demand curves combined with 'curves of constant satisfaction' or indifference curves. Edgeworth acknowledge that his treatment of the matter was similar to that of 'Auspitz and Lieben's beautiful and original reasoning'.[62] Edgeworth showed the optimum tariff to be one which shifts the domestic offer curve to a point located on the elastic portion of the foreign country's offer curve, where the latter curve is tangent to the highest indifference curve attainable by the home country. More formal treatments of the matter were provided by Bickerdike (1906) and Pigou (1908), and again in the 1940s by Kaldor, Scitovsky, Kahn, de Villiers Graaff, etc.

Edgeworth was a free-trader, and whilst he accepted in principle the few exceptions to the free-trade argument, his position was similar to that of Marshall on the severe limitations of their practical application. In his view, any departure from a free-trade policy, however nicely calculated and valid the restrictive measure might be, would open the way for illicit protection and abuse. Thus when Bickerdike came out with his own precise formulation of the optimum tariff argument,[63] Edgeworth applauded the effort but warned of the practical danger involved in its use:

> Mr Bickerdike has accomplished a wonderful feat. He has said something new about protection . . . the direct use of the theory is likely to be small. But it is to be feared that its abuse will be considerable. It affords to unscrupulous advocates of vulgar Protection a peculiarly specious pretext for introducing the thin edge of the fiscal wedge . . . Let us admire the skill of the analyst, but label the subject of his investigation POISON.[64]

Edgeworth, like Mill and Sidgwick, was steeped in the utilitarian ethic. He could not countenance the deliberate manipulation of trade taxes to exploit selfish national advantages, and particularly recoiled at the prospect of tariff wars (i.e. retaliation and counter-retaliation) that would be unleashed by such selfish international behaviour: 'For one nation to benefit itself at the expense of . . . others is contrary to the highest morality . . . But in an abstract study upon the motion of projectiles *in vacuo*, I do not think it necessary to enlarge upon the horrors of war.'[65]

TECHNOLOGICAL CHANGE AND THE TERMS OF TRADE

Technological change is now regarded as a key determinant of international trade in manufactures. The idea that technological change has important consequences for international trade is, of course, not a new one. The classical economists and several lesser-known writers showed a lively interest in many aspects of the interrelation between trade and growth; but it was what they had to say on one aspect of the matter – namely, the impact of technological change on the terms of trade – that attracted the attention of the early neoclassical economists, including Edgeworth. Mill's views, in particular, stimulated Edgeworth's analysis of the problem.

Mill considered two types of technological improvement: one that resulted in the creation of a new export commodity, and one that had the effect of lowering the cost of production in an existing export commodity.[66] He concluded that, in the former case, the innovating country's terms of trade would improve, but deteriorate in the case of a cost-reducing improvement; and that the deterioration in the terms of trade would be proportionately greater than the reduction in cost if the elasticity of foreign (reciprocal) demand was less than unity. Thus if the productivity growth occurs in the existing export industry, then it is possible for the deterioration in the commodity or net barter terms of trade to be so large as to outweigh the effect of the physical increase in output, and therefore leave the country worse off than before. This phenomenon is, of course, well known in the modern literature as 'immiserising growth' – a case analysed by Edgeworth who reaffirmed Mill's result, claiming that it was 'sufficiently supported by common sense'. He provided an explicit statement of the welfare implications of the result, and pointed out that the welfare loss to the innovating country may continue to hold even if the export commodity is consumed by its own citizens as well. Thus, 'the exporting country is damnified by the improvement; and by parity of reasoning may be benefited by a restriction of its exports'.[67] Here is a case, then, where although the rest of the world gains, free trade may be harmful to an innovating country and commercial policy may be required to retain the benefits of expanded production.

Edgeworth established the condition for immiserising growth by a simple model of complete specialisation both in consumption and production – i.e. each country produced and exported only one good which it did not consume, relying on imports from the other country to satisfy its consumption needs. In a restrictive model such as this, the foreign elasticity of demand is crucial and the condition for harmful growth is obvious: a foreign elasticity of demand less than unity. Joseph Shield Nicholson objected to Edgeworth's proposition on the ground that it was based on a highly restrictive and special model, and argued that if (a) money was introduced, (b) residents of the innovating country consumed some of their export commodity, and (c) the assumption of labour immobility in the export industry was dropped (so that labour could be shifted out of export production), then the Mill–Edgeworth conclusion would not necessarily follow.[68] In reply to Nicholson, Edgeworth defended the generality of his result and, in effect, denied that it depended on his restrictive model.[69] A few years later, Bastable contributed to the controversy on the side of Edgeworth and further developed the latter's reply to Nicholson. He supported Edgeworth's claim that money made no difference to the analysis, and proceeded to show that conditions for 'damnification' could be established in terms of a model of incomplete specialisation in consumption, provided the innovating country faced an inelastic foreign demand. Bastable summarised the theoretical argument thus: 'Where the gain from the improvement was greater than that from foreign trade, detriment to the country exporting the article now made cheaper was impossible. It is only where the benefit from improvement is smaller than the advantage of interchange that loss could result from it.'[70] At the practical level, however, Bastable believed that the innovating country's prospects of real-income losses were fairly remote; for in the real world of many trading countries, each facing competition from close substitutes produced by several other countries, it was unlikely that any single country would face an inelastic foreign demand for its products.

The Mill–Edgeworth proposition was endorsed by Bertil Ohlin,[71] but it was only in the 1950s with the revival of interest in the problem of trade and economic development that the issue resurfaced. The standard term for the phenomenon, 'immiserising growth' was coined by Jagdish Bhagwati in 1958 but, as Corden recalled, 'Harry [Johnson] was the first to revive the case and explore it in rigorous modern terms.'[72] The theoretical issues involved in the problem were analysed on several occasions by Johnson and Bhagwati,[73] and in 1960 they clarified the Edgeworth–Nicholson controversy on the subject;[74] yet Södersten observed, 'they have had difficulty in obtaining simple answers to it. For this they should perhaps not be blamed because it is a rather involved problem and, by the way, perhaps not very important from a practical point of view'[75] – a judgement nicely reflecting Bastable's opinion. Modern theorists tend to the view that technological progress in a country's export industry may in fact improve the country's welfare if measures other than the commodity terms of trade (such as the factoral terms of trade) are considered.

EFFECTS OF FREE TRADE

Edgeworth was involved in an exchange with Bastable and Loria on the theoretical and practical implications of a suggestion by Henry Sidgwick that the removal of protection on manufactures could cause some workers either to emigrate or remain permanently unemployed – a proposition accepted by Edgeworth.[76] Sidgwick's hypothetical example was based on the operation of diminishing returns and increasing costs in agriculture. Under such circumstances, agriculture would be unable to absorb workers thrown out of employment by cheaper imports of manufactures, and therefore it was undesirable to adopt free trade. Both Edgeworth and Nicholson concurred with this conclusion which challenged the classical view that no large, freely mobile factor (such as labour) could suffer from tariff removal. Nicholson noted that although Sidgwick's proposition was contrary to the 'popular view of English political economy', it was nevertheless true that the removal of trade restrictions could force manufacturing workers into agriculture with 'disastrous results'.[77]

It was Edgeworth's support for the Sidgwick–Nicholson proposition, together with his suggestion that if a country's export industry was subject to increasing cost, its comparative cost ratio would become equal to that of its trading partner (at which point the value of mutual trade would stabilise), that invited objections from Loria and Bastable. Loria disputed Edgeworth's two propositions on the ground that if the countries' comparative cost ratios did indeed coincide, then all trade would cease, and consequently there need not be unemployment under the conditions envisaged by Edgeworth.[78] Bastable agreed with Loria, stating that:

> As trade arises out of differences in the comparative cost, it would seem to be a necessary inference that should these differences cease to exist, the trade which results from them would also come to an end. This doctrine which has been, I cannot but think, the accepted doctrine of Ricardo and his followers, is impugned by Professor Edgeworth.[79]

There was therefore no danger of unemployment from trade expansion following tariff reduction. On the contrary, Bastable asserted, free trade would

> permit of greater efficiency in production, and therefore under a state of freedom will assign to the labourer a greater amount of wages, whatever be his comparative gains when measured against those of other classes.[80]

Edgeworth's reply clarified the issues and apparently achieved a reconciliation of views. The clarification was on two points: (1) Diminishing returns to labour in agriculture, combined with a low elasticity of factor substitution due to the existence of a specific factor or a 'non-competing' labour group, imply that injury was likely to befall such a specific factor from tariff removal. (2) Trade would not cease when comparative cost ratios became equal; at that point, 'it would no longer pay to specialise any more; . . . the expansion of trade would cease – the trade would not stop, but become steady'.[81] Perhaps what Edgeworth had in mind was that in a two-good Ricardo–Mill Model, trade would cease only when the ratios of the two countries' productivity were the same in one industry as in the other and if relative real wages-rates adjust accordingly in both countries.

Bastable and Loria did not carefully distinguish between the conditions for trade and the conditions for specialisation; and this was the source of their confusion. They both seemed to believe that the condition for trade (i.e. a difference in comparative cost ratios) was the same as the condition for specialisation (i.e. for each country to specialise in the production of the commodity in which it had a comparative advantage). In other words, they implied that comparative costs alone would uniquely determine the pattern of specialisation. The mistake stems from their neglect of the demand conditions and thus the possibility of partial specialisation under the specified production assumptions. Bastable later conceded his error and also accepted Edgeworth's view that under 'this special state of things, i.e. when free, or indeed anv movement of labour and capital from manufactures to agriculture was impossible . . . the injury inflicted on manufactures by the introduction of free trade is great'.[82]

3.3 Pigou and Bickerdike

The early writings of Arthur Pigou and Charles Bickerdike on tariff theory were stimulated by the tariff reform controversy (1903). From this there emerged some notable theoretical developments, i.e. Pigou's treatment of trade, income distribution and factor movements, and Bickerdike's derivation of the optimum tariff formula.

PIGOU ON PROTECTION AND INCOME DISTRIBUTION

During this period Pigou wrote one article and two books on the theoretical issues involved in revenue and protective tariffs. In *Protective and Preferential Import Duties* (1906) he had something interesting to say about trade and income distribution. Basing his argument on the existence of 'non-competing' groups, Pigou asserted that tariff protection could increase the real income of a factor used intensively in the protected industry. To free traders who normally ignored non-competing groups, Pigou put the question:

> Is it not the better view that the great divisions of the industrial world, land, capital, brain-power, trained hand-labour muscular labour, are non-competing in the sense that, against those who would pass from one to another, there is a great gulf fixed?[83]

Pigou noted that these non-competing groups were usually combined in non-uniform proportions. A protective tariff which increases the output of industry A and reduces that of industry B can increase the proportion of the (altered) total product going to the factor used more intensively in A. Moreover, Pigou argues, even if the tariff reduces the real national dividend (income) as a whole, the absolute return to the favoured factor or non-competing group may be improved by the tariff. He says: 'The increase per cent in the share of the dividend obtained by the favoured factor might exceed the shrinkage per cent of the dividend itself.'[84] Pigou derived this conclusion from his assumption on factor immobility and varying factor proportions in production; but this anticipation of the Stolper–Samuelson treatment was preceded by Nicholson's 1897 analysis, as Chipman noted.[85]

In the same work Pigou also noted the implications for international factor movements of restrictions on trade in goods. Thus he asserted (without providing a proof) that free trade equalises factor prices internationally. A tariff which raises the share of one factor in the national dividend (real income) will create incentives for the international movement of the disadvantaged factors. The factor most likely to move will be capital, for national immigration controls restrict the freedom of movement of labour. Thus if a tariff increases the share of national income going to labour, immigration of labour may not occur, but capital, may leave the country and thus frustrate the redistributive effect of the tariff.[86]

PIGOU VERSUS BICKERDIKE ON OPTIMAL TARIFFS

In 'The Theory of Incipient Taxes' (1906) Bickerdike set out to answer the question, 'whether a country by means of taxes can get more favourable terms of exchange with foreigners in such a way as to have a net advantage after allowing for the disadvantages involved in turning production from its natural course?'[87] His answer, which he developed both in the 1906 paper and his 1907 review of Pigou's *Protective and Preferential Import Duties*, gave birth to the famous theory of the optimal tariff.

In his geometric and algebraic analyses Bickerdike used surplus concepts and the diagrams developed by Marshall and Edgeworth. He defined a country's net advantage from an incipient (or 'a small enough') tax on exports or imports and proved that except in one peculiar and unlikely case (i.e. when supply and demand for the traded commodities were inelastic in both countries), the use of such trade taxes would always increase a country's economic welfare. National gains depend only on the condition that the country possesses some advantage in international markets, either as a buyer or seller or both; and no doubt thinking of Great Britain, Bickerdike says: 'No great country is an absolutely insignificant quantity in the eyes of those who buy from it and sell to it.'[88] The gains are likely to be larger, the greater the elasticity of demand for imports in the taxing country. Bickerdike showed that trade taxes could produce benefits for the nation as a whole, not merely for individual interests or groups. He clarified the conditions under which maximum gain was possible and observed that the exclusion of tariff revenues would not affect his results. He approved of the rise in prices attendant on tariff imposition as it caused a desirable transfer of income 'from the rentier class to the community'.

Pigou's approach was altogether different. At that time (i.e. before he wrote *The Economics of Welfare* which distinguished between private and social costs and benefits) Pigou conceived of the national dividend (national income) as the sum of private dividends, and felt that any restriction on free individual bargaining (e.g. through protection) would lower aggregate real income. Pigou accepted the infant-industry argument, observing: 'Of the formal validity of List's argument there is no longer any dispute among economists.'[89] But with respect to a developed industrial country, tariffs were of no avail in securing additional long-term gains. Tariffs could of course be used to raise a given amount of revenue, and it was for this purpose that Pigou considered the respective merits of protective and non-protective duties.

Bickerdike objected to this narrow concentration on the fiscal aspect of the problem and the unwillingness to accept the possibility of improved national gains owing to the divergence of individual interests from the national interest. 'Is there no general rule,' queried Bickerdike, 'that each individual in making his own best bargain in international trade to some extent prejudices the position of his fellow countrymen, and that the maximum national advantage is not found in unrestricted individual freedom? If this is so, it would seem that a certain amount of revenue would be incidentally raised by a tariff designed primarily to maximize the advantage of international trade.'[90]

Pigou concentrated on the direct effect of a protective duty – the effect on domestic prices, the distortion of consumers' choice and the misallocation of resources – and minimised the indirect effects, notably the possibility of securing better terms of trade by means of it. In contrast, Bickerdike thought that the terms-of-trade effect was the major influence to be considered in any reckoning of the national gains, and developed the analysis of the optimal tariff to make the point;[91] and further (given Pigou's interest in raising a given revenue), that such a tax may be superior on efficiency grounds (i.e. in static welfare terms) to either an equal-yield income tax or equal-yield domestic production tax. What Pigou failed to see was that the distortion costs of the tax contemplated by Bickerdike might be more than outweighted by real-income gains from a country's ability to influence international prices.

Pigou, in his rejoinder, challenged the theoretical basis of Bickerdike's analysis and conclusions, arguing on Marshall's authority that it was illegitimate to treat a supply curve as equivalent to 'a particular expenses curve' – a fault Pigou detected in Bickerdike's procedure of integrating a supply curve to obtain total cost.[92] However, 'it was a charge which Bickerdike successfully met' as Jha observes.[93] Citing the writings of Cunynghame, Edgeworth and Pigou himself, Bickerdike replied that since it was generally agreed that an increase in the scale of production could either raise or lower the particular expenses curve, the assumption that the particular expenses curve was constant and therefore the same as the general supply curve was an equally valid one to make. Moreover, Bickerdike argued, there was no reason why the doctrine of consumers' surplus should be accepted whilst the corresponding simple measurement of costs and producers' surplus may be rejected.[94]

Edgeworth, as we have seen, regarded Bickerdike's analysis as a notable theoretical development, and later gave a masterful treatment of the argument applying Bickerdike's model to the stability problem: that is, he showed that Bickerdike's conclusion could be derived 'by the condition that the equilibrium of trade with which we are concerned is stable',[95] i.e. that the slope of the home country's reciprocal demand curve is greater in absolute value than that of the foreign country. On the basis of his 1906–7 analysis of the effects of trade taxes, Bickerdike some years later set forth the conditions for foreign exchange stability (for a regime of fluctuating exchange rates) and thereby provided the first formal framework for the 'elasticities approach' to exchange-rate devaluation.[96] The elasticities approach will be discussed in Chapter 8 (section 8.4).

3.4 Barone, Auspitz and Lieben, Pareto

(I) Enrico Barone (1859–1924)

COMPENSATION PRINCIPLE

Barone's contribution to the development of neoclassical theory was in many directions: the theory of the firm, marginal productivity theory and general equilibrium, the theory of the optimum allocation of resources in a socialist or centrally planned economy,[97] welfare economics and international trade theory. His writings on welfare economics, in particular the early sketch of the 'compensation principle', stimulated efforts to derive criteria in connection with the optimality of free trade. He was, in other words, a pioneer in the 'new welfare economics' – a welfare economics free from interpersonal comparisons of utility that was revived by Nicholas Kaldor and

Sir John Hicks in 1939.[98] The new welfare economics introduced the idea of compensation so that community indifference curves could be used. Given that some people will gain and others lose by free trade, the compensation principle attempts to find a criterion by means of which one can say that one situation is 'better' than another.

Barone first considered this problem in connection with the question: What would be the welfare effects of policy changes in a collectivist (non-competitive) regime? He wrote:

> Some individuals will be benefited, others will suffer loss; the loss to the latter will be decidedly greater than the advantage to the former, in the sense that even taking all their gain from those who have gained in the change (which takes them back to their former condition) and giving it to those who have lost by it, the latter, even with such an addition, remain in a worse situation than originally: or, indeed, what comes to the same thing, some of the latter with such an addition might be brought back to their former situation, but all of them certainly could not.[99]

Without making value judgements, but if the possibility of compensation exists, one can compare two situations and conclude that one is better than the other, e.g. a move from autarky to free trade. Can the gainers 'bribe' the losers and still be better off? Barone was doubtful that this could be achieved in a non-competitive economic system – a belief similar to that of Pareto's.

PARTIAL-EQUILIBRIUM ANALYSIS

Barone developed a partial-equilibrium analytical framework (the now familiar back-to-back diagram) which he applied to international trade in order to establish welfare results. The rigorous analysis of partial-equilibrium relations goes back to Cournot (as noted previously). Marshall used partial-equilibrium demand and supply diagrams for the analysis of some problems of domestic trade. But it was Marshall's pupil, Henry Cunynghame, who first applied (1904) such diagrams to trade between two countries.[100] The prices prevailing in each country were expressed in a common currency unit and the two diagrams placed back-to-back to share a common price axis. Cunynghame used the diagrams to illustrate the theory of international values and in particular to integrate costs of transporting commodities between countries into the traditional analysis.

Four years later (1908) Barone used similar diagrams, not only to illustrate international equilibrium but also, in addition, to say something about the welfare implications (i.e. the gains from trade).[101] He indicates how both countries gain when trade is opened up as compared with autarky. If in two countries, A and B, the pre-trade price of a particular commodity in A exceeds the price in B plus transport cost, country B will export that commodity to A upon the freeing of trade. Equilibrium will be established when country A's imports are equal to country B's exports and prices are equalised except for transport costs.

By identifying areas under the demand and supply curves bounded by the pre-trade prices, Barone concludes that in country A the gain to consumers exceeds the loss to producers, and in B the gain to producers is greater than the loss to consumers. There is thus a net gain to each country which Barone locates as the triangles enclosed by the demand and supply curves in A and B.

Barone's use of surplus analysis is different from that of Marshall's, but he arrives at very nearly the same result as that produced by modern theorists using the same construction. Barone's technique explicitly allows for any change in the terms of trade, either in the movement from protection to free trade or vice versa. However, when he goes on to examine the welfare effects of tariff imposition, he omits the tariff revenue accruing to the government and considers only the effects on consumers and producers. He thus concludes that a country can never gain from the imposition of a tariff.[102]

Years later, Stephen Enke referred to Barone's oversight and showed how a country might gain from the imposition of a tariff by maximising 'the algebraic sum of its nationals' suppliers' and consumers' surpluses plus its own revenue from duties'.[103]

The Cournot–Cunynghame–Barone diagram was also used by Schüller and Haberler and is now frequently displayed in textbook treatments of trade and tariffs. Equally widely used is a variant of the diagram designed to show the economic effects on one country if it imposes a tariff on one of its imports, on the assumption that the terms of trade are unaffected. Max Corden was perhaps the first to use such a model.[104]

FREE-TRADE EQUILIBRIUM AND THE GAINS FROM TRADE

Barone made an even more remarkable contribution to modern international trade theory: the diagrammatic representation of an economy's free-trade equilibrium and the gains from trade – a prototype of the diagram that now features in all elementary trade texts. Barone accomplished this in a long footnote accompanying the text of his 1908 treatise *Principi di economia politica.* Two diagrams were used to represent what he called, in one example, 'a curve of production indifference' and, in the other, 'a taste indifference curve' – transformation and indifference curves, in modern parlance. These two curves were then combined in a third diagram to illustrate an economy's trading equilibrium and gains from trade according to the theory of comparative costs.

This neoclassical method of modelling an economy's equilibrium under autarky and with trade only came into vogue in the 1930s through the works of Lerner, Viner and Leontief – at least twenty-three years after Barone had first figured it out. Barone's hitherto unacknowledged role in fashioning this invaluable pedagogical device has recently been brought to light and to the notice of the profession by Andrea Maneschi and William Thweatt.[105]

(II) Auspitz and Lieben

Rudolf Auspitz (1837–1906) and Richard Lieben (1842–1919) – two Austrians, the first the owner of a sugar refinery, the other a banker – were widely acclaimed developers of early neoclassical theory in a book published in 1889.[106] Their analysis of economic surplus was based on Dupuit's notion of 'relative utility' and therefore not grounded on cardinal utility. Theirs was the second (after Jules Dupuit, 1844) precise definition of consumer's surplus. In demand theory, Auspitz and Lieben were also the first formally to identify complementarity (i.e. the relationship that exists when the utility of one good depends on how much of another good is being consumed) with the sign of the cross derivative $\partial^2 U/\partial q_i \partial q_j$. Thus commodities i and j are defined as complements if $\partial^2 U/\partial q_i \partial q_j > 0$ in a utility function $U = U(q_1, \ldots q_n)$ where the qs are the amounts consumed.

OFFER CURVES AND INDIFFERENCE CURVES

Auspitz and Lieben drew indifference contours (the way they are now drawn) which they called 'curves of constant satisfaction' (*kurven Konstanter Befriedigung*). These curves bear a resemblance to Edgeworth's 'no gain from trade' curves; but since they had apparently not read Edgeworth they must be regarded as independent discoverers of the indifference curve concept. Their work probably had some influence on Irving Fisher. They also devised curves similar to Marshall's offer curves,[107] i.e. total demand curves in terms of money values based on the assumption that money has constant marginal utility.

They combined these curves to show for each country the gains from trade (indicated by the vertical distance between the free-trade equilibrium point and the two indifference curves) and the welfare effects of a single duty on imports.[108] Since the analysis is restricted to the case of a single commodity, the authors' construction is akin to the analytical model used by Cournot, Cunynghame and Barone.

As a method of measuring gains from trade or losses from trade restriction, Viner finds it 'superior to Marshall's because of its use of the indifference curve as an element in the measurement'.[109] Auspitz and Lieben also used this method to state an early version of the optimum tariff argument which, as we noted earlier, Edgeworth in his usual courteous manner duly praised – although Pareto, then (1892) a firm free trader, took exception to it.

(III) Pareto

OPTIMALITY CRITERION

Vilfredo Pareto (1848–1923) was, of course, the great pioneer of modern welfare economics and the optimality criterion named after him[110] – a situation in which it is impossible to increase the welfare of one individual without decreasing that of another. Although not universally accepted, the criterion has exercised an enormous influence on contemporary welfare analysis, including the normative side of international trade theory. Indeed, much of the extensive literature on welfare criteria has been concerned with matters arising in trade theory. The optimality criterion relates to the simultaneous achievement of optimum efficiency in production and exchange when certain well-known marginal conditions are satsified.

Pareto optimality describes the essential welfare properties of a general equilibrium system of competitive markets and thus relates to the traditional concerns of writers on the gains from trade. The argument for free trade has always been that with appropriate compensation, free trade results in an improvement in economic welfare. It puts the world out on the global production-possibility frontier. The theoretical underpinning for this belief is provided by the Pareto optimality criterion; for it is easily shown that free-trade equilibrium achieves a Pareto optimum or, conversely, that a Pareto optimum implies or denotes a free-trade equilibrium.[111]

For neoclassical economics in general, consumer theory and the theory of general competitive equilibrium are fundamental. They deal, in Pareto's words, with 'the opposition between men's tastes and the obstacles to satisfying them';[112] and it was Pareto who first synthesised it all by drawing together the theoretical threads spun by Cournot, Walras, Edgeworth, Auspitz and Lieben, etc. His personal input into the synthesis, the woven fabric, is impressive enough: the perception that the theory of general competitive equilibrium can dispense with the notion of measurable utility (in contrast to Edgeworth's view that interpersonal comparisons of utility could be made on a more or less firm objective basis), and that provided certain conditions are fulfilled, such an equilibrium yields a maximum of ophelimity or welfare.

PARETO'S PROBLEM

Pareto occupies a prominent niche in the pantheon of neoclassical economists and it is therefore of interest to hear what he has to say on some points in trade theory.

Pareto had a problem with Ricardo's famous analogy between the benefits of international trade and the gains from individual barter where two persons specialise and exchange hats and shoes. Pareto took this to mean that Ricardo's illustration of the mutual beneficiality of free trade was premised on complete specialisation in production by each country. In that case, argues Pareto, it can be shown that Ricardo's conclusion (that free trade increases the world's welfare) is not generally true. Only if the total output of each good is increased after specialisation will Ricardo's conclusion hold good; otherwise, for example if specialisation leads to a reduction in the world's output of one of the goods, even though the output of the other good has increased, it is impossible to say whether specialisation has increased or decreased world welfare without taking tastes into account, i.e. demand, as specified in a utility function. Pareto constructed hypothetical arithmetical examples to show that specialisation could indeed lead to such a result and thus Ricardo's presumption must therefore be false.[113]

Pareto's observations have merit as a rebuttal of the proposition that complete specialisation is necessarily mutually beneficial as compared to no specialisation or partial specialisation; but as Viner points out quoting textual extracts, Ricardo never placed any emphasis on complete specialisation in his model of comparative cost. Moreover, Pareto's counter-example of unprofitable specialisation would not be observed in practice since it was not a competitive equilibrium: that is, specialisation would not be carried to the point where the reduction in the value of one country's output was uncompensated through free trade[114] – i.e. citizens will normally obtain their desired level of the other good through imports, thus raising utility.

Pareto had obviously not read Mill on this point. If he had, he would have noticed that Mill provided (admittedly with the help of a special demand assumption) conditions for full specialisation in both countries and also for cases where one country would not be fully specialised.[115]

Pareto's problem is nowadays resolved by way of the concept of an efficient point in activity analysis. Such analysis proves that the value of world output is maximised only if every country maximises the value of its own output, as indicated above. Indeed, a free-trade equilibrium in the classical model corresponds to the model of competitive equilibrium that is Pareto-optimal.[116]

GENERAL EQUILIBRIUM

Pareto was the first to build a general-equilibrium model of world trade and production. Adopting a closed-economy Walrasian framework, he added extra equations to balance the additional variables required for the solution of trade equilibrium. The counting of endogeneous variables (unknowns) and equations, however, gives no guarantee of the existence of a solution and, as Haberler observes, Pareto 'did not get beyond a more or less formal equation system which can hardly be used for purposes of analysis'.[117]

General-equilibrium models of classical trade theory were developed in the 1930s and 1940s (by Yntema and Mosak).[118] These models were fruitful precursors of others to follow, in that they explored the implications of multi-commodity, multi-country trade and advanced the discussion of stable and unstable international markets beyond the Marshallian treatment.

THE DEFINITION OF COSTS

Pareto, like Barone, objected to the classical economists' treatment of costs as 'real' or labour costs, especially when these were defined in terms of 'abstinence' or 'sacrifice' (e.g. Cairnes). Pareto preferred to work with money costs instead of real costs, but recognised that for many interesting problems in trade theory some real-cost notion of costs was necessary. He held, however, that scarce factors of production were combined to yield the highest level of utility or *ophélimité* and it was preferable to define costs of production (*coûts en ophélimité*) both in terms of subjective disutility and in relative terms, as alternatives forgone. By so doing, a fixed factor of production, like land, that incurred no subjective disutility could be treated as an 'indirect cost' (i.e. opportunity cost, in terms of forgone output) and all the other costs referred to by the classicals as 'real costs' could be labelled the 'direct costs'.[119]

Viner seemed to have accepted this clarification of the meaning of 'real costs', but Caves writes that 'neither Viner nor Pareto makes it clear what significance the result has'.[120] Later, the Austrian notion of opportunity cost replaced the use of real costs in trade theory. This brought the analysis of international value in line with general value theory.

PARETO ON PROTECTION

In his analysis of tariffs, Pareto does not use surplus analysis or the partial-equilibrium diagrammatics of Barone but arrives at the same conclusion as Marshall and Barone. A tariff causes consumers' loss to be greater than producers' gain and therefore 'we can *grosso-modo*, and as a first approximation, conclude that every protective tariff is the cause of a destruction of wealth within the country which levies this duty on a good'.[121] Conversely, the removal of a tariff by causing a transfer of resources from the import-competing industry to the more efficient export industry augments wealth, since under free trade the same or a greater consumption bundle can be obtained at lower factor cost. The gains are even greater if the contracting import-competing industry is subject to increasing production cost and the export industry enjoys decreasing costs.

Pareto is critical of the infant-industry argument for protection. He admits that an *a priori* case can be made out for temporary protection, but in his usual terse, crisp style says, 'there is no known example of it'. 'All the industries born under a system of protection have always sought more and more protection, and the day has never come when they declared they could do without it.'[122] He thus accepts the argument in principle but condemns it in practice – a position not dissimilar to that of his English counterparts.

When he considers the social effects of protection his attitude is less hostile, but this serves to reveal how confused he was on the issue. Here we have an example of the confusions and ambiguities characteristic of his writings.[123] Consider the following passages:

> Industrial protection in agricultural countries, and free trade in an industrial country, both have the effect of developing industry . . .
>
> From all the preceding it can be seen how complex is the practical and synthetic problem of knowing whether protection is preferable to free trade, or vice versa . . .
>
> . . . in every era and for every country, protection is detrimental and free trade advantageous.[124]

With remarkable frankness, Pareto confessed his own confusion. In a footnote he revealed that he had declared in 1887: 'the social effects and their economic consequences . . . are the primary issues involved and, in my opinion, the only ones which could sometimes raise serious doubts about the more or less considerable usefulness of free trade, in certain cases'.[125]

It is possible to rationalise Pareto's confusion over the issue of free trade versus protection at the time he wrote (1906) in terms of the evolution of his own personal political opinions. Terence Hutchison provides the clue: 'Pareto started as an ardent economic liberal, campaigning for free trade . . . and propagating the kind of ardent Cobdenite sentiments which he would later have treated with the deepest contempt.'[126]

However, there was one positive result of political experiences and frustrations working on a mind as acutely sociological as Pareto's: a thoroughly modern-looking socio-political theory of tariff formation – the general notion that in a democracy tariffs are shaped by rent-seeking behaviour of interested parties (lobbyists and politicians). The concerns of this study go back to Adam Smith's comments on mercantilism as a rent-seeking society; but Pareto was exceptional among the early neoclassical economists in taking an interest in it.[127] Pareto also had something to say about the income-distribution effects of protection a few years after Bastable's famous chapter on 'International Trade and Income Distribution'.[128]

4 The Tariff Reform Debate (1903)

INTRODUCTION

In 1852 Queen Victoria remarked to her uncle, the King of the Belgians, 'Protection is quite gone.'[1] A generation later, however, a chorus of voices rose up in Britain against the continuance of the policy of free trade. At the time Victoria wrote, the British economy entered a period lasting twenty years of unparalleled prosperity. Leading economists attributed the mid-Victorian boom to the enlightened policy of free trade. In 1865 John Stuart Mill referred to the 'flush of prosperity occasioned by free trade'. William Stanley Jevons, in the same year, ascribed the buoyant economic conditions to 'the unprecedented commercial reforms of the last twenty years'.[2]

The onset of the depression in agriculture (1874) and the milder general recession shattered confidence in the immutability of British industrial progress and triggered a reaction against free trade. It altered perceptions of Great Britain's situation in the world economy. The challenges to free-trade doctrine and the debate on the state of the British economy ranged over matters such as the growth of foreign competition, the rise of protectionism, the competitiveness and efficiency of the British economy, imperial preference and the role of the Empire; and the implications of all these factors for Great Britain's superpower status and its industrial future. The views of the economists were canvassed, and many were eager to participate publicly in the debate. The national controversy erupted at a time when the economists were themselves involved in an often fierce debate over the nature and purpose of economics – a debate which was intensified by Marshall's efforts to seek a consensus and thereby establish the academic status of economics as a recognised, scientific discipline. The economists found themselves in disarray when confronted with the Tariff Reform issue. Although a majority was behind the free traders, the protectionists' case was ably represented by several academic economists, particularly the economic historians. The free traders won the national debate; and although divisions within the ranks of the economists were exposed, international trade theory benefited in terms of a sharpening of the analysis.

There were two phases to the debate: (1) The Fair Trade Movement of the 1880s and (2) Joseph Chamberlain's Tariff Reform campaign of 1903. The earlier phase was a trial run, a warm-up to the more serious 1903 challenge to free-trade orthodoxy and practice in which the economists on each side were ranged in front of, behind and at the side of the politicians, publicists and vested interests. We shall focus on the economists' involvement in the 1903 Tariff Reform debate, but before doing so it will be helpful to survey briefly the historical background and indicate the highlights in the controversial saga.

As indicated above, the reaction against free trade in Great Britain stemmed from the 1874 agricultural depression and the less severe general depression lasting from 1873 to 1896. Some economic historians baulk at the use of the terms 'general depression' and 'Great Depression' to describe this period. They dispute the connotation, since it suggests that the period was somehow special in terms of the pronounced downturn of leading economic indicators and that Britain and several other countries faced a uniform pattern of economic problems unlike those experienced in the preceding and subsequent decades. However, the phrase 'general depression' remains serviceable as a description of the opinion of contemporaries and will do in the present context. The world decline in the price of wheat stemmed from the rapid expansion of the American rail network which substantially reduced the cost of moving wheat to the ports. Similar developments occurred in Eastern Europe where the vast Ukrainian wheat fields were connected to the Crimean ports. In addition, the iron-clad steamship reduced transatlantic freight rates. Partly in response to the depression but also for budgetary reasons connected with the finance of defence expenditures and the belief that protection was an effective method to spur industrialisation, tariff barriers went up around the world. British farmers felt they had good grounds for complaint against the rigours of free trade, and industrialists badly hit by foreign – in particular German and American – competition claimed to have been disadvantaged by 'one-sided free trade' owing to the failure of other countries to commit themselves to free trade. The United States never adopted free trade, but up to the eve of the Civil War in 1861 the southern states had succeeded in moderating the worst excesses of American tariff policy, so that by 1857 the United States had the lowest tariff level since 1816. At the end of the Civil War, however, the urgent need for federal revenue and pressure from manufacturing interests led to an increase in customs duties culminating in the highly protectionist McKinley tariff of 1890 and Dingley tariff of 1897 (on wool, iron and steel and other manufactured items).[3]

The Cobden–Chevalier commercial treaty (1860) between Great Britain and France marked the final triumph of British free-trade diplomacy. It led over the next sixteen years to a whole series of commercial treaties embodying the MFN (most-favoured-nation) clause involving France, Belgium, the German *Zollverein*, Italy and Great Britain. However, in the 1880s, as defensive measures against the depression in agriculture, France imposed tariffs on grains and in 1892 the Méline tariff was enacted which made France highly protectionist. Until the agricultural depression, Bismarck and the Prussian junkers were free traders. The external tariff of the *Zollverein* was set to raise revenue and the protective element was minimal. The altered economic conditions prompted the famous alliance of 'rye and iron' (i.e. the political compact between the Junkers and the iron magnates) which was backed by Bismarck, who added his own call for protective tariffs to safeguard German trade.[4] The change in policy was signalled by the resignation of Rudolf von Delbrück, the free-trade Prussian minister and chief architect of German economic policy. The Tariff Act of 1879 (adopted on 12 June 1879 introduced duties on agricultural products, iron and other industrial goods, and increased the tariff on textiles after fourteen years of free trade. In 1885 Germany became even more protectionist. Italy, Austria–Hungary and Russia followed the protectionist powers – notable exceptions to this trend were Holland, Denmark and Switzerland.

In the British Empire, the colonies with responsible governments were at least as protectionist as Germany. Customs duties were at first imposed primarily to raise revenue, but they became increasingly protective as the manufacturing interests exerted pressure on colonial legislatures. In 1846 an Act of the British parliament allowed the colonies to withdraw the preferences they had hitherto been forced to accord British goods. They were conceded the right to enact their own tariff legislation and therefore free to erect barriers against imports of goods from the mother country. In Canada, Alexander Galt's tariff of 1859 raised duties on manufactures to around 20 per cent, designed to provide funds for railway development. Sheffield manufacturers complained nevertheless that the measure was blatantly protectionist. The Canadian tariff was the first in a long list of such colonial enactments – South Africa (1866–7), Victoria (1877), etc.

At the time of the Great Exhibition of 1851, it was natural for Britons who thought about the country's role in the world economy to succumb to the comforting belief that the existing international division of labour would endure indefinitely, i.e. other countries would continue to provide Britain with food and raw materials in exchange for manufactured goods. Indeed, it was the scenario envisaged by Ricardo in his attack on the Corn Laws as distinct from the predictions of his formal model of comparative advantage. But there were those (e.g. Malthus, in particular) who, even in Ricardo's time, doubted this optimistic vision of Britain's role. Several writers, often on impressionistic or intuitive grounds but sometimes also on the basis of comparative-cost logic, expressed fears that Britain's industrial and trading supremacy would be eroded in the course of time by the spread of industrialisation abroad aided by the diffusion of technology, the appeal of protectionist arguments and the greater resource potential in some foreign countries. The consequences for Britain, such writers felt, would inevitably be a retardation of the rate of economic growth, falling export shares in world markets and even increasing penetration of the home market for manufactured goods.

From the 1880s there were unmistakable signs that these fears were not simply pessimistic fantasies but living reality, reflecting a fundamental and irreversible shift in the pattern of international specialisation and trade.

Great Britain lost her position as the leading manufacturing power to the United States in the 1880s, and by 1900 was also overtaken by Germany in terms of percentage shares of world industrial output. In pig-iron and steel production – regarded by contemporaries as a vital indicator not only of industrial prowess but also of military and naval might – Britain's dominance came to an end, and by 1905 slipped to third position after the United States and Germany.[5] The pace of technological innovation faltered after 1870. Productivity fell from 1.87 per cent per annum between 1860 and 1880 to 0.25 per cent per annum until 1914. From the 1870s there was a deceleration in the overall rate of economic growth from 3.5 per cent to 1.7 per cent per annum by the turn of the century. The commodity composition of British exports and their principal market destinations made them vulnerable both to protectionism and changing demand patterns. The staples (coal, cotton, iron and steel) still accounted for more than 70 per cent of British exports in 1880. After running at the rate of 3.3 per cent during the mid-Victorian boom years, the rate of growth of British manufactured exports fell to only 1.6 per cent per annum between 1873 and 1899, and there was a relative decline in British exports to Europe and the United States. British imports slowed slightly but continued at a rate (4.5 per cent) much in excess of export growth.

The sluggish growth of British exports, not only to Europe (which reflected protectionism) but in markets like Latin America, the Middle and Far East, was due to German competition. Partly as a consequence of structural and factor-endowment changes in the late nineteenth-century world economy, increased output abroad, the rise of protectionism and intensified competition, the British share of world trade in manufactures fell from 37 per cent in 1883 to 28.4 per cent in 1900. but to some extent it reflected underlying structural weaknesses of the British economy itself: a marked failure to match the levels of investment in human capital undertaken by international competitors – even before the turn of the century, both Germany and the United States were spending higher proportions of GNP on education and training. This failure meant that Britain remained heavily reliant on existing product ranges and techniques of production, and therefore met with relative lack of success in technologically advanced goods (chemicals, industrial equipment, electricals, cameras, etc.) – the products of the so-called 'second industrial revolution'.

From the evidence revealed in his detailed study of human capital formation in nineteenth-century Britain, Jeffrey Williamson (1981) concluded that 'it may well be said that the "failure" of British industry in the late 19th century can be laid at the doorstep of inadequate investment in human capital . . . compared to her main competitors in world markets'.[6] This suggestion has recently been supported by a superb econometric study of the comparative advantage basis of UK trade in manufactures over the period 1910–35 (including a tentative study of the earlier period 1870–80) based on the human-capital version of the Heckscher–Ohlin theory (Crafts and Thomas, 1986).[7] Ever since Leontief's pioneering study of the factor content of US trade it has been clear that a test of the H–O theory can validly be used to infer the factor-endowment characteristics of trade between two or more countries. This point was understood by Marshall (1919), who asserted, on the basis of a modified version of classical trade theory, that 'one of the best indicators of the nature and extent of a country's leadership is found in the character of goods which she exports, and of those which she imports'.[8]

Crafts and Thomas found that the UK trade pattern over the period 1870–1935 exhibited the characteristics of 'having a comparative disadvantage in goods intensive in the use of human capital', and that 'the pattern of exporting manufactures intensive in the use of unskilled labour appears characteristics of the United Kingdom in her "pre-eminent" period right through to the 1930s'. The authors concluded that 'Britain's handicap in the latter part of the century was a scarcity of the human capital which was an essential input to the technologically progressive product-cycle industries that dominated the Second Industrial Revolution.'[9]

Historians are far from unanimous on the interpretation of the factors behind Britain's relative economic decline from the last quarter of the nineteenth century, despite the wealth of accumulated information. Evidence is still being heard, and the final verdict is yet to come in on what has been called that 'critical inquest into the state of the British economy'.

Those involved in the political and economic debate were bereft of some of the vital data bearing on the issue and they lacked, of course, our perspective. The debate stimulated research into various aspects of the economic problem. At the turn of the century, that part of trade theory known as the theory of commercial policy was fairly well developed, and the economists therefore had a very serviceable tool of analysis; but both the theory and its empirical applications benefited from the need to provide answers to the questions thrown up by the debate. But, as in all great critical national controversies, the agenda of the debate was far wider than the usual boundaries of international trade theory and policy. It was set within the context of the growing foreign rivalries and imperialism of the 1880s. For the economists who participated in it, the debate was therefore an occasion to ventilate their prejudices, fears and ideological dispositions; in addition, it afforded them an opportunity to offer advice on technical matters within their professional competence. Before moving on to the economists' perceptions of, and answers to, the question before the public, brief account must first be given of how tariff reform became a political issue.

TARIFF REFORM AS A POLITICAL ISSUE

In 1879 (the year German tariff policy changed) Gustav Schmoller noted: 'The times of boom, of increasing exports, of new openings of overseas markets, are the natural free trade epochs, while the reverse is true in times of foreign slumps, of depressions, of crisis.'[10] This observation has since become part of the conventional wisdom, and it aptly applies to the anti-free-trade agitation in Britain under the banner of 'Fair Trade' during the 1880s. The leading figure in the movement was Farrer Ecroyd. In an 1881 article, he claimed: 'Our manufacturers are more and more excluded from the markets of the civilised world, not by fair competition, but by oppressive tariffs.'[11] He proposed: (1) the imposition of retaliatory tariffs (10 per cent) on all foreign manufactured goods in order to secure tariff reductions on British exports and to safeguard the British share of international trade; (2) that raw materials be admitted duty free; (3) the imposition of a 10 per cent duty on foreign foodstuffs whilst allowing duty-free entry of Empire food products. Farrer Ecroyd claimed that his proposals were not protectionist, but were designed to enable British manufacturers to capture a larger share of the domestic market and stimulate Empire trade. He expected food and manufactured goods' prices to be increased only slightly.

In 1881 a National Fair Trade League was formed. The movement gained support from manufacturers suffering from foreign competition (e.g. West Riding woollen and worsted clothing manufacturers) as well as landlords and some members of the Tory party. The Royal Commission on the Depression of Trade and Industry (1885–6) supported free trade, but a minority report recommended the 'fair trade' solution by invoking the unemployment argument. 'Safeguarding', 'reciprocity' and 'fair trade' were the slogans of the movement; but the fair traders failed to win mass support for their programme. They lacked the leadership capable of focusing the issues at the political level, and, in addition, changes in national political and economic circumstances pushed the free trade issue into the background – the Home Rule for Ireland issue and the trade revival in the late 1880s. Ironically, it was Joseph Chamberlain (the advocate twenty years later of Imperial Preference and general protection) who most tellingly undermined the credibility of the fair traders' proposals by emphasising their consequences for an urban working-class population, i.e. the rise of food prices. This he did in his capacity as President of the Board of Trade, 1880–85.

The story of Chamberlain's conversion to tariff reform and his crusading campaign to rouse national sentiment in favour of imperial preference, protection for British industry and social reform, is well known, and only the highlights need to be recounted here.

Chamberlain launched his 'raging and tearing' campaign in Birmingham on 15 May 1903. He called for the abandonment of Britain's longstanding adherence to the policy of general free trade in favour of a system of imperial preference designed to achieve three objectives: (1) imperial economic unity; (2) the provision of reveue to finance expenditures on social reform (e.g. old-age pensions); and (3) the reduction of unemployment through the protection of British industry.[12] Four months later, Chamberlain resigned as Colonial Secretary from Arthur Balfour's cabinet in order to have a free hand in his battle against free trade. He and his supporters in the Tariff Reform League conducted the campaign at public meetings up and down the country, in the daily press and in innumerable periodical articles and books. The defenders of the status quo did likewise.

The tariff reformers failed to convince the public; in fact, as a writer recently put it, 'the people were not interested',[13] and the Liberal landslide victory at the 1906 elections put an end to the political battle. But the issue remained unresolved, and the arguments continued right up to the outbreak of war in 1914. Britain's departure from free trade had to wait until the slump of the 1930s.[14] How the economists responded to the national controversy, what arguments they used to justify their various positions, is the subject of the next section.

JEVONS'S WARNING (1865)

The first thing to notice when considering the economists' involvement in the tariff reform controversy is the fact that they were not unprepared for the subject of the debate. As long ago as 1865, in a book which attracted much attention, William Stanley Jevons warned his readers of the certain threat to Britain's industrial, commercial and military supremacy owing to the rapid exhaustion of the country's coal reserves. Coal-reserve constraints within the next half-century or so would check Britain's industrial progress, its population growth and general living standards.

Comparative advantage in manufactures would shift to other countries better endowed with natural resources (principally coal) and Britain would slip from first place among the ranks of industrial powers. Jevons backed up his discomforting prognostication with a wealth of statistical analyses on depletion rates, estimates of coal reserves and price projections for coal. From the evidence he concluded that: 'We cannot long continue our present rate of progress . . . So far, then, as our wealth and progress depend on the superior command of coal, we must not only stop – we must go back.'[15] He predicted that as coal reserves vanish, undermining Britain's comparative advantage in manufacturing, 'America will tend to supplant us in the European market for iron and other crude materials, and in all parts of the world in the market for textiles and useful manufactured articles in general'.[16] There was also a potential threat from countries in the Empire, as they industrialised. Was relief then to be sought in a retreat back to protection? Jevons could hardly sanction such a drastic change of policy; for as a writer recently put it, for Jevons, 'free trade was an unquestioned and almost unquestionable article of faith'.[17] Jevons did in fact recognise that it was an unpleasant choice: 'It would seem,' he said, 'that we have placed ourselves in a painful dilemma; we must either retract . . . the principles we have so recently adopted, or else we must submit to see our material resources exhausted in a shorter period than could have been thought possible.'[18]

His own investigation implied that the unwavering pursuit of free trade would hasten Britain's eventual decline as a manufacturing nation: 'Take away that resource [coal] and our expectations from free trade must be of a very minor character.' Yet he would not counsel the abandonment of free trade (through, for example, the imposition of an export tax or ban on coal exports).

Jevons's position remained steadfast years later when the effects of the post-1874 depression were being felt: 'Freedom of trade,' he wrote, 'may be regarded as a fundamental axiom of political economy; . . . though even axioms may be mistaken . . . We may welcome bona fide investigation into the state of trade, and the causes of the present depression, but we can no more expect to have our opinions on free trade altered by such an investigation, than the Mathematical Society would expect to have axioms of Euclid disproved during the investigation of a complex problem.'[19]

THE ECONOMISTS AND TARIFF REFORM

Jevons's faith in free trade was shared by the next generation of mainstream economists; but an influential and vocal minority supported tariff reform. In 1903, it has been said, the entire country was called upon to take sides 'over an abstract not to say highly technical economic theory'[20] – the theory of commercial policy as it was called, or, more specifically, a choice between free trade and protection.

Needless to say, the outcome was not determined solely or even mainly on that simple basis. Nevertheless, arguments from international trade theory did figure prominently in the debate, as Chamberlain's dramatic political initiative did put Free Trade firmly 'in the dock'. As usual in such momentous national debates, economic arguments were combined with much rhetoric and play on national fears and sentiments. This ploy was particularly marked in the case of the tariff reformers who often deployed economic arguments in support of wider political and strategic objectives, e.g. imperial unity and security, social reform, etc. The free traders (including the majority of economists) had an easier time. Since by common consent the free-trade policy was innocent unless proved guilty, the defenders could rely on the traditional argument developed over the previous hundred years. But they were sometimes forced to deal with the broader issues raised by their critics. In facing up to this, they were stimulated into further theoretical developments which led to a much clearer definition of assumptions and conditions under which a free-trade policy would achieve a particular outcome in terms of economic welfare.

In this account we are concerned only with the economic arguments as they related to international trade theory; and in this connection shall examine the contributions of Marshall, Giffen, Pigou, Bastable (free-trade advocates), and Ashley, Cunningham, Hewins, Price (tariff reformers). In general, free trade found support among the theoretical economists, whilst the most ardent advocates of protection were the economic historians; but there were exceptions – for example, Clapham (historian) supported free trade, but Price (economist) dissented from his colleagues.

Throughout the summer months, almost from the start of the Tariff Reform campaign in May 1903, William Hewins, first Director of the London School of Economics, published a series of anonymously signed articles (seventeen in all) in *The Times* in support of Chamberlain's proposals.[21] Hewins became a protectionist at the time of 'Fair Trade' agitation when he expressed deep concern about the effects of foreign competition which he felt posed a serious threat to British industrial supremacy, employment, prosperity and Britain's world-power status. He described himself as a 'constructive imperialist' and felt that tariffs were necessary to revive British industry and consolidate the Empire.

Hewins's arguments for protection were usually non-economic ones, as for instance his attempt to turn the traditional infant-industry argument into a 'senile' industry argument for protection, claiming that protection 'in the modern sense is meant the use by the Government of special forms of regulation or restraint, particularly import duties and analogous fiscal expedients, in order to encourage or to maintain essential industries which must be determined by the requirements of public policy'.[22] Similarly he tried to argue, contrary to traditional reasoning, that protection would increase economic welfare, on the ground that 'the protectionist policy, properly administered, will bring about a balance of economic activity, involving a higher maximum of efficiency to the community as a whole and a more equitable distribution between the economic groups'.[23] Hewins's meaning here is clear, but the statement is very unspecific in terms of economic content. Evidently, Hewins is here dwelling on the political and social benefits of protection and playing down the role of net economic welfare gains. Protection may, indeed, bring about a better 'balance of economic activity', but no economist can seriously argue that the policy brings about 'a higher maximum of economic efficiency' (under the standard assumptions of full employment, factor mobility, etc.). Trade policy, no doubt, has the capacity to change the free-trade domestic income distribution, but the question of the 'equity' of the altered income distribution surely involves non-economic considerations, and therefore a matter of socio-political judgement. Hewins's stance was thus vulnerable to criticisms on purely economic grounds.

Marshall declined an invitation to answer Hewins's criticisms of free-trade policy in the columns of *The Times*. However, on 15 August 1903, *The Times* published a letter signed by fourteen leading economists rejecting Chamberlain's proposals and affirming support for free trade. The letter, which became known as the 'manifesto of the fourteen professors', was drafted by Edgeworth, and the signatories included Marshall, Cannan, Bowley and Pigou.[24] A summary of this letter is warranted, since it has been called 'a very important historical document showing the attitude of British economists to the question of commercial policy and its relation to recent theoretical developments'.[25]

The economists expressed their sympathy for Chamberlain's aims, i.e. imperial unity, but objected to the fiscal means (i.e. preferential tariffs) for attaining that objective. Specifically, they feared that 'any system of preferential tariffs would most probably lead to the reintroduction of protection into the fiscal system of the United Kingdom'. Protection would be attended by ineradicable evils both material and moral, among the latter being 'the loss of purity in politics, the unfair advantage given to those who wield the powers of jobbery and corruption, unjust distribution of wealth, and the growth of sinister interests'. Refuting the protectionists' arguments, the economists made five observations:

(1) They denied that an increase in imports meant more unemployment.
(2) A tax on food imports would be unlikely to raise wages; what it would most probably do would be to lower real wages.
(3) An import tax on wheat would injure British consumers since its price would rise; the injury would be less, to the extent that 'a small proportion of the burden being thrown permanently on the foreign producer'. But they regarded this lightening of the burden as 'very improbable' under existing circumstances.
(4) It was impossible, they believed, to devise any tariff regulation which could simultaneously protect British agriculture and expand Colonial food production without injuring British consumers.
(5) To the argument that although the public would suffer from higher food prices they would secure an equivalent benefit from the distribution of the tariff revenues collected by the government (e.g. through more social expenditures), the economists countered with the observation that the argument ignored the welfare loss from the interference with the free circulation of goods, i.e. the detriment caused by 'diverting industry from the course which it would otherwise have taken'. In addition, the government tariff revenues gain would be small compared with consumers' losses, since consumers would have to pay nearly the whole tax on all imported wheat, whilst the government would only collect the taxes on foreign wheat.

The economists' manifesto was an attempt to mount a solid, authoritative front against Chamberlain's proposals; but it backfired. It particularly enraged the tariff reformers; and far from stifling academic dissent, it actually intensified the controversy. It served to revive the old antagonisms over the role of 'facts' in economic analysis and policy which raged during the 1890s; and since Hewins had revealed that there were at least two sides to the question, the manifesto destroyed the appearance of consensus that the authors wished to convey to the public at large.[26]

Langford Price, a former pupil and protégé of Marshall, was one of the few economists of non-professorial rank asked by Edgeworth to sign the manifesto. Price declined and sent his letter of refusal to *The Times*, whose editor printed it just below the manifesto. In his letter to Edgeworth, Price alleged that the manifesto was a misleading statement since the details of tariff reform were not then known, yet the economists dwelt at length on the costs of the proposed policy without mentioning the costs of the status quo. He called for a Royal Commission to investigate the matter.[27]

William Ashley, the noted economic historian and occupant of the newly created chair of Commerce at Birmingham University, deplored the fact that 'a majority of British economists have signed a pronouncement intended to veto any serious reconsideration of the commercial policy of this country'.[28]

Up to the time of the economists' manifesto, Price, who had adopted a conciliatory stance in the methodological dispute, now felt free to voice his dissent from free-trade, *laissez-faire* orthodoxy in more forthright language. He severely criticised Pigou's *The Riddle of the Tariff*, and in 1906 had another swipe at the manifesto, declaring that at a time when serious cracks were appearing in the theoretical foundations upon which 'the free trade dogma' was raised, 'an appeal was made by interested politicians to an authority to which they had not been accustomed for some while to pay much deference, and professors were invited to confirm the populace in their traditional beliefs. Free trade was presented as correct economics.'[29]

The economic historians – Hewins, Ashley and Cunningham – were of course the principal critical dissenters from the free-trade orthodoxy represented by Marshall and his followers, and they intensified their onslaught after the appearance of the manifesto. Referring to the economists' démarche, Cunningham voiced popular feeling when he observed: 'The professors who protested that there could be no change of circumstances which made it desirable to reconsider the trading policy of the country did much to discredit the scientific character of the doctrine they taught.[30]

The dissenters were much influenced by the German Historical School (Ashley studied with Schmoller in Berlin), Arnold Toynbee, Cliffe Leslie and, on matters of trade and protection, by Friedrich List. They were particularly impressed by List's ideas on 'productive powers' and 'stages of development' and the relation of these to tariff policy. Thus Ashley admitted that Chamberlain's proposals would increase food prices in the short run, but that was a small price to pay for the revival of British industry which would be the long-run benefit of protection. List had convincingly maintained, he said, that 'the question of the productive powers of a country and their possible development is far more important than that of present values; it might be well worth while to incur a loss for a time in order to secure a more than proportionate future gain'.[31] Cunningham agreed with List's analysis of the role of free trade in the maintenance of Britain's industrial and commercial hegemony and the reasons which led other countries to defend their nascent industries through tariff protection; but Cunningham declared that circumstances had altered for England and hence free trade was 'no longer the appropriate policy for the nation to follow'.[32] Ashley agreed with this position. He held that economic theories were only true relative to time and circumstances, i.e. economic 'laws' and doctrines were always relative and hypothetical. Economic theories reflected economic circumstances and conditions, and what was sound economic advice at one time might be totally inappropriate for another age. Conversely, old doctrines deemed to be erroneous by modern canons of economics might, in fact, have had value and relevance in their time. The policy of free trade was clearly unsuited for Britain's present stage of evolution, and hence protectionism in some form could not be ruled out as an alternative simply on the ground that Adam Smith and Ricardo had rejected it for their time and circumstance.

The employment argument for protection figured prominently in the writings of the dissenters, and much use was made of it by Chamberlain and his supporters both in the press and in public meetings. Protection, it was felt, would be a defence against displacement of labour caused by import penetration, as well as a device for securing regular employment of labour. In this context, the mobility of labour and full employment assumptions of orthodox theory were called into question. Ashley, for instance, contended that one of the principal benefits of a programme of protective tariffs and imperial preference would be a guarantee of regular and secure employment for the working classes. Such attempts to link tariff reform with unemployment conflicted of course with the professors' explicit denial that a rise in imports brought a corresponding fall in domestic employment. Despite Charles Booth's suggestion that 'the interests of the mass of the people, and of the poorest not the least, are found in regularity of employment more than in cheapness of food',[33] the TUC was more alarmed at the prospect of an increase in the price of food, and lent its support to the free traders.

At the height of the Tariff Reform campaign the Prime Minister, Arthur Balfour, presented a memorandum to the Cabinet (13 August 1903) entitled *Economic Notes on Insular Free Trade* which was published a month later. This was an attempt to find a *via media* between the contending factions within his own (Unionist) party; but apart from its political purpose, the memorandum raised some interesting questions in the theory of trade policy. Balfour turned out to be a 'retaliationist', i.e. he wanted to use tariffs as bargaining weapons, not for protective purposes, and summarised his position in the slogan: 'Freedom to negotiate that freedom of exchange may be increased.' He indicated that his position on the tariff issue was prompted by the question, 'whether a fiscal system suited to a free trade nation in a world of free traders remains suited in every detail to a free trade nation in a world of protectionists?' He concluded that the answer must be 'No', and consequently affirmed 'that we should openly and avowedly announce that this country no longer considers itself debarred by economic theories from making the best commercial bargain it can with other countries'.[34]

Economic theory in Marshall's time was certainly hostile to the idea of using tariffs in the manner recommended by Balfour; yet the principle and practice of doing so was endorsed by John Stuart Mill as early as 1829. Mill wrote:

> A country cannot be expected to renounce the power of taxing foreigners, unless foreigners will in return practise towards itself the same forbearance. The only mode in which a country can save itself from being a loser by the duties imposed by other countries on its commodities, is to impose corresponding duties on theirs.[35]

Tariff bargaining was, from the 1860s onwards, a normal process in European commercial diplomacy; but in such negotiations Britain's hands were tied, since it had no reductions to offer on account of its free-trade policy.[36] This was the weakness referred to in Balfour's memorandum. The modern principle of the 'second best' as applied to the economic theory of tariff bargaining does indeed provide an economic justification for Balfour's position within the strict limits of neoclassical postulates on welfare maximisation.[37]

MARSHALL'S MEMORANDUM

Marshall was apparently 'quite excited' about Balfour's memorandum, and in the same month that the economists' manifesto appeared, he took the opportunity of addressing some of the issues when asked to do so by the pro-free-trade Chancellor of the Exchequer, C. T. Ritchie.

Marshall's memorandum – described as 'one of the finest policy documents ever written by an academic economist', and 'an analytical masterpiece' – was subsequently published in revised form in 1908.[38] In it Marshall discussed the changing international position and prospects of Great Britain, and surveyed British trade policy in the light of the economic changes of the preceding sixty years. Marshall's convictions as a unilateral free trader come across strongly in this memorandum. We have already dealt with his position on the question of protection in general (Chapter 3), and need only take brief note of the reasons why in his opinion protection was not a practical option for Great Britain in 1903.

However, Marshall is not complacent. He identifies sources of weaknesses undermining Britain's competitiveness in world markets, but is quite clear that protectionism is not the answer. More fundamental changes are required (e.g. in the attitudes of management and labour). Among the developments which have altered the international economic environment of British industry, Marshall surveyed the following:

(1) Intensified competition and industrial growth abroad have resulted in the relative economic decline of Britain compared with the United States and Germany.
(2) Modern technology – 'the progress of the arts and resources of manufacturing' – has benefited Britain less than any other country. British industrialists have been slow in innovating and adopting new techniques.
(3) Industrial processes and technology upon which British industrial ascendancy was built have been diffused abroad and some countries have even improved upon such processes and techniques.
(4) The growth of foreign trade cartels and protective tariffs have tended to narrow the market for British manufactures.

Despite these unfavourable developments Marshall believed that

Britain still possessed considerable advantages over competitors, i.e. its abundant capital, cheap coal and favourable climate for the production of fine cotton yarn – 'a thing for which other nations have an elastic demand, and are at present almost wholly dependent on England'.[39]

Marshall felt that sales in the home market could compensate for the loss of exports markets due to tariffs in industrial countries. Some of the advantages of economies of scale would be lost, but no serious injury was likely to be inflicted on British industry. Nor was there any danger in the immediate or near future from the tariffs of underdeveloped, including Colonial, countries.

Protection was not a feasible solution to the problems facing Britain, and political pressure to go along the protectionist road must be resisted. No lasting advantages could be gained from imperial preferences, attempts to 'tax the foreigner' or retaliatory action against hostile tariffs; nor was there any theoretical and practical justification for the so-called 'senile' industry argument for the protection of British industry. Britain could not hope to arrest and reverse its relative industrial decline by the method of protection or tariff retaliation. At a time of rapid technological change and intense commercial rivalry, it was absolutely essential for Britain to keep 'her markets open to the new products of other nations and especially those of American inventive genius and of basic systematic thought and scientific training', for that was the surest way of 'increasing the alertness of her industrial population in general, and her manufacturers in particular'.[40]

Marshall emphasised in another passage the urgent need for a positive British response to the challenge of technology and competition – a response that a mere change in commercial policy could not hope to elicit:

> England will not be able to hold her own against other nations by the mere sedulous practice of familiar processes. These are being reduced to such mechanical routine by her own, and still more by American, ingenuity that an Englishman's labour in them will not continue long to count for very much more than that of an equally energetic man of a more backward race . . . England's place among the nations in the future must depend on the extent to which she retains industrial leadership. She cannot be the leader, but she may be a leader.[41]

Elsewhere in the document, Marshall expressed his confidence that under free trade Britain would be able to retain her place among the leaders because of the country's tradition of 'unrestricted freedom of movement', or 'viability' – an attribute essential to industrial success.

Marshall's memorandum, written in layman's language – his own preferred style – was a persuasive reaffirmation of the free-trade case in the new century. There is little or no mention of any theoretical point, although it is obvious that behind his survey and recommendations lies solid analysis, e.g. the estimate of the elasticities of demand for British exports and the supply of imports. Marshall himself was responsible for the development of much of the analytical techniques used by his contemporaries, and when he re-wrote the memorandum was certainly aware of the contributions to the theory of trade and protection by people like Edgeworth, Cunynghame and Bickerdike. These writers, as we have seen, explored the possibilities of State intervention in international trade and found theoretically plausible instances where such intervention could be beneficial. None of this appeared in Marshall's memorandum. He knew that free play was made of those economists' writings by tariff reform propagandists who often twisted and slanted them to suit the flow of their rhetoric and polemics. Marshall decided not to play that game and to stick to the 'facts', leaving the finer points of pure theory on one side as being irrelevant to the central issue of the debate. Marshall himself admitted elsewhere: 'It is very difficult to defend Free Trade on absolute a priori reasoning . . . it is based on a study of details.'[42] He would have agreed with what Pigou said of Balfour's *Economic Notes* – Balfour's fault was that he failed to 'bring . . . these undisputed or indisputable hypothetical reasonings into relation with the actual facts of the present circumstances of England'.[43] However, by failing to give due recognition to these 'undisputed hypothetical reasonings' (i.e. the possible benefit from tariffs), Marshall laid himself open to the charge that his defence of free trade was not an impartial one.

FACTUAL EVIDENCE

Marshall relied on facts; so did other free-trade writers, most notably Sir Robert Giffen, the leading official statistician of the day. Giffen in particular did much to remedy the paucity of statistical information available to the public at the time of the debate.

Wide margins of error were detected in the extant official data, which led to calls for more comprehensive and reliable coverage. There were, for instance, no regular balance of payments figures; only the balance of trade accounts were published and these excluded, of course, data on factors that were recognised as bearing significantly on the international economic position of the United Kingdom – i.e. the growth of 'invisible' earnings and overseas investment. The official publication of unemployment figures started as a result of the tariff debate; so too did the compilation of data on production. Under the Census of Production Act 1906, the first Census of Production was undertaken in 1907. The Act provided that manufacturing output and employment data were to be classified so as to be consistent with the 'headings in the Import and Export Lists'.

Giffen undermined the case for tariff reform by his statistical work which controverted the protectionists' claim that (1) tariffs were responsible for the industrial success of the United States and Germany; (2) tariff retaliation would be an effective defence against foreign competition; and (3) Britain's export performance and rate of economic growth were being crippled by foreign competition. Giffen criticised the protectionists for attempting to show 'that the United States is prosperous'; but, he pointed out, that is not what they have to prove. 'What they have to prove is that it is more prosperous than it would have been under a free trade regime, a statement in which statistics cannot help them.' 'The assumption that foreign manufacturing has largely increased by means of protection,' he wrote, 'is one of those wild assumptions which constantly crop up . . . but for which it is never possible to find a scintilla of evidence, and which are entirely opposed to broad facts regarding which there can be no dispute.'[44]

Giffen was convinced that protectionist policies were incompatible with the conditions of modern industrial production. Such policies were particularly ineffective in 'new countries' with small domestic markets. Referring to Australian experience under protection, he confidently predicted that protectionist politicians would disappear from the scene 'in a generation or so; . . . the breed, I am confident, is very nearly extinct, because the modern atmosphere and conditions, not theory, are making the policy next to impossible'.[45] Giffen's prediction turned out to be wrong, of course. Australian politicians continued to urge protectionist policies, and the 1929 Brigden Report (the work of a committee of eminent Australian economists set up by Prime Minister Bruce to examine the workings of the tariff) concluded: 'The evidence available does not support the contention that

Australia could have maintained its present population at a higher standard of living under free trade.'

Giffen constructed balance of payments figures to demonstrate that Britain's international economic position gave no cause for alarm, and certainly did not justify protection. The balance of trade figures did indeed show a rising deficit, but that was more than compensated for by a large positive balance on 'invisible' trade (i.e. earnings from shipping, insurance, banking, etc.). Some British industries (iron and steel, textiles, shipbuilding) suffered from a certain lack of competitiveness in overseas markets, Giffen admitted; but the remedy was for those industries to increase their efficiency and productivity. For British industry in general, the free-trade recipe was best; it would spur some industries to increase their efficiency and would 'encourage those industries which have a comparative advantage'.[46]

Empirical work bearing on the tariff controversy was also carried out by A. L. Bowley and A. W. Flux. Bowley provided the empirical counterpart of the 'terms of trade' concept widely used in the theory of international values. His 1903 estimates of the British terms of trade revealed that 'over sixteen years, goods exported have risen about 4% in price, while prices of imports have fallen 9%. This looks like profitable business.'[47] Jha comments: 'Such a statement would have silenced any advocate for a change in fiscal policy.'[48]

Bastable claimed that an Imperial Customs Union, as proposed by Chamberlain, 'would divert two-thirds of the foreign trade of the United Kingdom into the Colonialist direction'. Britain would suffer, since 'the cheapest sources of supply for many articles of prime necessity are outside, not within the Empire'. The scheme, he declared, 'rests on the false economic idea that trade between members of the same political body is better than trade with foreigners . . . The true line of progress lies in greater freedom of commerce for and within all countries.'[49]

FINAL THOUGHTS

At the conclusion of this chapter on the British tariff controversy, one is prompted to ask the following two questions: (1) Did the tariff reformers address the real issues? (2) Was the free trade solution the appropriate one for Britain at that time?

Answers have, of course, been suggested by economic historians. This is not the place to debate the matter. Suffice it to say that the most frequently recurring responses say 'No' to the first question and 'Yes' to the second; but the reasons are not altogether consistent. In retrospect, Marshall's judgement as set forth in his memorandum has been upheld; retaliatory tariffs, permanent tariffs on manufactures and imperial preference would not have worked to Britain's advantage, and as one writer puts it, 'protection and preference would not have done much to revive the fortunes of British industry or to ensure rapid growth in the future',[50] or, as another suggested, 'tariff reform might really have over-committed British industry to traditional markets'.[51] What about the tariff reformers' strategy? Here, we are told that they helped to create 'new forms of conceptualizing the economy', but they failed to spell out how that conception conflicted with Britain's traditional role in the late-nineteenth-century world economy, i.e. as the 'manager' of the gold standard and leading creditor nation, both of which were dependent on free foreign access to the British market. Thus, it has been said, the tariff reformers neglected to attack the pillars of the free trade system – they were 'singularly reticent about pursing the relation between free trade, the gold standard and foreign investment beyond rhetorical generalities'.[52] And again: 'What defeated Chamberlain in the last analysis was the City of London, which still dominated the British economy.'[53]

But if Britain's economic problem was really 'structural' in nature, in that 'the sources of weakness in the economy of Edward VII were still paramount in the economy of Edward VIII',[54] it is difficult to see what difference free trade made; or, for that matter, what difference tariff reform would have made.

5 Two Arguments for Protection

5.1 Schüller and the Idle Resource Effect

In 1905 the Austrian academic economist, Richard Schüller, published an argument for protection based on the normal existence of idle natural resources in all countries.[1] Years later, Haberler provided a trenchant refutation of it, but commented that Schüller's argument 'ranks with justice as one of the most profound arguments for tariffs'.[2]

Schüller discussed the disruptive effects of free trade, particularly the adverse effects on employment. Manufacturing industry could be ruined by competitive imports and that could occur ever though foreign producers were only slightly more efficient than domestic manufacturers. Human misery and economic waste may be involved before unemployed workers find acceptable jobs in new industries, if indeed they ever find such jobs. A low tariff may be required to protect jobs in domestic manufacturing industry.

Schüller adopts a partial-equilibrium approach, and shows, given the elasticities of home and foreign demand and supply curves, that only small tariff-induced changes in prices are necessary. He considers the loss of consumer surplus involved in tariff imposition, but judges that the increase in the production of the protected output will more than compensate for such loss. Thus:

> The smaller is, firstly, the spread between the highest and the lowest costs with which the home demand for the good can be satisfied by home production, and the smaller is, secondly, the comparative advantage of foreign producers in the case of goods which under free trade would not be produced at all in the home country . . . the greater is the increase in output due to a tariff relative to the loss on the side of consumption caused thereby, and the more favourable, therefore, are the effects of the tariff upon the total income.[3]

He reckons the increase in domestic production as an increase in total national income and takes note of the objection that if more of the protected output is produced, less production must necessarily take place in other industries – hence, there will be no net effect on national income, only a shift in the composition of total output; but Schüller asserts that this objection is not generally valid.

At this point, he makes an interesting observation: in all countries, factors of production, particularly natural resources, are never fully utilised; hence, a suitably small tariff can result in the employment of destitute workers and idle natural resources. 'In no country,' says Schüller, 'are natural economic forces – fertile soil, deposits of coal, ore and minerals, water power – fully made use of; rather, they are in all countries available for an expansion of branches of production for which they are needed.'[4] Free traders cannot therefore appeal to some general principle which suggests that all existing productive factors must find employment, since the existence of unemployed resources violates the conditions for economic optimum; also, free traders are wrong when they maintain that tariffs result only in a change in the output mix but never an increase in total output. On the contrary, says Schüller, moderate tariffs can help to bring about a better use of existing productive resources. Tariffs can bring back into production idle natural resources and so increase national output (income) and welfare. In addition, moderate protection may induce the import of capital (foreign investment) or the immigration of labour – all tending to increase total national production.

Schüller believed he had found a new, theoretically valid argument for protection; but later writers, including Mackenroth and Haberler, spotted the flaw in it.[5] Schüller failed to take into account the cost of utilising the so-called 'idle resources' in terms of the forgone use of other factors. The opportunity cost of activating the idle factors may be greater than the value of output created, so that on balance it may be better to leave the resources idle. A certain amount of unutilised resources is inevitable in a dynamic, growing economy. Market adjustments will leave some 'specific' factors temporarily idle; and while such transitional adjustments may result in private losses to the owners of specific factors, the community as a whole gains from the more efficient deployment of available resources. Haberler concludes: 'the existence of unutilised means of production is no argument whatever for tariffs'.[6]

5.2 Manoilescu and Wage Differentials

In 1929, the Romanian economist and Minister of Trade and Industry in his country's prewar government, Mihail Manoilescu (1891–1950), made a case for protection of industry in poor countries which attracted considerable interest.[7] His case for industrial tariff protection rested on imperfections in the labour market of an underdeveloped country that disfavoured industry, i.e. the existence of permanent differences in money wages between industry and agriculture due to differences in marginal productivity – 'the productivity of capital and labour'. Ricardo's comparative-cost principle loses its universal validity when, as so often happens in underdeveloped economies, a country's comparative advantage in terms of labour costs is in sectors of relatively low value productivity per unit of labour. The advantage of free international trade exists only for industrial countries (i.e. rich countries), not for poor countries whose exports consist of agricultural products.

Manoilescu produces a variety of statistical evidence supporting the view that capital and labour are always more productive in industry than in agriculture and consequently average incomes tend to be higher in industry. However, because the structure of internal costs and prices is distorted between industry and agriculture in a way that handicaps industry, poor countries find themselves 'over-importing' industrial products in exchange for agricultural exports. Industry has to pay a wage rate in excess of the opportunity cost of labour in the economy, i.e. in excess of the marginal product of labour in agriculture. There is too little labour at too high a price in industry – factors are inefficiently allocated between the sectors – so not enough will be produced in manufacturing and too much will be produced in agriculture. This results in inappropriate specialisation and trade under the Ricardian assumption of constant costs. On this reasoning, Manoilescu argues that agricultural countries can benefit by imposing tariffs on industrial imports to offset the inappropriate market encouragement to imports. The rise in the price of imported goods which protection entails will allow domestic industrialists to expand production and thereby facilitate the movement of workers from low-productivity agriculture to high-productivity industry. Protection to industry will enable the country to get manufactured goods at lower labour-time costs by domestic production than via imports.

CRITICISMS

Do intersectoral differences in wages provide a valid argument for protection? Critics at the time wanted to know more about the reasons for the existence of wage differentials, but felt in any case that numerous qualifications must severely limit the validity of the new doctrine. Viner pointed out that the wage differential might be due to what he called, following Taussig, 'equalising differences in wages', i.e. differences in money wages which merely equalise the 'net advantages' of different occupations. Thus the higher industrial wage might reflect the 'disutility' of greater economic costs incurred by labour in the industrial sector. In this case, there is no justification for protection, since specialisation according to money costs will then be in accordance with comparative real costs (measured in terms of 'disutilities') although not in accordance with labour-time costs, i.e. with wages and value of marginal products lower in agriculture.[8]

However, if the wage differential is due to trade-union activity, social legislation, custom or political and humanitarian considerations on the part of employers which prevent complete occupational mobility, then there may be a case for government intervention in trade. These impediments to labour movement may cause a genuine distortion – as Haberler notes, 'the price-ratio is not the same as the substitution-ratio'.[9] Here, Viner finds 'the one grain of truth which is embedded – but not displayed' in Manoilescu's exhaustive argument.[10] The free-trade solution will not provide a welfare maximum. Real income can be increased by a redistribution of the factors so as to bring private costs in line with social costs. The correction may be brought about through tariffs on industrial imports. But this is only a 'second-best' remedy, since although the production distortion is eliminated it appears on the consumption side. The ideal policy will be one which directly removes the distortion or imperfection in factor-market pricing. The 'first-best' policy means therefore free trade combined with a subsidy to the employment of labour in the manufacturing sector, i.e. a subsidy per unit of labour used in industry equal to the difference between the higher unit labour cost in industry and the lower labour cost in agriculture. Viner concludes that Manoilescu's attempt to defend protection 'has not been carried forward by this attempt' and that it confirms the conventional view that 'the existence of differences in wages does not suffice to overturn the doctrine of comparative costs'.[11]

Ohlin discussed the argument in terms of Cairnes's idea of non-competing groups (imperfect mobility) and conceded that free trade might lead to a lower national income than protection, but observed: 'It does not follow that the existence of artificial non-competing groups is a sufficient argument for protection. The more natural remedy is, of course, to increase the labour mobility.'[12] Haberler agreed with Viner and Ohlin, but in addition noted that Manoilescu's analysis could be extended in a dynamic fashion so that it 'approaches the infant-industry argument';[13] although it should be noted Manoilescu himself distinguished his plea from that of the infant-industry or 'educational tariff' case.[14] This is the case where (in the development of a manufacturing sector) a higher industrial wage is necessary to attract and retain skilled workers, an adequate supply of which may not be forthcoming because of market failure. But here again, the theory of domestic distortions provides no support for intervention in trade to remedy the situation – the optimal policy is a subsidy to labour training.

Manoilescu's case for protection was revived in the early postwar period in the context of the economic development of poor countries. It was restated in modern form by Gunnar Myrdal and W. Arthur Lewis; and Everett Hagen subjected it to rigorous analysis using a two-commodity, two-factor model with a constant wage differential. Bhagwati and Ramaswami discussed the argument in the light of the modern theory of domestic distortions and arrived at conclusions essentially the same as those of Viner, Ohlin and Haberler. The literature on the case (including several modern variants of it) was surveyed by Stephen Magee in 1973 and summarised more recently by Corden.[15]

6 Graham's Critique

INTRODUCTION

During the interwar years, a prominent critic of the Ricardo–Mill–Marshall model of trade was Frank Graham, a former student of Frank Taussig.[1] His complaint was over the question of dimensionality in the basic classical model – the assumption that many interesting issues about international trade could be adequately handled by means of an analysis based on two countries trading in two commodities. Graham rejected this reductionist procedure and believed that classical and neoclassical economists were led astray on substantive matters by generalising from the 2×2 case. Several of the propositions propagated by these writers as being relevant to complex trading relationships in the real world of many countries and many commodities, were in fact true only of simple bilateral trade of the England–Germany, cloth and linen variety considered by Mill. Graham called for a more realistic theory of international values incorporating many commodities and many countries; and in fact (using numerical examples) he did attempt such a generalisation, and showed how the results could be applied to a number of practical problems.[2]

Graham also had some interesting things to say about the theory of tariffs and argued that decreasing costs could justify protection – a contention which stirred controversy. He also disputed Marshall's position on demand shifts and the terms of trade. We proceed to a brief review of Graham's stand on the question of dimensionality and then consider his views on demand shifts and on tariffs and protection.

GRAHAM ON DIMENSIONALITY

In a lecture (at Princeton University) in April 1976, Ronald Jones admitted: 'For the past twenty years I have taken seriously the kind of question concerning dimensionality that was posed so forcefully by Graham.'[3] Earlier (1950), Lloyd Metzler felt that Graham's critique and proposal for an alternative theory constituted 'a major contribution to international economics . . . a substantial innovation, and perhaps one of the most important innovations since the classical theory was first presented'.[4] What, then, were the important theoretical issues involved in Graham's critique? One point was about the determination of the terms of trade and the adjustment process involved when shifts in international demand occurred.

Following Mill, the early neoclassical economists explained the determination of the terms of trade by means of the equations of reciprocal demand, i.e. in terms of offer curve analysis in a two-country, two-commodity constant cost model. Within the limits set by the comparative cost ratios in both countries, an equilibrium trading ratio would be established by the forces of reciprocal demand, i.e. each country's demand for the export product of the other country. This contrasts with the explanation of the determination of domestic prices. In the long run, relative prices within a country are determined largely by costs of production. Labour cost fixes internal relative prices through its influence on supply. Demand conditions do not determine relative prices (say of X and Y) but they do affect the actual output mix, i.e. under constant costs, the relative price ratio is determined solely by costs. Demand conditions determine only the allocation of available capital and labour between the two branches of production and hence the relative quantities of X and Y which are produced.

Graham accepts the classical model of production and the domestic pricing process as summarised above. What he takes exception to is the account given of the process governing the determination of international prices. He believes that the ratio of international exchange is determined largely by costs of production (opportunity costs) as in domestic trade, and that demand conditions play only a minor role. Therefore, for Graham, there is no essential difference between the theory of domestic prices and the theory of international prices as far as the adjustment process is concerned. The Mill–Marshall theory of reciprocal demand (offer curve) as applied to the determination of international relative prices relies on changes in the terms of trade as the fundamental means of adjustment to a shift of international demand. But, says Graham, this hypothesised process of international adjustment must be flawed, since the terms of trade are empirically stable. The source of the error lies in the totally unwarranted assumption that the equilibrium terms of trade necessarily lie between the cost ratios in either country, or, even more far-fetched, that they lie *strictly* between the cost ratios in each country as some classical writers asserted. Graham calls such an intermediate terms of trade a 'limbo' price ratio, one not anchored by costs of production. Graham himself holds a contrary view. He believes that the equilibrium terms of trade are, as a rule, equal to the pre-trade equilibrium price ratio of one of the countries with at least one commodity produced in common by more than one country, and that intermediate or 'limbo' price ratios are the exception.

The relevant feature of a 'limbo' price ratio is that shifts in world demand triggered by changes in tastes (nowadays shown by shifts in the indifference curve) result in price changes only, with production and supply remaining constant in each country. Thus if 'limbo' price ratios were the norm rather than the exception then we would observe violent fluctuations in international prices because of the volatile nature of demand. But since international relative prices are empirically stable, 'limbo' price ratios do not exist in reality.[5]

To illustrate his thesis, Graham considers the case of 3 goods and 2 countries and then that of 3 countries and 2 goods in which an intermediate commodity or country (a 'common country') serves as a link between the countries' cost structures. It is here that Graham makes a contribution, universally recognised as an important one, in raising again the question of dimensionality in trade models.

Take the case of 3 goods and 2 countries. If one good is produced in both countries – this good is thus a marginal or 'intermediate' commodity – adjustment comes about through a movement of labour into and out of this industry (in the two countries) rather than as a result of a change in the terms of trade. For instance, a change in tastes that results in a balance of payments deficit for one of the countries, would be eliminated by a shift of production and a reallocation of labour in the two countries, with no permanent gold movement in either direction and with no change in relative prices (or terms of trade) between the two countries.

Next, consider the example of 3 countries and 2 goods where one country's cost ratio is intermediate between the other two countries – Graham calls this the 'common country'. If the world price ratio coincides with this country's cost ratio, then shifts in world demand would be accommodated by labour and production changes in the 'common country' rather than by changes in the terms of trade. As you add more countries and goods the probability of there being a 'common country' and/or 'intermediate commodity' is increased. That is why the terms of trade are empirically stable; they are a reflection of opportunity costs.

In the real world of many commodities and countries, some of the commodities will be marginal in certain countries, i.e. some commodities produced at home may be either export or import goods; additionally, there is bound to be some intermediate country whose domestic cost ratios for at least two of the goods are approximately the same as world price ratios. Accordingly, any disturbance (e.g. change of tastes, demand, or balance of payments disequilibrium) will be offset by adjustments of output. World supply adjusts to demand, although resources cannot move from one country to another.

In general, the adjustment to international disturbance does not differ from the parallel process in domestic trade; hence the classical economists and their followers were wrong to make a distinction between international and domestic values. The multilateral model of comparative advantage that Graham discusses yields the following conclusion: despite the international immobility of factors, cost conditions fix the exchange ratios between most commodities by virtue of the existence of 'common commodities' and 'linked competition' as described above. Graham asserts: 'The world integration of prices is also an integration of national relative cost structures.'[6]

It is interesting to note that, like Graham, Nassau Senior a century earlier seemed to have claimed that demand variations had no practical effect in the long run. An equilibrium price ratio determined exclusively by reciprocal demand was the exception rather than the rule. The pattern of international specialisation, influenced as it was by productivity differences was, he held, remarkably stable. Thus, costs of production determine value in international trade. Senior habitually thought of international trade in monetary terms, and was fully conscious that in the real world trade takes place in many commodities among many countries.[7]

Graham's critique was constructive in that (1) it stimulated useful analyses of the relative roles of demand and cost factors in international trade, and (2) inspired economists to explore more fully the properties of multi-country and multi-commodity models.[8]

Now, as we saw earlier, Mangoldt, Edgeworth, Bastable and Viner contributed to the task of extending to higher dimensions the classical 2×2 model of comparative advantage, but the question that interested Graham – what factors were involved in the international adjustment process – was only partially resolved by these writers. An exaggerated importance was given to demand (through the application of the device of reciprocal demand curves) in the determination of the terms of trade. But some of the writers criticised by Graham did not suffer from monadic myopia to the extent suggested by Graham. Marshall, for one, fully recognised the role of supply factors in terms-of-trade movements – the offer curve does not depend on demand alone; and whilst it is true that Edgeworth initially derived the offer curve with reference to the case of fixed supplies of commodities, he later gave a graphical account of the underlying production changes involved in Marshall's curves, in these words:

> A movement along a supply-and-demand curve of international trade should be considered as attended with rearrangements of internal trade; as the movement of the hand of a clock corresponds to considerable unseen movements of the machinery.[9]

This was made explicit in Meade's 1952 derivation of the offer curve which made use of both the production-possibilities frontier (supply) and the social indifference map (demand).

Graham's result is possible even within the simple classical model when (1) the two trading countries are of unequal size; (2) one country's tastes are heavily biased in favour of one of the commodities; and (3) the two commodities are consumed in fixed proportions. In these cases, one of the countries may produce both commodities with the possibility that the terms of trade will be reflected in that country's cost ratio. Indeed, case (3) is the assumption made by Graham in some of his examples – all demands have unitary price and income elasticity.[10] But as Chipman observes, this 'practically guarantees the extreme solution',[11] i.e. terms of trade equilibrated to the cost ratio in one of the countries.

Graham's conclusion (for the multi-country case) depends on the existence of an intermediate or 'common' country whose cost ratio is the same as the international terms of trade. But the location of this marginal country depends crucially on demand conditions. Hence, contrary to Graham's belief, one cannot dispense with demand.[12] Graham's theory was therefore not, as he asserted, a complete refutation of classical doctrine; rather, it constituted a modification. Since Graham wrote, a consensus has arisen about the matter (in respect of multi-commodity, multi-country trade), neatly summarised by Ronald Jones: 'a disturbance to trade may be met primarily by price changes, on the one hand, or production changes, on the other'.[13] Jones adds, further contradicting Graham, that 'limbo' price ratios may occur.

It may be urged in defence of Graham that he repeatedly stated that he was dealing with 'normal' not 'market' values. If the theory of normal values means a long-run theory explaining the stability of values over time, then Graham's analysis is not widely off the mark. For instance, Graham assumed a high degree of mobility of productive factors within countries, and recognised that demand conditions might play an important role in determining the international terms of trade when factors of production were not mobile, as they would be in the short run.[14]

DEMAND SHIFTS AND THE TERMS OF TRADE

As mentioned in the section on Marshall, Graham disputed Marshall's solution to the problem of demand shifts on the net barter terms of trade. The controversy is now purely of historical interest. It merely serves to illustrate one aspect of Graham's general critical attitude to the concept of reciprocal national demand. By a 'shift in international demand' Graham understood a uniform change in the quantity demanded of a country's imports at given terms of trade. Marshall, however, felt that any shift of international demand must entail some movement of the terms of trade, and he therefore defined a shift of demand as a uniform change in the amount of one country's export good offered in exchange for a given amount of the other country's export good.[15]

Commentators usually say that the source of the controversy was the failure to define more precisely the phrase 'increase in demand'. This is correct, since the two types of demand shifts lead to the same conclusion, except that this fact was obscured by Marshall's practice of working with cases where the elasticity of both reciprocal demand curves exceeded unity. Graham used this diversion to score a point against Mill and Marshall. Marshall was, however, the wrong target, since in the *Principles* Marshall defined a demand shift in exactly the same way as Graham did: 'When we say that a person's demand for anything increases, we mean that he will buy more of it than he would before at the same price.'[16]

Graham's attack on the idea of reciprocal demand was not pointless, however. It conveyed an important message, namely that we must not confuse 'demand for commodities' with 'demand by countries', as we are apt to do when we apply the concept of reciprocal national demand (limited to two countries and two commodities)

> as if trade . . . were . . . between national entities, in national bales of goods, rather than between individuals buying and selling, as traders nationally undistinguished, individual commodities in a market competitive in every respect except in the mobility of factors of production across national boundaries.

Graham continues:

> When instead of discussing the *total* reciprocal demand (supply) of the various products in an integrated trading system, the classicists split demand (supply) into irrelevant national parts, with assumed reciprocal national demands for fixed sets of commodities of mutually exclusive composition . . . they were indulging in pure fantasy.[17]

Graham's point is that in a multilateral trading system, the appropriate focus ought to be upon all countries' demands and supplies of particular commodities.[18]

Graham's emphasis on the supply side, and the importance he attached to the possibility that international prices might reflect the actual cost ratios in some country, brought him into conflict with another classical bit of conventional wisdom, i.e. to the effect that a country might improve its terms of trade by levying a tariff – except in the case of a small country unable to exercise any influence over world prices. Contrary to Torrens and Mill, Graham maintains that the opportunities for rigging the terms of trade are extremely limited, if not non-existent:

> In the world as it is, with many countries producing commodities in common, and with most or all commodities *somewhere* on the margin of producers' indifference as regards various other commodities, the chance of shifting the normal international ratio of exchange through the imposition of protective duties is always small.[19]

There is therefore little or no scope for securing national gains at the expense of others. Foreign producers discriminated against by the home country's tariff policy may become competitors with the country's export producers. What Graham fails to recognise is that for many products with inelastic demands (typically products that figure in trade between less developed and industrialised countries) the theory of reciprocal demand is indispensable. One only has to recall the massive increase in oil prices engineered by OPEC in the 1970s which dramatically altered the terms of trade between oil-producing and non-oil countries.

THE GRAHAM PROTECTION CONTROVERSY

Graham argued that decreasing costs could justify protection. A country with a comparative advantage in an industry subject to decreasing returns to scale and a comparative disadvantage in an increasing returns to scale industry, may lose from free trade when trade leads to a reallocation of resources (labour) from the increasing returns industry to the decreasing returns industry. Gross domestic product evaluated at constant commodity prices falls (i.e. output per man falls in both industries), indicating a welfare loss. Consequently, the country may be worse off with free trade than under autarky, and may be able to improve its free-trade welfare by means of tariff protection.[20]

Although Graham's contention was not a new one, it provoked extensive criticisms, most notably from Frank Knight,[21] but also from Haberler and Viner. The criticisms, many of which were not really relevant to Graham's basic contention, were about the empirical relevance of external economies, failure to note the distinction between internal and external economies, the incompatability of internal economies with standard notions of competitive equilibrium, the irreversibility of returns to scale, the confusion between average and marginal costs in Graham's pricing rules and whether scale economies were to be associated with industry generally or with specific products, etc.[22] Upon these grounds Graham's case was summarily dismissed in judgements typified by the following: 'the basis for the kind of protection defended by Graham is all but completely destroyed'; 'little or nothing remains of it'; '[Graham's] thesis reduces to little more than a theoretical curiosity'.[23]

Nevertheless, from these criticisms there emerged two clarifications which proved useful in subsequent discussions about the role of economies of scale in international trade: (1) external economies may depend on world output rather than national output, i.e. 'international' returns to scale resulting from an increased international division of labour;[24] and (2) market structure and the equilibrium allocation of resources depend on the precise nature of the economies of scale, i.e. assumptions about the behaviour of firms depend on what forms the economies of scale take.

Graham presented his case using a two-country model incorporating one factor of production (labour) producing two commodities, whose costs are expressed in terms of output per unit of labour time. The argument as it stood failed to convince his contemporaries – Caves notes that Graham's arguments and numerical examples were 'grossly insufficient for establishing' his case.[25] But the question about the logical consistency of Graham's case was not seriously addressed until many years later when Jan Tinbergen gave a geometrical proof of it, utilising for that purpose the comparatively new technique of the production-possibilities frontier combined with indifference curves – an analysis which improved on Graham's exposition in respect of the evaluation of real national income. Tinbergen's reformulation (validation) of Graham's case seems to have clinched the matter – Caves observed (1960), 'Trade theorists now generally concede [Graham's] point'[26] – and the controversy subsided.

Recent developments in international trade theory – specifically, the increased attention now given to the effects of increasing returns to scale and non-competitive behaviour on international competition – have led to renewed interest in the 'Graham protection controversy'. Several papers have addressed the issue either explicitly or briefly in more general contexts, resulting finally in a more thorough analysis than this classic externalities model has hitherto received. What new interpretations emerge from recent theoretical innovations?

It turns out that Tinbergen's reconstruction of Graham's case is not the definitive answer. It is now seen to be incorrect. Murray Kemp points out: 'Tinbergen's treatment is wrong in essentials.' This has been supported by Wilfred Ethier and Arvind Panagariya.[27] Tinbergen's error pertains to the shape of the production-possibility frontier, especially near the axes. He draws the production-possibility frontier concave to the origin near the decreasing-returns-industry axis and convex to the origin near the increasing-returns-industry axis. But as Herberg and Kemp (1969), also Panagariya (1981) show, if the technology is such that production functions are homothetic or homogeneous then the production-possibility frontier is convex near the decreasing-returns-industry axis, concave near the increasing-returns-industry axis and has a single inflection point.[28] This slip misled Tinbergen into drawing the inference that temporary protection would reverse the free-trade equilibrium and lead to complete specialisation in the increasing-returns industry.[29] Panagariya also mentions that Tinbergen fails to recognise the divergence between social and private marginal products (the externality distortion) at the competitive equilibrium.

In the modern treatments, external scale economies are output generated, i.e. each firm's output depends on the industry output. This implies that the firm perceives its production to be subject to constant returns to scale. Price therefore equals average cost. Even when economies of scale occur at the firm level (scale economies internal to the firm), average-cost pricing may still prevail if markets are contestable (entry to the industry is free). Competitive equilibrium then requires a single firm earning zero profit – free entry or threat of entry enforces average-cost pricing.

Turning to the substance of the case, we find that there is a variety of possible types of equilibria. Assuming tastes are represented by a Mill–Graham utility function identical in both countries (a constant fraction of income is spent on each commodity), the most likely outcome in a two-country world will be for the larger country to export the good subject to industry-level increasing returns. The small country is likely to specialise in the decreasing-returns industry as a result of the opening of trade. This is Graham's case, the country with a comparative advantage in wheat.

Before trade, the small country will be underproducing the increasing-returns commodity (since firms cannot internalise all the benefits from increased production). If free trade causes output in the increasing-returns sector to fall, this will increase the distortion caused by underproduction, and drive the economy further away from the Pareto-optimal allocation, i.e. the economy suffers a welfare loss. This also results in a decline in the economy's average productivity. Yet a loss is not inevitable, since the economy gains from trade, i.e. the gains from importing the increasing-returns commodity at an even lower cost, and securing for the commodity it exports (the decreasing-returns commodity) a higher price than under autarky. The smaller the 'small' country is, relative to the larger country, the greater the likelihood that it will gain.

But the impression one gains from reading Graham is that he is discussing the case of two countries of nearly equal size. Ethier characterises the Graham case as 'the case of two approximately equally matched countries confronting each other in a situation where one must gain and one must lose'.[30] Nevertheless, gains from trade are possible as long as the world output of the industry with scale economies exceeds the national output under autarky.

On the other hand, if we apply the Graham conjecture to the case of an open economy facing a given world price, we see that his argument is considerably strengthened. Here, if the country specialises in the decreasing-returns industry, welfare maximisation would seem to require a permanent tax-cum-subsidy measure to encourage expansion of the increasing-returns industry and contraction of the decreasing-returns industry. Graham argued for tariff protection; but modern economists tend to favour production and/or consumption subsidies to deal with country-specific externalities, as in the present case. However, given the existence of multiple equilibria in the presence of increasing returns to scale, some circumstances may in fact call for tariff protection as the optimal policy.

Granted that Graham's argument has intrinsic merit (i.e. with respect to sector and country-specific economies of scale), is it relevant to international competition in the modern world? Should a government seek to promote domestic production of goods that yield positive externalities? Does it matter in an integrated world economy which country succeeds in becoming the producer of externality-generating goods? A significant strand of the modern literature gives a negative answer to each question. In many instances of industrial/financial services competition, external economies are not country-specific – they are international in scope; hence, some say, the relevant concept is 'internationally decreasing costs'. The appropriate way to think about industries linked with external economies is in terms of externality-generating industries at the *international* level. These industries, it is alleged, are the major sources of economies of scale which are diffused to individual firms throughout the world by multi-stage production and trade in intermediate inputs.[31] Making the point that it is in everyone's interest that industries be concentrated so as to reap the gains from scale economies, Krugman says 'it is important that the industries be concentrated, not where they are concentrated'.[32] Essentially the same suggestion was made by Viner over fifty years ago in connection with the Graham controversy. If the theory of international trade and increasing returns is conceived in this manner, 'it would, incidentally, invalidate Graham's argument for protection', according to Ethier.[33]

7 Trade and General Equilibrium

7.1 The Approach to General Equilibrium

THE 1930s WATERSHED

The transformation curve (or concave production-possibility frontier) was introduced into trade theory by Enrico Barone in 1908, but for various reasons his contribution went unnoticed. Twenty-two years later, Haberler reintroduced the construction under the label of 'production substitution curve'. It was a diagrammatic representation of a country's maximum attainable set of outputs for two commodities from a given supply of productive factors, and described the rate at which commodities could be substituted for each other not only under constant opportunity-cost conditions, but also under increasing and decreasing casts as well.[1] Under increasing costs (the assumption frequently made) the production-possibility frontier is drawn strictly concave to the origin, i.e. the production possibility set is convex, reflecting the law of diminishing marginal productivity.

For Haberler, the great advantage of the approach was that it dispensed with the need for a labour theory of value, or a real cost theory or indeed for any other specific theory of costs. It enabled relative commodity prices to be analysed under conditions of variable factor proportions in a more straightforward manner than was possible with the real cost approach espoused by Taussig and Viner. It restored simplicity to the original Ricardian doctrine of comparative costs by making obsolete the use of ill-defined concepts like 'bales' and 'units of productive power' introduced by Marshall, Edgeworth, and others to deal with the analytical problems posed by a multiplicity of productive factors.[2]

Although others had utilised the concept of opportunity costs before him, Haberler with his training in the Austrian School was the first to see its potential as a simple but versatile tool for modelling production in trade theory. With the transformation curve device, costs are measured subjectively, not by the absolute amount of labour and other factors required to produce a given output but by the alternative output forgone – i.e. the cost of a commodity is the amount of another commodity which might have been produced by the same resources. Under increasing costs the exchange ratio, or the ratio of internal relative prices, of two commodities will vary with the relative demand for the commodities, i.e. the ratio at which the two commodities exchange against one another in the market will equal the ratio of their marginal costs.

Haberler's brilliant display of the production-possibility frontier triggered a remarkable outburst of seminal papers by Lerner (1932, 1934), Leontief (1933) and Viner (1931) which not only revived the lacklustre image of trade theory, but also lifted it to a new plateau from which it was able to advance with speed and assurance.[3]

In 1931 Viner presented a paper (at the London School of Economics) in which he combined the transformation curve and 'consumption indifference curvers' (community indifference curves) to represent free-trade equilibrium and the gains from trade, in a diagram that is now all-too-familiar to beginning students in international economics – 'the sacred diagram of the international trade economist', as some call it.[4] This was followed by four equally fundamental papers – three in quick succession by Lerner, and one by Leontief.

The first was Lerner's 1932 paper, 'The Diagrammatical Representation of Cost Conditions in International Trade',[5] written whilst an undergraduate after only two years of part-time study. By a skilful use of geometry he integrated Marshall's offer curve, the production possibility curve and the indifference map to illustrate the free-trade optimum, and developed a way of depicting increasing and decreasing opportunity cost curves. He proved that increasing returns imply specialisation by at least one country. Lerner was the first to devise a global production-possibility schedule by aggregating transformation functions of several countries at equal marginal cost ratios. In his article on demand conditions in international trade (1934) he analysed various conditions affecting the demand for imports: e.g. satiety and over-satiation.

In his 1932 paper, Lerner had justified the use of community indifference curves for depicting equilibrium conditions on the ground that even though no inference could be drawn with respect to the assessment of an absolute level of community satisfaction, 'the behaviour of the community with respect to these curves is exactly comparable to that of an individual with respect to his true indifference curves'.[6] In the 1934 paper he acknowledged that the procedure of aggregating over individuals had still to be vindicated, and showed the possibility of dispensing with community indifference curves in the evaluation of welfare levels. Lerner hinted at what later became known as the 'weak axiom of revealed preference'; for the community, 'too, can be said to prefer that which is acquired by the community to that which might have been acquired in its stead.'[7] Lerner simply aggregated the net market demands of all consumers to find the market-clearing prices for all goods. In the same paper, Lerner commented on the analogy between monopolistic (export) pricing and the effect of tariffs on the terms of trade whenever a country faced a less than elastic foreign demand for its products.[8] However, as Robert Mundell observes: 'The relation is not exact . . . because monopoly equilibrium differs from the optimum tariff equilibrium in that it does not discriminate between home and foreign consumer prices.'[9]

In December of the previous year, 1933, Lerner gave a proof of factor-price equalisation, the account of which was not published until 1952 – a few years after Samuelson's celebrated geometrical and mathematical proofs (1948, 1949).[10] Here, in an elegant, clear and succinct version of the proof, Lerner demonstrates for the first time how the production-possibilities curve can be derived from the Edgeworth–Bowley box diagram, the conditions under which factor prices may or may not be equalised as a consequence of trade, and an analysis of the significance of factor-intensity reversals. This was a significant achievement, for as Mundell observes, it 'requires an integration of the theory of international income distribution with the terms of trade, the theory of comparative advantage and factor endowments, and the corresponding conditions of international demand and supply . . . a knowledge of Euler's theorem and the marginal productivity theory of distribution as applied to a two-sector model'.[11] All this understanding Lerner demonstrated with a flourish and astonishing mastery in 1933.

Haberler had suggested that the gains from trade could be indicated, if not measured, by means of his production-possibility curve. In a classic 1933 paper which did much to establish the concept of community indifference curves for analytical purposes, Wassily Leontief combined Haberler's curve with a system of indifference curves to make the idea more precise. Leontief makes the important assumption that community indifference curves do not intersect; but he does not consider the question how they may be obtained from individual preferences.[12]

During these years, too, Lerner published another famous paper, 'The Symmetry between Import and Export Taxes', which fully clarified and resolved a disputed point in the theory of trade policy between Edgeworth and Bastable. The question was, were taxes on imports and exports symmetrical, in the sense that they had identical real effects? Marshall, Bastable, Pigou and the classical economists, stressing as they did the barter nature of all trade, took it for granted that the two taxes were symmetrical. Edgeworth alone evidently held the contrary view and criticised Bastable for failing to see the difference between the two types of taxes. Edgeworth, however, later retracted his criticism of Bastable, but maintained that the difference between the imposts was true only of 'taxes in kind'. Edgeworth's error was due to the fact that he failed to see that the difference was not about how the taxes were levied, but how the proceeds were spent. Edgeworth mistakenly interpreted the result of his method of shifting the duty-imposing country's offer curve as indicating a real difference between the two types of taxes.[13]

Lerner established the correct results by means of the ingenious device of a geometrical pencil formed by the two different price radiants to the offer curves – a difference created by the tax, whether on imports or exports. Only the commodities on which the tax proceeds are spent create a difference – e.g. the more spent on imports, the less favourable the impact on the terms of trade.[14] With balanced trade, the revenues collected by the two taxes are the same. An export tax on one good has a real effect similar to an import tax on the other good. Similarly, equilibrium remains unaltered if an import tariff is substituted in place of an export tax. Would the symmetry proposition continue to hold in a monetary economy? Mundell has recently argued that the result must be qualified when the central bank's assets and relative changes in home and foreign price levels are taken into consideration, and concludes that his analysis 'suggests that the symmetry theorem Lerner proved applies strictly to the barter world of two commodities on which his proof rests'.[15]

A DIGRESSION ON VINER

At this point it may be permissible to digress for a moment from the chronological narrative to offer some further general remarks on Jacob Viner's work in international economics. This is certainly appropriate in a book on doctrinal history – a field Viner made his own; and, perhaps more important, because, as Samuelson said,

'There has never been a greater neoclassical economist than Jacob Viner'[16] – a judgement many would endorse.

Some of Viner's contributions to international economics have been mentioned in various parts of this book. Together with others not specifically noted, they stand as memorials to the workings of a brilliant and scholarly mind over the entire field – from trade theory and policy to international monetary economics. In general economic theory his interests were equally universal; and in two areas his writings were path-breaking: (1) the 1921 paper on the marginal conditions for maximisation of an imperfect competitor's profits, including the concept of the kinked-demand curve, and (2) the derivation of the long-run cost-curve envelope in the famous 1931 article on 'Cost Curves and Supply Curves'. In international economics, besides the several contributions mentioned in the present book, one analytical piece is worthy of mention: his 1950 book, *The Customs Union Issue.* Here Viner pioneered a field of study that has itself become a specialist area in international economics, encompassing both theoretical and empirical aspects of the subject-matter. Viner introduced the terms 'trade creation' and 'trade diversion' (production effects) and concluded that a customs union which resulted in a partial reduction of trade barriers was not necessarily beneficial to the world as a whole, since it combined elements of freer trade with features of greater protection. As Viner's analysis was developed by other economists (e.g. Meade, Lipsey, etc.) it soon became clear that what Viner was exploring was, in fact, one of the most important practical applications of the theory of the 'second best'.

Viner's impact on international economics came not only or mainly from his technical pieces, but largely from his writings on doctrinal history: i.e. his classic *Studies in the Theory of International Trade* (1937) and the brilliant articles on mercantilist thought and Adam Smith. Through these he made a permanent mark on the subject. It is by his *Studies* that Viner is remembered today by specialists in international economics. In this work, Viner applied his remarkable erudition and meticulous scholarship to the colossal task of clarifying and integrating a large and diverse literature spanning more than three centuries. Moreover, Viner related the historical discussions to contemporary theoretical debates on substantive issues. He thus conveyed to his readers a sense of engagement in a living, on-going intellectual quest or enterprise. Classical theory was no fossilised relic of an uninteresting bygone age. It had meaning and relevance for modern concerns. Viner's magisterial review and evaluation of the literature is partly responsible for the continuity of the basic approach to international trade theory. It also undoubtedly raised the status of international economics as a unified academic discipline in political economy. Other works which came out in the 1930s or thereabouts tended to have the same effect (e.g. Haberler's treatise, and the histories of trade theories by Angell and Wu); but Viner's work was principally responsible for the changes mentioned. Leading writers in the field now feel it incumbent upon them to refer to earlier literature when exploring new approaches to old problems.

Finally, some comments on Viner's views on policy matters. His opinions changed over the years, perhaps for several reasons: the impact of the Great Depression and the Keynesian revolution; his experience as a policy adviser at the US Treasury during those momentous years; his later interest in the problems of economic development and, most significant, the fact that the postwar world had changed – it had become, in his words, 'a world of planned economies, of state trading, of substantially arbitrary and inflexible national price structures, and of managed instability in exchange rates'.[17]

For most of his career Viner was an ardent advocate of free trade and a stout defender of the classical theory;[18] but in his later years he saw that altered conditions made the classical assumptions patently unrealistic, in particular the assumption of flexible prices determined in competitive markets. Owing to monopolies and government intervention, prices had become rigid and distorted, with the result that relative prices could no longer be taken as indices of relative real costs; consequently, the classical theory was largely irrelevant and 'the logical economic foundations for the routine application of free trade are absent; . . . free trade becomes almost as irrational as random interferences with trade'.[19]

Similarly, Viner felt that the classical mechanism of monetary adjustment was rendered obsolete by modern developments – market forces alone could not be relied upon to correct balance of payments disequilibria. He conceded that one genuine innovation of the Keynesian revolution was the emphasis on the role of income elasticities in the adjustment mechanism, the influence of which was unduly neglected in accounts of the older theory.

Viner thus came to terms with the modern world – in that sense he was a realist; but he also confessed that temperamentally he was an intellectual conservative. He could not bring himself to abandon the whole corpus of classical thought. Classical welfare theory was still serviceable, if only to demonstrate the inconclusiveness of the welfare arguments presented in support of trade restrictions and government intervention generally. But, as Eugene Rotwein comments, this only serves 'to underscore his [Viner's] belief that on various welfare grounds, the extent of the validity of the classical position is itself inconclusive'.[20]

HABERLER'S CONTRIBUTION

Haberler's prominent role in the formulation and development of the modern theory of international trade was widely recognised when an English translation of his 1933 treatise on trade theory and policy appeared in 1936. Even as late as the 1960s his book continued to be widely read and quoted.[21] A notable feature of Haberler's work was the way he integrated monetary and real theory – the monetary aspect was treated first and references were frequently made to the monetary mechanism when dealing with the pure theory. The monetary sections are indeed refreshingly modern; in fact, as Thomas Willett suggested in 1982, these sections 'can still be read with profit by modern economists'.[22] Among his analytical contributions to international monetary economics are: the analysis of the transfer problem; the introduction of the concept of supply and demand curves for foreign exchange; purchasing power parity; and the monetary and asset market approaches to exchange-rate determination. His influence was equally felt in the many areas of trade theory and policy that he developed and refined – an influence barely recognisable today, since they were all speedily absorbed in the wider, more dominant Heckscher–Ohlin framework.

In his book, Haberler introduced the useful concept of 'specific' factors of production which he attributed to Wieser.[23] This was used to deduce the curvature of the 'substitution curve' (production-possibility curve) – an explanation similar to that commonly used today to account for the shape of the curve in terms of factor-intensity differences: i.e. products can be classified in terms of their relative K-intensity or L-intensity in production. Haberler said that the distinction between specific and non-specific – the latter being capable of employment in a number of different uses – was first mentioned by Friedrich von Wieser, his teacher at the University of Vienna. Some factors of production are, at least to some extent and especially in the short run, 'specific': either they can be used only for one particular purpose – i.e. they are completely immobile among industries – or they would yield so much less if transferred to another use (machinery, for example, being used as scrap-iron) that in fact they are not transferred. At the international level, specificity may arise because of obstacles to movement (e.g. national immigration controls or prohibitive transport costs, etc.).

Haberler's approach was vulnerable to criticism on account of its two assumptions, as Viner first noted: (1) fixed factor supplies, and (2) factors indifferent as between different employments. Viner's criticism related to the welfare issue – the alleged superiority of the real-cost welfare criterion over Haberler's approach; but his observation was taken up by other critics and used as evidence that Haberler's opportunity cost theory was not truly a general equilibrium approach.[24] Samuelson, for instance, referred to Haberler's twin assumptions as 'empirically gratuitous'.[25] Factor supplies are variable when they depend on real factor rewards. If product prices change, then factor rewards will change and so will factor supplies. In principle, under this more general assumption, the exchange ratio between two commodities will not equal the slope of the production-possibility curve traced out as product prices and factor supplies change; although, given a particular supply of factors, the equality between the commodity price ratio associated with that factor supply and the opportunity cost ratio can still be indicated on the curve. Nor can one expect to see equality between the commodity price ratio and the opportunity cost ratio when factors are not indifferent between alternative employments, even though factor supplies are fixed.

It was primarily this ambiguity concerning the set of possible outputs, and therefore the location of a definite transformation curve, that critics of Haberler's approach had in mind when they said of it that it was not a full general-equilibrium model. However, the analysis of familiar trade problems under the assumption of variable factor supplies opens up 'a veritable Wonderland of possibilities', as Murray Kemp warns those who attempt it.[26] Haberler later (1950) set out precise conditions under which the production-possibility frontier was well defined, and insisted that 'I never regarded the opportunity-cost theory as anything but a simplified general equilibrium approach', and again, 'the opportunity cost theory is a convenient approach, a first approximation to a general equilibrium theory'.[27]

The objections raised by Viner and others to Haberler's approach were finally stilled by the subsequent development of trade theory by

Lerner, Leontief, Stolper, Samuelson and Rybczynski among others, which incorporated Haberler's concepts within the Heckscher–Ohlin framework. The decisive moment in this integration came 'after Rybczynski . . . explored the production implications of changes in relative factor supplies', as Robert Baldwin recalls. As a result, Baldwin notes 'the usual simplified form of the Heckscher–Ohlin proposition requires (among others) the same assumptions that Haberler made'.[28]

Haberler's exposition of the theory of comparative costs was a masterful achievement, as was his clear and comprehensive evaluation of the various arguments for protection. Observing that 'economists are nearly as unanimous in favour of a liberal trade policy as are Governments in favour of the contrary',[29] he set out in true scientific earnestness to discover what was valid and what was nonsense in the protectionists' perennial pleas. Haberler's celebrated 1950 paper on 'Some Problems in the Pure Theory of International Trade' initiated a line of enquiry concerned with optimal trade policy in the presence of domestic distortions (divergences between private and social marginal costs) caused by external economies, factor immobility or factor-price rigidity, which was later more fully developed by Bhagwati and Ramaswami (1963) and Johnson (1965). Haberler's purpose was to show that free trade did not necessarily imply *laissez-faire.* The case for free trade still holds (excepting the optimal tariff argument) even when the various simplifying assumptions associated with it are removed, although domestic *laissez-faire* may have to give way to policy interventions. Meade's (1955) work on trade and welfare as well as that of Hagen were also pioneering pieces in the development of this literature on policy intervention in open economies.

Haberler called for further efforts to develop the pure theory of international trade; in particular, he said, the theory of imperfect competition 'must be applied to the problems of international trade', and referring to the progress made in that field by Chamberlin and Joan Robinson felt that 'it will soon be possible to do this in a systematic way'.[30] But the hoped-for development was long delayed and is only now being tackled. Together with Viner's classic *Studies*, Haberler's book did much to enhance the intellectual status of international economics in the 1930s. The other book published around this time which had a powerful, indeed revolutionary, impact was of course Bertil Ohlin's *Interregional and International Trade.*

7.2 The Heckscher–Ohlin–Samuelson Model

OHLIN'S THEORY

Since the spring of 1922 Ohlin had formulated his factor endowment theory of trade based on a mutual interdependence (or multiple-market) theory of pricing.[31] For the first time, the analysis of factor markets became integrated into trade theory. Ohlin's new approach was much influenced by the work of two of his teachers: Eli Heckscher and Gustav Cassel. From Cassel he acquired a version of the Walrasian system of general equilibrium, and from Heckscher the view that international trade flows could be explained in terms of the relative scarcity or abundance of different factors of production, if both countries had access to the same technology; and the further idea that factor returns would be equalised by free trade in goods alone if there was a difference in the factor-input combinations for different goods. Heckscher in turn acknowledged his indebtedness to Knut Wicksell for the analysis in terms of factor endowments.[32]

Ohlin built on this Swedish approach and combined elements of his own. He felt that the theories of international trade, interregional trade and location shared enough common characteristics that made them amenable to unified treatment under the rubric of a general locational analysis of spatial pricing, migration and capital movements. In fact, Ohlin declared: 'The theory of international trade is nothing but *internationale Standortslehre*.'[33] The hoped-for integration of international trade theory into locational analysis has, however, not occurred. Regrettably, in the view of location theorists, the space factor and costs of transporting commodities between countries (or transfer costs, in general) have never been satisfactorily integrated into the competitive general-equilibrium theory of international trade – in 1960 Richard Caves omitted the economics of location from his survey of trade theory on the ground that 'trade and location theory have not been successfully juxtaposed'.[34] The scant regard, until recently, for the role of non-traded goods was partly connected with the usual assumption of 'no transport costs' – although in the case of non-tradeable services, transport cost is infinite. Yet it is pretty obvious that differential transfer cost between individual trading countries is not a negligible factor, despite recent developments in containerisation and jet transport facilities.

Ohlin endeavoured to construct an operational factor-proportions theory of general-equilibrium multi-country trade, and realised that such a theory would have to incorporate 'distance' and other trade-resisting variables that affect location; for he knew it to be quite evident that geographical distance adversely affects trade flows. The fact that integration between location theory and international trade theory has not actually taken place is perhaps due to the partial-equilibrium mould of much of locational analysis. Samuelson (1981) confesses: 'I share the widespread feeling that location theory has never fulfilled its exciting promise (and its promises)';[35] and some time ago Haberler predicted that only when location theory 'succeeds in developing a system of general equilibrium will the theory of international trade become merely a special case within such a general framework'.[36]

Ohlin emphasised the role of increasing returns to scale as a cause of international specialisation and trade.[37] Such economies of scale, he pointed out, can supplement the incentives created by cross-country differences in factor endowments and, even in the absence of such differences (including tastes and technology), can give rise to lasting and mutually beneficial trade. Analytical convenience was decisive, however, in the retention of the assumption of constant returns in much of trade theory, at any rate until very recently – witness Samuelson's comment: 'The phenomenon of increasing returns negates the nice convexity properties that are so beloved by us lazy mathematical economists hell-bent for elegance of formulation.'[38] Relaxing the assumption of a constant-returns technology, means, of course, confronting the issue of market structure; in particular, the analysis of imperfect competition. For, as is well known, except only under special circumstances (e.g. where total demand is large relative to the potential economies of large-scale production), perfectly competitive markets cannot prevail where returns to scale are non-constant. Nevertheless, Ohlin joined Haberler in calling for a useful theory of imperfect competition in international trade; but as Samuelson notes, 'that call has thus far not evoked a very exciting response'.[39] The signs are, however, that things may be changing, as evidenced by the recent spate of important and useful writings on imperfect competition, increasing returns and international trade.

Ohlin's model is a multi-factor one; he recognises not only three basic factors of production considered in neoclassical writings – land (or natural resources), labour and capital – but also varying *qualities* of the first two of these factors. Labour, for example, is divided into three groups: unskilled labour, skilled labour and technical labour.

He also recognises that there are international differences in the qualities of labour in all three classes. Ohlin explains the reasons for differences in prices and comparative advantage between countries and adopts two simplifying assumptions (for the two-factor case): (1) that the technology of production is the same in both countries, and (2) that 'the productive factors enter into the production of different commodities in very different proportions'.[40] Like Haberler, he considers the possibility that endogenous changes in relative factor returns (brought about, for example, by international trade) will eventually alter the available supplies of some of these factors, i.e. capital and the various types of labour.

Ohlin uses his general model to deduce certain fundamental propositions concerning the causes and consequences of trade. Trade will take place between two countries (or regions) if the domestic ratios of money costs of production of two commodities differ under autarky:

> The first condition of trade is that some goods can be produced more cheaply in one region than another. In each of them the cheap goods are those containing relatively great quantities of the factors cheaper than in other regions. These cheap goods make up exports, whereas goods which can be more cheaply produced in the other regions are imported. We may say, therefore, that exports are in each region composed of articles into the production of which enter large quantities of cheap factors.

If two countries have the same production functions, the same taste patterns for the two goods and the same endowments of primary factors, then their autarky price ratios will be the same and there will be no opportunity for gainful trade. If, however, tastes differ between them, but in all other respects the two countries are identical, then price ratios will differ inasmuch as in each country the commodity towards which demand is biased will be relatively dearer in autarky. Asymmetrical taste patterns will then generate mutually profitable trade; for each country will then find it advantageous to import the commodity for which its demand is more intense.

Similarly, Ohlin shows that differences in factor endowments or the occurrence of increasing returns are sufficient to generate viable trade among countries. Of all the factors liable to cause differences in autarky price ratios Ohlin considers differential factor endowments as the most important. Countries tend to export those commodities requiring more of their relatively abundant factors (i.e. low-priced factors) and import commodities intensive in the use of their scarce, hence high-priced, factors. Free trade in goods thus compensates for (or relieves) factor scarcities in the trading countries.

In a discussion of the effects of trade on factor supplies, factor returns and the structure of demand and taste patterns, Ohlin takes up Heckscher's proposition about the absolute equalisation of factor returns under free trade. Ohlin finds, however, that there will only be a partial equalisation; and he mentions factors which prevent complete equalisation – i.e. when some factor of production is found only in one country, the positivity of transport costs, and if specialisation leaves one country with an unproduced good.[41] Free trade in goods is thus a partial substitute for the free migration of factors.

THE HECKSCHER–OHLIN THEORY: ANTECEDENTS AND BASIC FEATURES

Ohlin regarded his new theory as the first decisive break with Ricardo's law of comparative costs. In his keeness to emphasise the novelty of his factor-endowment approach, he even refused to use the phrase 'comparative advantage'. His strong criticism of the classical theory is partly explained by his dislike of the labour theory of value. Of course, his theory was not a rejection of comparative advantage, but merely a restatement of it along neoclassical lines as part of a more general theory of the causes of trade.[42]

As a complete model of the forces governing international specialisation Ohlin's theory was certainly path-breaking; but antecedents to the theory can be found in earlier writings. Ohlin himself finds that the factor-endowment basis of trade patterns was 'first touched upon, not by the English classical school, but in French works', and he cites Sismondi's 1803 work, *De la richesse commerciale*, and the writings of Samuel Mountifort Longfield, Ireland's first professor of political economy.[43] Viner retorted with a string of quotations from the writings of the English classical economists (Ricardo himself, Malthus, McCulloch and Cairnes), selected to make the point that the classical economists 'did not wholly ignore the question of what forces determine international specialization, and when they did touch on it, their adherence to the doctrine of comparative costs did not prevent them from dealing with it on lines similar in essentials to those followed by Ohlin'.[44]

No one believes, however, that the extracts quoted by Viner are anything more than mere fragmentary, albeit brilliant, insights – but, nevertheless, hypotheses disjoined from the writers' basic paradigm or theoretical scheme. One nineteenth-century writer who fully anticipated the essentials of the Heckscher–Ohlin theory was the American economist, Stuart Wood. George Stigler called attention to Wood's work in the development of the marginal productivity theory of distribution (before Clark, Wicksteed and Flux). Wood's marginal productivity theorem was part of his theory of general equilibrium and he applied that theory to interregional and international trade, advancing in the process a sophisticated form of the H–O theory based on differences between countries (or regions) in terms of the relative supplies and prices of capital and labour. Robert Mundell more recently referred to Wood's pioneering contribution and declared that Wood's priority was even more remarkable than Stigler suggested: 'Stigler could not have been aware, in 1947, of the breakthrough by Samuelson or, of course, Lerner in factor-price equalization theory' – implying that Wood also anticipated the latter theory as well.[45]

Ohlin's judgement that members of 'the English classical school' contributed little or nothing to the development of the factor-endowment hypothesis has recently been challenged by Simon Power. Like Viner, he is concerned to show that 'the Heckscher–Ohlin concept has a far longer history than Ohlin was aware of', and in particular that British economists including Josiah Tucker, Smith, Ricardo, Torrens and McCulloch were all aware of the concept.[46] Now, this is true; and no doubt Ohlin was at fault in dismissing the writings of the British school on this point. However, again, the reflections of the British writers and others are so closely related to particular commodities or types of trade, notions about absolute advantages, locational factors, etc., that the essence of the H–O hypothesis does not stand out clearly alongside the more traditional explanations.

These early statements and conjectures are no doubt alternative explanations of trade; but they are not yet like the true H–O proposition. Even though many of the writers referred to come up with the factor-endowment result – a fairly obvious deduction for one disposed to absolute advantage reasoning – including the idea of variable proportions, the accounts are often superficial, generally falling short of any deeper analyses as to why the factor-endowment explanation should provide the basis of trade in general. It was

Heckscher and Ohlin who first established a sufficient reason for profitable trade premised on the simple but key assumption of identical production functions (identical technology) among countries. Thus even if technology and taste patterns are the same in all countries, a difference in relative factor endowments between countries combined with a common technology in which different goods require different factor-input proportions is a minimal or sufficient condition for gainful trade. The writers mentioned by Power fail to carry the argument this far. If the H–O hypothesis were so clearly stated by earlier writers, why is it that Marshall (the great respecter of tradition) and Edgeworth failed to recognise it in the classical literature?

The Heckscher–Ohlin theory made its appearance at an opportune time.[47] The time was ripe for the reception of such a theory by the new enthusiasts for general-equilibrium theory. In particular, it was quickly seized upon by Samuelson, who re-shaped and refined it in a series of articles in the late 1940s and early 1950s to produce what now appears in the textbooks as the standard $2 \times 2 \times 2$ H–O model of trade – the most popular model of production relationships in an open economy. Indeed, Samuelson's imprint on it is so marked that it is often referred to as the Heckscher–Ohlin–Samuelson model. Samuelson achieved that much because, as a leading practitioner of general-equilibrium theorising, he was uniquely equipped to appreciate the potential it afforded for giving substance (or structure) to the notion of general equilibrium – an area he discerned as being ripe for development.

The 1930s was a watershed between the old and the new (or modern) neoclassical economics. In the 1930s, there was growing dissatisfaction with the Marshallian tradition which led to Hicks's *Value and Capital* (1939) and Samuelson's *Foundations* (1947) and the consequent reconstruction of economic theory in a general-equilibrium framework. A research programme was initiated concerned with the existence, uniqueness, stability and Pareto-optimality properties of a competitive economy in general equilibrium.

In the field of international trade, the general theories of Heckscher and Ohlin offered a splendid opportunity for Samuelson to display the analytical techniques and propositions he had fashioned. The two-factor H–O theory (in contrast to the classical one-factor model) enabled the analyst to deal with the functional distribution of income within countries and the allocation of factors between industries. It also suggested new questions, such as the effects of capital accumulation and international factor movements on trade. Moreover, the 2-factor H–O model was intrinsically more revealing than the Ricardian model about production relationships and the structural characteristics of an exchange economy, since it fully recognised 'mutual interdependence' and 'simultaneous determination' in commodity exchanges among economic agents. Trade and economic structure were tightly knit together, and this went well with the new vogue (initiated by theorists like Lerner, Haberler and Leontief in the 1930s). In short, the factor-endowment theory considerably widened the scope for the application of the full techniques of marginal analysis (comparative statics) to trade theory. The core ingredients of the simple Heckscher–Ohlin theory were assembled from the basic relations of the general equilibrium of a two-sector economy upon which special assumptions were imposed so as to obtain sharp conclusions or unambiguous qualitative results.

Thus, in a perfectly competitive economy in which two commodities are produced with two factors utilising production functions characterised by constant returns to scale and diminishing marginal rates of substitution between factors, minimum unit cost depends only on factor prices, not on the level of output. Assuming perfect mobility of factors and adopting the marginal productivity theory, it follows that the price of each factor will be equated to the value of its marginal product and that the price of each factor will be the same in both industries. Then if a positive amount of each commodity is produced, competitive output-market assumptions guarantee that the price of each will equal its cost of production. It then follows that there is a one-to-one relation between the commodity price ratio and the factor price ratio. Further, if the factor endowment ratio is fixed and an assumption is made about the invariance of relative factor intensity, then the ratios in which the commodities are produced will be fixed, since their aggregate factor requirements must just absorb all of the available factor supplies.

THE STOLPER–SAMUELSON THEOREM

Using this framework, extended to a free-tree world of two countries each producing both goods, Samuelson provided meaningful sufficient conditions to prove two theorems – the Stolper–Samuelson theorem and the celebrated factor-price equalisation theorem. These results are well known, so no extensive discussions need be provided.

In a 1941 article with Wolfgang Stolper, Samuelson re-examined an old problem in the theory of trade policy: can a tariff effectively raise the real return to a large factor such as labour? In the first clear resolution of the problem, expounded with the aid of a simple diagrammatic and algebraic analysis of the Heckscher–Ohlin model, Stolper and Samuelson indicated that protection will unambiguously increase the real wage if labour is the scarce factor of production, and concluded: 'We have shown that there is a grain of truth in the pauper labour type of argument for protection.'[48] The statement of the theorem was prompted by the US trade unions' traditional concern about competition from cheap foreign labour, and was possibly also related to the prewar Australian debate on protection. The analysis clarified the logical structure of the Heckscher–Ohlin theory and paved the way for the factor-price equalisation theorem and numerous other results in simple general-equilibrium models of trade. In effect, it launched the Ohlin–Samuelson research programme.

A crucial assumption made by Stolper and Samuelson was that a tariff would raise the relative domestic price of importables: i.e. the terms of trade do not change – an assumption later challenged by Lloyd Metzler. The rise in this relative price brings about a rise in the price of the 'scarce' factor relative to all commodity prices. Thus, in a relatively labour-scarce country that imports the labour-intensive good, the real wage of its workers will be increased in terms of the price of capital or the price of any good by the imposition of an import duty.

Stolper and Samuelson eliminated the index-number problem that previously bedevilled attempts to arrive at a clear-cut answer: Do you evaluate income at the free trade or post-tariff prices? – given that protection will change all prices and money incomes. They also resolved the apparent paradox contained in the result that factor propertions (e.g. the ratio of capital to labour) in both industries respond in the same direction, despite the fixity in the overall factor-endowment ratio. The solution is found in the fact that the overall endowment (capital/labour) ratio is a weighted average of the two industries. As the relative outputs of the two industries change, so do the 'weights' – the expansion of the protected industry must give it a heavier weight. Stolper and Samuelson used the production box (the counterpart of the Edgeworth–Bowley consumption box) to derive their proof – the first published account of its construction; although, as noticed previously, Lerner had used it earlier in 1933. With the aid of the Edgeworth–Bowley box diagram (for a single country) they showed how the production–possibilities curve could be derived, and how factor proportions varied along the curve.

The Stolper–Samuelson conclusion depends only on the direction of change of the commodity price ratio after tariff imposition. It does not depend on the validity of the Heckscher–Ohlin theory; for instance, it does not depend on the assumption that countries share the same identical technologies. Nor does it depend on factor prices being completely equalised through commodity trade. What can affect the cogency of the proof, however, is the possibility mentioned by Metzler that when demand effects and foreign repercussions are included (i.e. the effects of the tariff on the terms of trade), the relative domestic price of importables may perversely fall – contrary to the Stolper–Samuelson assumption.[49]

Today, however, the theorem is commonly interpreted as a standard result independent of the tariff context in which it was first formulated. The theorem suggests that there is a unique relation between the commodity price ratio, the factor-price ratio, the real returns of factors and the structure of production (if no joint production prevails). Thus the relationship holds for any change in the domestic price ratio; this changes the real return to the factor used intensively in producing the commodity affected by the price change. In this more general context, the essence of the Stolper–Samuelson theorem is immune to the Metzler-effect.[50]

FACTOR-PRICE EQUALISATION AND RYBCZYNSKI THEOREMS

In 1948 Samuelson astonished the profession with his proof of the factor-price equalisation theorem – a corollary of the Heckscher–Ohlin theory.[51] Economists were almost completely unprepared for the result. What floored them was the use of the key Ohlinian assumption that the two countries shared identical technologies (or identical production functions) – the importance of which was insufficiently appreciated hitherto. Professional reaction is understandable, for three reasons: (1) Heckscher's work was not published in English until the following year, 1949;[52] (2) most economists were unaware of Lerner's 1933 proof – not published until 1952; and (3) Ohlin's denial that factor-price equalisation would ever be complete under free trade. He did assert that there was a tendency towards equalisation, but his statement was hedged about with many qualifications that obscured the underlying logic.

Two crucial assumptions (among others associated with the H–O theory) are necessary to establish the proof. (1) Both countries continue to produce positive amounts of the same two goods after free trade – the assumption of incomplete specialisation. This assumption requires that both countries' endowments lie within the same 'cone of diversification', to use Chipman's apt phrase,[53] which rules out the possibility of a factor-intensity reversal. (2) A two-good, two-factor model: factor-price equalisation will not necessarily occur when the number of goods is not equal to the number of productive factors. These are, of course, sufficient conditions (not necessary ones), and in a sense provide a weaker proof of the theorem.

A year later (1949), Samuelson followed this up with a more detailed statement of the theorem. In 1953 he made a comprehensive study of the theorem with a more general H–O model of many factors and many commodities in which he attempted to prove the uniqueness of the relation between a given set of commodity prices (a p-vector) and the corresponding factor prices (a w-vector).[54] If the commodity price-factor price relationship is unique then factor price equalisation is the only equilibrium solution. This will be the case where there are two goods and two factors, for then p and w are both two-dimensional vectors; hence, if both countries continue to produce the same two goods with free trade, then the equalisation of p implies the equalisation of w. This means that the schedule of production possibilities is convex. Mathematically, the convexity condition requires the unique inversion of the vector function $p = \mathrm{f}(w)$, where both p and w are n-vectors, into $w = \mathrm{f}(p)$; then, the equalisation of p certainly implies the equalisation of w – this is the convexity condition. The convexity condition breaks down, however, when factor-endowment ratios diverge widely, hence increasing the possibility of factor-intensity reversals and complete specialisation. If factor endowments are very dissimilar, both countries cannot produce both commodities. Factor price equalisation will hold for a group of countries whose factor endowments lie within the same cone of diversification. However, there will be 'cross-over' points (where critical factor-endowment ratios occur) at which factor intensities reverse themselves. Countries in such areas (i.e. on one side or the other outside of a particular cone of diversification) prevent worldwide factor price equalisation. As Mundell observes: 'The real world is characterised by factor-price equalisation zones rather than a single worldwide zone where universal factor-price equalisation can be achieved.'[55]

Just before Samuelson's article on prices of factors and goods in general equilibrium appeared, the third principal pillar in the H–O structure was put into place – the Rybczynski theorem. Tadeusz (Tad) Rybczynski (then at the LSE), using a simple diagrammatic technique proved the following theorem: if the supply of one factor increases with the supply of the other factor constant, the absolute output of the good which uses the increased factor less intensively must diminish so as to keep the relative price of the goods constant.[56] This theorem has spawned countless subsequent treatments of the trade and closed-economy effects of economic growth, factor movements and technical change. This exploration of the production effects of changes in relative factor supplies served another purpose as well, namely, to suggest the compatibility of the H–O model with the work done in the 1930s by Haberler, Lerner and Leontief. This integration is now taken for granted; but as Baldwin reminds us, it only took place after Rybczynski's work brought about 'a clear understanding of how, when technology is everywhere the same, intercountry differences in relative (fixed) factor supplies are reflected in the shapes of their production-possibilities curves' – i.e. a bias in the shape of the transformation schedule imparted by relative factor endowments.[57] The simple H–O model with its assumptions of identical, homothetic taste patterns and no factor-intensity reversals was revealed as isomorphic with the Haberler–Lerner model.

TRADE THEORY AS GENERAL EQUILIBRIUM ANALYSIS

Samuelson's suggestions regarding the conditions for factor-price equalisation (particularly his 1953 paper) stimulated developments both in pure mathematics and economic theory. Many properties of the two-sector economy (particularly on the supply side) became better known to trade theorists, and the attempt to move to higher dimensions posed problems that attracted the attention of mathematicians and mathematically-oriented economists (e.g. Gale, Nikaido, Kuhn, Chipman, Jones, McKenzie, etc.).[58] The postulate regarding the determination of factor prices by commodity prices goes beyond the Walrasian principle that prices are simultaneously determined, to the deeper question concerning their interrelations.

In this sense, the search for a multi-factor, multi-good model was a potentially promising one; thus Samuelson's quest was concerned with discovering equilibrium conditions for a trading world faced with a given set of commodity prices – a more interesting problem than that concerned with (for the most part) stating the conditions for full Walrasian equilibrium.

The investigations revealed several important relations useful in other branches of economic theory: for example, (1) cost-minimising behaviour; (2) the equivalence condition defining the one-to-one correspondence between commodity prices and factor prices; and (3) the inverse or implicit function theorem. The exploration of these relations stemmed from Samuelson's work on factor-price equalisation. He saw the problem as being central to the cost-production duality in general equalibrium and also as a logical extension of the mathematical theorems on implicit functions.[59]

The technical apparatus of economic theory was extended (particularly in the handling of general-equilibrium relationships) by these investigations. Ronald Jones in 1965 emphasised the dual relationship between the Stopler–Samuelson and Rybczynski theorems, i.e. the link between commodity and factor prices, on the one side, and output-factor endowment relations at constant output prices, on the other. The duality relation between the two theorems was also noticed by Samuelson, out of which came a new finding: a population increase will raise the output of the labour-intensive product. It was in this connection that Samuelson introduced the 'reciprocity relation' or theorem, neatly expressed as:

$$\frac{\partial X_j}{\partial V_i} = \frac{\mathrm{w_i}}{\partial p_j}$$

where X_j and V_i denote the output of commodity j and endowment of factor i respectively; p_j is the price of commodity j and w_i the price of factor i. In words: the jth output response to an ith input increment (keeping all other endowments and commodity prices constant) equals the ith factor-price response to the jth commodity price increment.[60] This remarkable result applies to any general-equilibrium model regardless of the number of factors or commodities. Jones notes that this relationship has been extremely useful in simplifying the theory of foreign investment, in particular, analyses of optimal tariffs and direct investment.[61] Henry Wan observes: 'Both the reciprocity theorem and the factor-price equalisation theorem were then shown to be implications of a general-equilibrium model under constant returns and without joint products.'[62]

THE LEONTIEF PARADOX AND THE EVALUATION OF THE OHLIN–SAMUELSON RESEARCH PROGRAMME

Coincidentally, the very year Samuelson's classic 1953 article on prices of factors and goods in general equilibrium appeared – the crowning achievement of his work on the H–O theory – Wassily Leontief published his paradoxical findings on US trade patterns: the manufacture of US exports required a higher proportion of capital to labour than the manufacture of import-competing goods. Until that time, the standard H–O theory held great sway among trade theorists (certainly as a pedagogic device) and was widely regarded as affording a complete and satisfactory explanation of the sources of comparative advantage and hence of the observed pattern of trade.

The revelation that the United States, according to its measured trade pattern, was scarce in capital compared with labour, contradicted the general impression that the reverse was true. Subsequently, Leontief-type tests were applied in experiments to determine the factor-intensity ratios of other countries' exports and imports. But since in about half of the studies undertaken theoretical predictions were at variance with the empirical result, confidence in the two-factor H–O theory was badly shaken. The paradox therefore led to a re-examination of the assumptions of the theory, especially the non-reversibility of factor intensities in production, but also attempts at enlarging or altering the simple theory to include such factors as tariffs, human capital, knowledge capital, natural resources, monopolistic competition, etc.

According to the 'naive falsificationist' criterion for the evaluation of scientific research programmes, economists should have rejected the Heckscher–Ohlin theory when the empirical content of its hypothesis on trade patterns was found to be empty (even perverse) by Leontief and others. To be sure, economists working in the applied field of international trade flows did respond by (1) developing new hypotheses, and (2) reacting in the way described.[63] But a group of leading theorists continued their allegiance to the empirically suspect factor-proportions theory. Why? First of all, what was refuted was the simple two-factor, two-commodity model (in terms of homogeneous labour and capital) not the general-equilibrium model in which it was embedded. Indeed, how can you empirically falsify a general-equilibrium model and the theorems derived from it? The simple $2 \times 2 \times 2$ model 'proved' strong theorems (Stolper–Samuelson, Rybczynski) but, with perhaps one exception, the effort has not resulted in any testable (falsifiable) hypotheses.[64] Undisturbed, theorists continued to explore the general-equilibrium model. But empirical analysts turned in another direction; indeed, back to Ohlin's more general model – what Ford calls his 'subsidiary model' – which focuses on economies of scale, multiplicity of factors, imperfect competition, etc.[65]

In the first attempt to evaluate the Ohlin–Samuelson programme in terms of Lakatos's methodology of scientific research programmes, Neil de Marchi came to essentially the same conclusions. The Ohlin–Samuelson programme resulted in fruitful work; novel 'facts' emerged from it – it was a 'progressive research programme'. As such it was perfectly rational for theorists to continue with it – 'under the wider theoretical perspective adopted by Samuelson it was entirely proper that Leontief's finding did not determine the direction of research'.[66] The charge that the Ohlin–programme represents an excessive preoccupation with formal structure, he dismisses as being beside the point.

Bert Hamminga, in another meta-theoretical evaluation of the Ohlin–Samuelson programme, characterised the aim of the programme's participants as that of increasing the plausibility of the theorem: theorists try to remove restrictive assumptions, thereby generalising the results. If a theorem holds in many worlds (i.e. higher-dimensional cases with weak conditions which can be described in the economist's language of production functions, utility functions, factor endowments, etc.) then the probability is high of the model being true in our real world 'without even considering at all what our real world exactly is like'. The less restrictive the assumptions, the more valuable the result. Hamminga supports his 'plausibility hypothesis' by quoting leading theorists to the effect that the removal of restrictive assumptions allows for more possible cases under which their theorems are still true, i.e. the theorems approximate 'true descriptions of the real world'. However successful theory development along these lines may be in terms of the theorist's own criteria of evaluation, very little is done in the way of deriving falsifiable hypotheses. Indeed, Hamminga points to a real irony in the situation. The more theory development proceeds along the 'generalisation' road (hence counted as the characteristics of a successful programme), the more difficult it becomes to devise empirical applications of the theorems suitable for estimation and testing: 'The Ohlin–Samuelson programme aims at deriving theorems with as few specifications as possible. Econometrists are on the lookout for suitable specifications; Ohlin–Samuelson participants aim at the removal of them.'[67]

Mark Blaug finds in the Ohlin–Samuelson research programme a good example to sustain his belief that much of economic theory is non-empirical, in the sense that the theorems give rise to no useful hypotheses. He asks: 'What would have been lost if the Leontief Paradox had put a stop to the H–O research programme?'[68] Very little, in effect, he answers; but grants that judgements may differ. His criticism ranges over many points: (1) The novel facts brought to light by the programme were less matters of fact than analytical connections between interntional trade and competitive exchange models. (2) The programme popularised the simpliste marginal productivity theory and encouraged the teaching of parables (e.g. the $2 \times 2 \times 2$ model with aggregate production functions). (3) It unified the treatment of domestic and international trade by means of a highly simplified general-equilibrium theory that 'promised more than it was capable of delivering'. Quoting Samuelson's claim that the factor-price equalisation theorem 'does convey insights into the process shaping world trade', Blaug remarks that this 'fond belief' is 'a contention reminiscent of the methodology of a priorism that he [Samuelson] professed to despise' – for Samuelson in his early days was a champion of 'operationalism' in economic theory.[69] Samuelson's claim for the empirical relevance of factor-price equalisation is similar to the one made for general-equilibrium theory by Professor Hahn – i.e. that it has 'great practical significance' for policy judgements on the free market – an assertion that prompts Donald Gordon to remark, 'This must be the ultimate in anti-empiricism.'[70]

The Leontief paradox may also be considered in the light of the Duhem–Quine thesis concerning the possibility of theory appraisal.[71] The Duhem–Quine contention is that it is not possible to falsify a single hypothesis in isolation from the auxiliary hypotheses which support the single-target hypothesis under empirical scrutiny. In scientific work, hypotheses come in clusters, revolving around some central theory that seeks to explain some phenomenon or aspect of reality. When we test a particular hypothesis from a theoretical group we are in fact testing a whole cluster of related hypotheses, and so when we find that empirical evidence tells against the particular hypothesis we cannot conclude that the hypothesis is false; only that the conjunction of the particular hypothesis with the set of auxiliary hypotheses belonging to that group has been disproved. One or more of the auxiliary hypotheses may be at fault, rather than the one in which we are interested. In the absence of independent empirical confirmation of all the related hypotheses belonging to a theoretical group, we must necessarily conduct our empirical investigations at the level of groupings of hypotheses.

Applying the Duhem–Quine methodology to the H–O model and the debate surrounding the Leontief paradox, the above argument suggests that when we test the H–O hypothesis on trade patterns we are necessarily also jointly testing a large number of supporting hypotheses. In the score or more of Leontief-type tests of the H–O hypothesis, no attention has been paid to the appraisal of the auxiliary hypotheses surrounding the maintained hypothesis of the data analyses. Consequently, on methodological grounds, no conclusion can be drawn either way about the empirical validity of the H–O hypothesis. The auxiliary hypotheses that escaped empirical scrutiny relate to the competitive exchange and production model: constant returns to scale, perfectly competitive markets, identical production functions – i.e. all countries have exactly the same technology – to name only the obvious ones. Moreover, in the tests thus narrowly applied, not enough care was taken to define the hypothesis subject to testing. The H–O hypothesis is a set of relations between trade on the one hand, and sectoral relative factor intensities and factor endowments on the other. Few, if any, investigators have succeeded in dealing with all three relations required by the theory. Instead, most of them, perhaps erroneously, have used empirical counterparts of two of these variables and have inferred the third (as revealed by the factor content of trade): for example, Leontief himself did not measure, but inferred factor abundance of one country from measures of trade and factor intensities. Moreover, no attempt was made to use independent data on factor endowments in the rest of the world. Thus, even within the restricted empirical framework, the tests can hardly be regarded as conclusive – to say nothing of the fact that no consensus can be formed as to what constitutes a valid test, when the theory itself is not well articulated for the case of many factors and many commodities.

There is no appropriate statement of the H–O hypothesis applicable to a multi-factor, multi-good, multi-country world, despite useful theoretical work towards that end. In the absence of any such precise statement, any enterprise of testing the theory empirically remains a will-o'-the-wisp. The generalisations to higher dimensions have not resulted in unambiguous falsifiable hypotheses – the point made by Hamminga. The fact is that the general-equilibrium model still determines or dictates the working hypotheses for empirical work – e.g. the assumption of constant returns to scale, balanced trade, identical homothetic preferences and factor-price equalisation. With the first postulate – constant returns to scale – trade is a linear function of endowments; but in the real world, non-linear relations are not only possible, but very likely. Departures from the competitive model may be the rule rather than the exception, i.e. trade may be characterised by monopolistic competition, scale economies, product differentiation and intra-industry specialisation. Such real-world factors and circumstances weaken the explanatory power of the simple H–O hypothesis. Thus far, the discussion on the appraisal of the H–O hypothesis has been at the meta-theoretical level. What about the current opinions and judgements of trade specialists on the recent empirical work?

TRADE FLOWS – EVIDENCE AND INTERPRETATIONS

Since its appearance in 1954 the Leontief paradox has been the bugbear, the 'Achilles heel' of the Heckscher–Ohlin model of trade. However, today, the paradox is less apparent and indeed may have disappeared since the early 1970s. A widely acclaimed attempt at resolving the paradox (i.e. the empirical anomaly *vis-à-vis* the model) is due to Edward Leamer (1980). Leamer says the paradox 'rests on a simple conceptual misunderstanding', and he shows that if the proper calculations are done, the paradox ceases to exist.[72] He starts by noting that Leontief's 1947 data showed that the United States was a net exporter of both capital and labour services, and also that the capital–labour ratio embodied in production exceeded that embodied in consumption. This occurred because US trade was unbalanced (there was a surplus on the balance of trade). Leontief applied the H–O hypothesis to a situation of balanced i.e. he compared the capital per man embodied in $1 million worth of imports with the capital per man embodied in $1 million worth of exports. But in a multi-factor world and unbalanced trade, Leontief's procedure (of calculating the factor contents of exports and imports separately) cannot reveal the true relative abundance of capital and labour. To deal with this situation in a correct manner, use must be made of an alternative version of the H–O hypothesis – namely, the Heckscher–Ohlin–Vanek theorem which states: A country will export the services of abundant factors and import the services of scarce factors; and what must be estimated, in the case of unbalanced trade, are the factors embodied in net exports. Factors embodied in net exports equal the excess factor supplies; hence net exports is the difference between domestic production and domestic consumption. A valid test must therefore be stated in terms of the factor ratios embodied in production compared with consumption, rather than in terms of exports compared with imports (as Leontief did); for with a trade surplus, a country can easily be a net exporter of the services of the factors with which it is relatively poorly endowed – e.g. the trade of a capital-abundant country may reveal its imports to embody a higher ratio of capital to labour than its exports. To estimate the true trade-revealed capital abundance, one must see (1) whether the country's production is more capital intensive than its consumption, or (2) if the capital intensity of net exports exceeds the capital intensity of consumption. Leontief's data showed that both of these were true of the United States in 1947, and Leamer concludes that 'therefore the United States is revealed to be capital abundant'.[73] There is no paradox after all.

But why, given its relative capital abundance, should the United States be also a net exporter of labour services? Brecher and Choudhri (1982) raised this question and showed that a country could be a net exporter of labour services only if its aggregate expenditure per worker (or per capita GNP) was less than in the rest of the world.[74] But there is overwhelming independent evidence that US per capita GNP exceeded world per capita GNP in 1947, even after making adjustment for the US trade surplus. Hence this finding contradicts the reformulated H–O–V hypothesis; and Leamer's observation that the United States was a net exporter of labour services is itself paradoxical. However, as indicated above, later empirical studies suggest a tendency for the US trade pattern to conform with the theoretical prediction in more recent time periods, e.g. in the study by Stern and Maskus (1981).[75]

Summarising the current state of the evidence on the Leontief paradox and its implications for the H–O model, Alan Deardorff writes that the paradox in any of its several forms 'seems to have disappeared by the early 1970s'; yet its persistence in the earlier decades 'continues to cast doubt on the overall validity and usefulness of the Heckscher–Ohlin model of trade'.[76] Deardorff further observes that Leamer's result, although supportive of the model, undermines the theoretical validity of the simple H–O hypothesis when trade is unbalanced.

Nevertheless, the accumulated empirical evidence does tend to support the view that net trade flows or the commodity composition of trade are related to cross-country differences in factor endowments broadly interpreted, i.e. human capital, unskilled labour, physical capital and natural resources. But the same data set may be compatible with other explanations, e.g. increasing returns to scale and non-competitive market structures, knowledge generated by firms through R&D and experience (technology), differences in domestic taxation, etc.; so that the factor-endowment explanation of trade is not indubitably proved by the same empirical observations. It is only one explanation for trade flows, and perhaps not the most significant. The theory from which the H–O hypothesis is derived claims that a difference in factor endowments is a sufficient cause for trade; but there are other sufficient conditions, as suggested above. Many analysts, however, seem to believe that differences in endowments constitute the single most important reason for trade. As a description of reality (particularly in relation to trade in manufactures), this position is clearly an untenable one. James Melvin recently expressed a similar scepticism about the empirical literature in these words: 'Why one would expect empirical results to show a relationship between endowments and trade patterns has always been a mystery to me.'[77]

Leamer starts his recent empirical study of the factor proportions theory of international trade by expressing the hope that his data analysis may perhaps convince the reader that the H–O–V model 'is surprisingly accurate, so much so that the model seems more useful than it did at the outset'.[78] However, what he does find by his cross-country regressions of net export commodity trade vectors on resource endowment vectors, is that trade is accurately represented as a linear function of endowments. But as one reviewer remarked: 'It leaves completely open the question whether it is the linear relation predicted by the H–O–V theory.'[79]

But all is apparently not well with the Heckscher–Ohlin–Vanek theorem, judging from the recent work reported by Keith Maskus (1985). In a complete empirical test of the H–O–V hypothesis and its corollaries with respect to US trade for 1958 and 1972, Maskus concludes: 'the H–O–V theorem does not receive support from the data used here'. Even with the application of the appropriate techniques, the H–O–V theorem was found to be inconsistent with independent data on factor endowments. Since each of his negative findings corresponds to some form of the Leontief paradox, Maskus believes that 'paradoxical outcomes may be the rule rather than the exception' in empirical applications of the theorem. Maskus guardedly notes, however, that his conclusions 'do not necessarily imply that differences in relative factor endowments across countries do not play an important role in the determination of world trade patterns'. Rather, the assumptions of the H–O–V version of the factor proportions theory are too restrictive for that version to offer accurate predictions concerning the factor content of the pattern of trade.[80] The scope for generalising the factor-content version of the Heckscher–Ohlin theorem in forms suitable for empirical verification seems promising, and some attempts have been made in that direction. It must be noted, though, that the Vanek–Leamer generalisation of the Heckscher–Ohlin hypothesis is concerned with predictions about the factor-content of trade patterns (i.e. the 'amounts of factor services embodied in goods traded'), not with the more traditional problem of explaining the commodity composition of trade (i.e. the explanation of trade flows in actual commodities). The former procedure is a definite shift of interest; but it corresponds with a commonly held view of the factor proportions theory, namely, that trade in commodities represents indirect trade in factor services. In general, however, the *communis opinio doctorum* is that work on the H–O model is a 'progressive research programme', since theoretical amendments widen the scope for the production of refutable hypotheses. In terms of Lakatos's methodological theory, the empirical work has stimulated the further development of trade theory along lines more consistent with empirical reality.

We now turn to a discussion of some of the interesting new developments in international trade theory, but note at this point that we have not touched upon the various hypotheses resulting from the empirical work stimulated by the Leontief paradox since these are well covered in most basic texts. One set of hypotheses relates to human capital, natural resources and skill groups, and the other to the role of technology (research and development, new products, product-cycle phenomena, etc.) in the determination of trade patterns – particularly the pattern of trade of the United States. The first set of hypotheses is consistent with a generalised H–O or H–O–V factor-proportions theory, whilst the second (in one particular instance) denies the relevance of comparative advantage as a determinant of trade, but in most versions the latter hypotheses seem to be indistinguishable from either Ricardian-type explanations or skills and human-capital factors as determinants of trade.

7.3 Recent Developments in Trade Theory and Policy

DIMENSIONALITY

Early attempts, starting in the 1950s, to extend the H–O–S theorem and its corollaries to higher dimensions introduced a heavy load of sophisticated mathematics into trade theory which undoubtedly improved the technical apparatus of economics. But this gain was counterbalanced by an even greater loss in terms of relevance, meaningful economic content and plain empirical probabilities. The pure theory of international trade appeared to be in danger of becoming just another branch of pure (or, more correctly, applied) mathematics. This regrettable trend resulted from misguided efforts to obtain or prove 'strong' propositions analogous to those obtained in the two-dimensional environment. Trade theorists and mathematical economists attempted to prove too much (via the obscure properties of input–output matrices) and the resulting failure was manifest in the incomprehensibly complex statements of the results. Reviewing this phase of theoretical work, Wilfred Ethier observes that it demonstrates 'a basic failure to break the chains of "twoness" when it is demanded that fairly strong properties survive'.[81]

In the 1970s, however, trade theory emerged from this theoretical dead-end. It was realised that dimensionality could be successfully incorporated if weaker, though no less interesting statements of the various theorems (or 'core propositions') were put forward. This had a liberating effect, as evidenced by the swift advance of higher dimensional theory over the last decade or so. Freed from the intolerable pressure to replicate the 2×2 results, trade theorists developed a generalised H–O–S model that yielded relevant, empirically plausible hypotheses directly applicable to a multi-factor, multi-good reality. The integrity of trade theory has been preserved; for the derivation of weaker propositions not only enhances the credibility of the theory but also suggests that the earlier stark insights may still be generally valid, if only in an average sense (in the form of correlations) or with reference to their applicability to some (not necessarily all) factors or goods, without identifying which goods or factors they are.

Some of the developments in this area may be briefly summarised. The fundamental proposition of trade theory – the principle of comparative advantage – can be stated not with reference to individual commodities, but in terms of a correlation between autarkic price differentials and net export volumes for different commodities: i.e. a country's net imports should be positively correlated with the comparison of its autarky commodity price vector and the vector of free-trade commodity prices. One drawback in the use of this procedure for the explanation of actual trade flows is, of course, that autarky prices are never actually observed. The Stolper–Samuelson theorem is not materially altered by an increase in the number of goods but only when there are many factors, and then the following statement applies: A rise in the price of one good must raise the real return of at least one factor and lower the real return of at least one other. Thus, every good is both a 'friend' and an 'enemy' to certain factors, to use the terminology of Jones and Scheinkman (1977).[82] The factor-price equalisation theorem remains basically intact when there are many commodities; but when factors outnumber goods, the most that can be claimed is a tendency towards equalisation.

THE SPECIFIC-FACTORS MODEL

One development has been the revival of interest in the specific-factors model which has its roots in the writings of Cairnes and Bastable. This model of production was developed by Haberler in the inter-war years; but its recent vogue stems from the formal mathematical treatment of it by Jones (1971), Samuelson (1971) and Mussa (1974).[83] Samuelson referred to it as the Ricardian–Viner model, since it combines the Ricardian analysis of rent (diminishing returns in agriculture, extended to all sectors) with the analysis of variable costs of production contained in Viner's classic article on cost and supply curves.

The properties of the specific-factors model contrast with the basic 2×2 H–O model, in that one of the factors (e.g. capital) is immobile between industries, so that its specific use in the two sectors means that it is a three-factor model (although each good is produced by only two factors). Clearly, in this model (where effectively the number of factors exceeds the number of produced commodities) factor-price equalisation is unlikely; trade will bring factor prices closer together, but not to the point of equality. The effects on domestic factor prices are also different from that suggested by the Stolper–Samuelson theorem. The Stolper–Samuelson theorem describes the effect of trade on a country's factor prices (the functional distribution of income): free trade will raise the relative price of labour as well as the real wage in a labour-abundant country, and decrease the real rental value of capital. This result follows from the assumption that factor prices are determined in national markets. The effect of a change in relative commodity prices on a particular factor depends not on the sector in which the factor is located, but what it implies for its national factor-market equilibrium. A productive factor, say, capital, may suffer a loss in real earnings even though there is a rise in the price of the product it helps to produce. This is liable to occur when the relative commodity price change causes the capital market to become depressed on account of the more intensive use of other units of capital in another industry.

In the specific-factors model, the earnings of mobile (or all-purpose) factors are determined by national factor-market equilibrium; but the real return to the mobile factor in each industry is equal to its marginal product in that industry. Changes in relative commodity prices always raise the reward of the mobile factor in terms of one good and lower it in terms of the other – e.g. the real earnings of the mobile factor fall in terms of the commodity whose price has risen and rise in terms of the commodity whose price has fallen. That is, the mobile factor, e.g. labour, will move towards the sector favoured by the price rise, thereby lowering the value of labour's marginal product in terms of that sector's good; while the reduction of labour supply in the other sector raises the value of labour's marginal product in terms of that other sector's good. Thus, changes in the real return to the mobile factor cannot be predicted without a knowledge of taste patterns, and we again encounter the 'neoclassical ambiguity' on this issue that was supposed to have been eliminated by the Stolper–Samuelson theorem.

Returns to specific factors move in the same direction (and to a magnified extent) as the prices of the goods they help to produce, i.e. returns change more than in proportion to the price changes. This theoretical result corresponds very well with observed reality. Owners of capital trapped in a depressed industry earn less than the economy-wide average rate of return on capital invested.

Mayer (1974), Mussa (1974, 1978) and Neary (1978) treated the specific-factors model as a short-run version of the standard H–O–S model.[84] Given enough time and allowing for the processes of depreciation and replacement to exert their effects, all factors are perfectly mobile. Therefore, the short-run behaviour of the economy can be described by the specific-factors model, but we still need the H–O–S model to determine its long-run equilibrium. The model has also been proposed as a more realistic framework for analysing the trade of developing countries.

The specific-factors approach exhibits many of the features of a fully specified general-equilibrium model, but the production structure of the former makes it a convenient mode for partial-equilibrium analysis of a particular sector. This and other properties of the specific-factors model make it a useful vehicle for suggesting empirical hypotheses, and to that extent it enhances the theory's relevance for practical policy-making. Thus, it provides a theoretical model for dealing with adjustment costs and other short-run problems when particular domestic sectors are forced to contract under the pressure of international competition and changing patterns of specialisation. The problem that economists call 'the Dutch Disease' – the case where the discovery of an exhaustible resource, e.g. oil, distorts a country's comparative advantage away from traditional manufactures in a manner which may be irreversible when the resource runs out (initially one sector depressed while others boom) – can readily be handled by the model, by virtue of the fact that a sector's 'profitability' is identified with the return to its specific factor.

In general, the specific-factors approach captures features of the real world that escapes the H–O–S model, and by showing how many of the strong theorems of the latter need to be modified, it helps to break the rigid mould of standard trade theory. Trade theory now has at its disposal a greater variety of models each of which can yield useful insights when applied to limited but appropriate problem areas.

INCREASING RETURNS, IMPERFECT COMPETITION, ETC.

Another major development has been the incorporation into trade theory of new work in industrial organisation theory. We now have an on-going research programme concerned with the analysis of trade and trade policy in a world characterised by imperfect competition, differentiated products and economies of scale. It took trade theorists half a century to respond to the call by Haberler, Ohlin, Lord Robbins and others for a more realistic theory of imperfect competition and increasing returns in international trade. The new analytical approach has implications for such issues as the volume and direction of trade and also the gains from trade that alter perceptions about what trade theory can convey. In addition, the new tools of analysis have already proved serviceable in dealing with some salient features of today's trading environment and policies; and to that extent, they have remedied the deficiencies of the conventional model.

The Heckscher–Ohlin–Samuelson model which dominated trade theory for over twenty-five years, besides its empirical failings, could not properly explain (a) multinational corporations, intra-firm trade and foreign direct investment in general; (b) intra-industry trade; (c) the consequences of trade liberalisation,[85] and (d) why a government should believe that through trade intervention it could appropriate for its country a larger share of monopoly profits or rent of the rent-yielding industries.

The new thinking in trade theory offers explanations in terms of imperfectly competitive market structures. What is at issue concerns the answer to the question: Is trade caused by differences or similarities between countries? The dissimilarities have traditionally been thought of in terms of differences in endowments, technology or tastes. These differences (or characteristics of countries) suggest that countries will export a different group of goods from those which they import. But the fact is that a large and growing share of world trade takes place among relatively similar countries (in terms of size and factor endowments) – a noticeable trend in manufactured goods trade since the end of The Second World War. In this intra-industry trade (even when measured with a high degree of disaggregation), countries export and import relatively similar products. Commodities embodying similar factor proportions (similar input coefficients in production) feature in two-way trade in horizontally differentiated products, i.e. products belonging to the same industrial category. Basic endowments and technological differences no doubt still shape the pattern of trade where there are cross-country differences in technology, income, skills and natural resources, as in North–South trade. But the intra-industry trade of the industrialised countries is not well explained by the factor-endowments model.

INCREASING RETURNS

At least since the time of Adam Smith it was recognised that by participating in international trade a country could reap significant economies of scale, and scale economies have long been associated with the infant-industry argument for tariff protection. A trade theory which assumed that all markets were perfectly competitive could recognise that potential technological externalities provide a case for trade intervention, and yet preserve its integrity. Firms could still be regarded as perfectly competitive, but could not perform optimally because of the technological externality represented by increasing returns. To fully admit the phenomenon of increasing returns into neoclassical trade theory generally would have meant facing the problem of complete specialisation, multiple equilibria, indeterminancy of production and the loss of the idealised world of perfect competition; hence the topic remained on the periphery of the theoretical field.

Analysts have recently redirected their attention to economies of scale in the form in which they had been traditionally treated, i.e. allowing increasing returns to scale to exist in industries, countries or the world, but external to individual firms; also, more boldly, they have tackled head-on the matter arising from increasing returns that are internal to the firm. The latter enquiry inaugurated, of course, the long-awaited integration of imperfect competition into the main body of trade theory.

Economies of scale linked to national levels of output can provide a basis for trade alternative to differences in factor endowments. That is, such economies alone can create a comparative advantage for a large country in a commodity which is produced under increasing returns to scale. Thus, if increasing returns exist at the national level, Markusen and Melvin (1981) show that country size can determine trade patterns.[86] The large country will tend to export the good which is produced under economies of scale even if relative factor endowments are the same in two countries.

What about increasing returns linked to the scale of world output? In this case, a firm's effectiveness in production (or the cost savings enjoyed) may depend on the scale of world demand for, and output of, its product. The expansion of world output of a particular commodity allows greater degrees of specialisation (division of labour) which give rise to cost savings by the firm through intra-industry trade in intermediate inputs. Thus, for example, the productivity of the British computer industry depends not only on the size of Britain's semicondutor industry, but also on the size of the US (or Japan's) computer industry. If external economies arise from the possibility of trade in intermediate goods subject to scale economies, then the pattern of trade is determined by relative factor endowments. If, however, increasing returns attach to the firm, such favoured firms will expand output, dominate the market, and we end up with imperfect competition – i.e. we face the issues of market power, monopoly rents and strategic behaviour.

A variety of models, borrowed from the industrial organisation literature, have been pressed into service to aid the analysis: the Chamberlinian model of monopolistic competition, the contestable market hypothesis of Baumol, Panzer and Willig (according to which incumbent firms are forced to keep prices low to avoid entry), and the Cournot model of industry structure. The resulting work has done much to incorporate into general-equilibrium theory features of differentiated products and monopolistic/oligopolistic competition.

The specification of consumer preferences (the demand for differentiated products) includes two forms of the utility function: one, the 'love-of-variety' approach, and the other, the Hotelling–Lancaster model. The first assumes that consumers are identical, and they like to consume a large number of varieties; they are better off, the wider the variety of products on the market. The second, the 'ideal-variety' approach, assumes that consumers themselves are differentiated in terms of their preferences, i.e. every consumer has an ideal product, perceived as being one which embodies the consumer's most desired combination of characteristics.

Despite their different specifications of demand, these monopolistic competition models are essentially similar, and they all tell the same story: in the presence of economies of scale and imperfect competition, intra-industry trade takes place, even between countries with identical factor endowments. Such countries can be expected to engage in considerable two-way trade, exchanging different varieties of the same basic product. The gross trade in manufactures is apparently driven by economies of scale and non-competitive market structures, while net trade is related to differences in factor composition.

INCREASING RETURNS, IMPERFECT COMPETITION AND GAINS FROM TRADE

What are the implications of the new wave of analysis for the gains from trade and commerical policy? Rather surprisingly, it adds to the list of trading gains and widens the scope for trade intervention policies. In addition to the exploitation of comparative advantage benefits (a more efficient allocation of resources), the following gains from trade are likely in the presence of increasing returns and imperfect competition:

(1) Trade increases product variety and raises consumer welfare. The opening of trade results in a decrease in the number of domestically produced varieties, but this is more than compensated for by the availability on the market of a wider range of both imported and domestic varieties.
(2) With each country producing only a limited subset of the products in each industry subject to scale economies, this increases efficiency in those industries (through longer production runs) and results in lower prices for all consumers.
(3) Trade may encourage rationalisation in firms where output per firm determines the extent to which economies of scale are realised. Trade that increases output per firm lowers average cost: i.e. individual firms move down their average cost curves.
(4) Trade has a pro-competitive effect. Trade can reduce the degree of monopoly power in the economy: i.e. it forces oligopolistic industries to become more competitive, thereby increasing the potential gains from trade.

With imperfect competition, market prices do not equal marginal social valuations and it is possible for trade to reduce welfare in a Pareto-optimal sense. Expansion of market size through trade, in a situation where markets are not contestable (i.e. where monopoly profits persist), may in fact serve to buttress monopoly power, leave consumers with a variety of products less suited to their needs and reduce welfare.

TRADE POLICY IN IMPERFECTLY COMPETITIVE MARKETS

The theories discussed above suggest new arguments for the use of commercial policy. The changing character of trade and the new theoretical models of imperfectly competitive markets widen the scope for the active use of trade policy to promote the interests of domestic firms against their foreign competitors. Three incentives for trade intervention have been identified:

(1) A government can change the variety of products available in the domestic economy through tariff policy. At the same time, tariffs can be used to increase welfare through the inducement they provide for the expansion of domestic firms which set prices above marginal costs.
(2) A country which consumes a good supplied by a foreign monopolist can improve its terms of trade through an optimal tariff. The domestic government can use the tariff to extract a portion of the rent (monopoly profits) from the foreign exporter. If there is a rival domestic firm, then the tariff policy can be used to shift profits from the foreign to the domestic firm; this is particularly attractive if the domestic firm can export and earn foreign monopoly rents, as in the example used by Barbara Spencer and James Brander (1981).[87] Besides tariffs, export subsidies may help a country's firms to capture a larger share of global monopoly profits and thereby raise national income at other countries' expense – a conclusion derived from a model where the foreign and domestic firms interact as a Cournot duopoly (each firm chooses its output level, taking the other firm's level of output as given).
(3) Trade policy can be used to achieve strategic advantages for the national economy.[88] Thus, a case can be made for the promotion, through protection and export subsidies, of certain domestic sectors which generate valuable 'spillovers' (R&D and experience) to the rest of society by way of technological innovation and external economies. Such trade intervention on behalf of certain key sectors may raise national income, since the producers in such sectors may not, in fact, be paid the full social value of their production.

Many economists, while welcoming the new analytical perspective, remain unmoved by the associated arguments for trade intervention. Critics detect a neo-mercantilist ('beggar-my-neighbour') slant in the policy implications of the new models. The arguments are exploitative – one country benefits at the expense of the rest of the world. We could face the Prisoners' Dilemma: if all countries simultaneously pursue selfish trade policies, all are likely to lose.

The ideas behind profit-seeking intervention in imperfectly competitive and strategic environments, it is claimed, are merely disguised optimal-tariff and second-best arguments for trade intervention, as commonly understood. The results of the partial-equilibrium models of monopoly and oligopoly in international markets are sensitive to changes in assumptions: for example, if firms compete in terms of price rather than quantity, if entry barriers are low, and if multinational firms are brought into the picture, then the interests of firms and nations diverge. The gains from government intervention may accordingly be rather limited and narrowly diffused. The allocation of resources still matter, critics say; and they point out that sectors promoted by interventionist policies must compete with all others for scarce resources.

In a recent review of current issues in trade policy, Deardorff and Stern conclude that they do not regard the new interventionist arguments as affording 'sufficient grounds for seriously compromising or rejecting outright the principles of free trade as the basis for trade policy'.[89] This, no doubt, sums up the opinion of the majority of neoclassical economists. However, one fact must be applauded: trade theory has taken a leap into the concerns of the real world. It is now dealing with issues that are relevant to those actually engaged in and directly affected by new trends in trade policy. In this sense, the rethinking of the analytical bases of trade policy is a useful step forward.

MULTINATIONAL CORPORATIONS, ENDOGENOUS TARIFF THEORY

Finally, two additional developments are worth mentioning briefly – multinational corporations and endogenous tariff theory.

Until recently, trade theory had little to offer by way of a convincing explanation of the multinational firm. The field was cultivated by business school economists who emphasised imperfect market structures, ownership-specific advantages (e.g. a patent, superior or secret technology, marketing skills, etc.) and transactions costs lower than would be the case in open, arm's-length markets. These factors, highlighted as being relevant to an understanding of the existence and activities of multinational firms (referred to by John Dunning as the 'eclectic theory'), cannot be analysed adequately with the traditional trade model that assumes perfect competition and the free access to the most efficient methods of production.

Equipped with their new models of trade in imperfectly competitive markets, trade theorists have returned to the subject of multinationals and have made useful contributions to the literature concerning the activities of such firms and their impact on patterns of trade. Helpman and Krugman (1985) show how monopolistic competition and firm-specific economies of scale can explain the presence of multinationals.[90] The firm requires a headquarters service to coordinate its production activities in several overseas plants. The 'head office' activity is a fixed cost of production that generates scale economies internal to the firm and simultaneously available to separate plants in different countries – i.e. the multinational firm enjoys multi-plant scale economies which are internalised. Ethier (1986) uses a general-equilibrium model for the purpose of endogenising the internationalisation decision (the exchange of information between agents) – a matter not explored in previous studies. Ethier shows how the results can be incorporated into general trade theory.[91]

Public choice theory and estimates of nominal and effective rates of protection have provided economists with an entrée into a field long dominated by political scientists – the political economy of protectionism. The rapidly expanding literature is concerned with theoretical and empirical analyses of how, in a democracy, tariffs and other trade measures are endogenously determined by a lobbying process in which opposing economic interests compete.

Findlay and Wellisz (1982) were the first to devise a general-equilibrium model of endogenous tariff formation using a 'specific-factors' framework.[92] Magee and Young (1987) explain the history of tariffs in the United States during the twentieth century with a formal two-good, two-factor general equilibrium H–O model incorporating two lobbies and two political parties.[93] However, many alternative hypotheses besides those suggested by the authors are possible. It is doubtful whether models like these can explain the average level of protection – a view recently expressed by J. Peter Neary.[94] Mayer and Riezman (1985) argue that the literature on lobbying theory is deficient, in that it does not explain why a rational lobby would prefer tariffs to other forms of protection (e.g. domestic subsidies), since the political process will favour subsidies to achieve a given degree of protection.[95] Targeted subsidies can be obtained at cheaper cost.

If what the models of lobbying and endogeneous tariff formation are saying is true (i.e. that there is an active political market for protection), is there any use for a normative theory of trade? Normative trade theory assumes the existence of a benign, omniscient government (or an 'efficiency-minded dictator') that guides trade policy in a manner calculated to ensure maximum national welfare. If that is not the way things are done in the real world, what is the point of policy-orientated normative theory or welfare-theoretic anlysis? Max Corden answers this question and concludes that normative theory provides 'one reference point for judging institutional arrangements'.[96] What the new literature on endogeneous protection does is to crack the apolitical mould of the theory of trade policy; but the impact is likely to be rather minimal. Endogenous protection theory is founded on a narrow conception of the concerns of political economy. Although conflict is recognised, the role of the state, relations of power and authority, social classes and disruptive change within historical settings, are excluded. The determinants of the level of protection are related to domestic factors without explicit reference to considerations of international political economy and global institutional arrangements – e.g. the use of trade policy to achieve foreign policy and national defence objectives, the constraints imposed by foreign retaliation and strategies of reciprocity, etc.

A wider perspective than that offered by public choice theory is required to deal with these issues. In the case of tariff history, for instance, Charles Kindleberger documents the inadequacies of hypotheses derived from public choice theory and orthodox trade theory in dealing with actual events and outcomes – for example, the response of various European countries to the fall in world wheat prices after 1880 – and remarks that what they offer by way of explanation is 'not a great deal'.[97] Economic history has a role here: it can check the tendency for theorists to get carried away by a single model.

8 Balance of Payments Theory

8.1 The International Adjustment Mechanism and the Transfer Problem

INTRODUCTION

In her authoritative 1969 survey of balance of payments theory, Anne Krueger observed that 'there is no theory of international monetary economics', only a cluster of theories bearing on particular aspects of international monetary problems.[1] The position remains the same since Krueger wrote; no all-embracing tightly knit theory has emerged. Despite a great deal of technical sophistication, we are still at the level of 'approaches' (at least three) when it comes to the analysis of international monetary problems. This seems at first sight a trifle odd, since as John Chipman reminds us: 'The emergence of economic science in Great Britain in the seventeenth to nineteenth centuries was to some extent an offshoot of the development of the theory of adjustment of the balance of payments.'[2]

It says something about the complexity of international monetary problems – inevitably always firmly located within the policy domain – that centuries of vigorous debate (e.g. the extensive English discussion on the foreign exchanges and the balance of payments in the 1620s, the Bullion debate and the Currency-Banking School controversy in the early 1800s, the debate between Keynes and Ohlin over German reparations, etc.) have not resulted in a simple, unified theoretical framework comparable to that displayed in the pure theory of trade.

The reasons for this state of affairs are not hard to find: (1) Theoretical issues in international monetary economics often arose out of urgent and complex matters relating to policy, wherein it was difficult to distinguish normative from positive aspects; thus value judgements intruded into the analyses, although of course out of these policy-oriented debates were forged some of the most enduring analytical concepts in economics. (2) Different conclusions arose from different assumptions (often implicit) and differing scenarios (e.g. varying assumptions about the level of employment and prices, capital mobility, etc. produce widely different results). (3) Changes in policy regimes often require different models each with its own special assumptions. (4) In the analysis of international monetary equilibrium, analysts were frequently tempted to engage in comparative-static comparisons of international equilibria without paying careful attention to the dynamic monetary processes implied by their models. The real and monetary aspects of balance of payments adjustment were sometimes not properly sorted out, with the result that writers jumped to conclusions valid under the barter theory of trade but which were problematic when the macroeconomic processes involved in moving between equilibria were considered – this was particularly evident in the Keynes–Ohlin debate on reparations. (5) The interface between myth and reality was sometimes blurred: for example, in connection with how the Gold Standard worked from 1871 to 1914. (6) The wide variety of international currency arrangements over the last hundred years defied attempts to construct a single mode of analysis.

All this does not mean, of course, that there was no traditional theory, no working model used by the neoclassicals; on the contrary, disagreements sprung precisely from the use of and interpretation of a single model: the international adjustment mechanism described by Cantillon, Vanderlint and Gervaise and finally formalised by Hume in 1752 as the price-specie flow mechanism.

With this preliminary anticipation of divergent views, let us review the main currents of thought on the international adjustment mechanism and related topics since 1870.

As indicated in Chapter 1, practically all the ingredients of later approaches to balance of payments analysis were present in classical writings. Thus when Marshall began writing his *Principles of Economics* (1890), the Hume–Ricardo–Thornton–Mill adjustment mechanism was the well-understood conventional theory, and the international gold standard was in operation. By 1879, most of the world, including the United States, was on the gold standard system. In Great Britain, the system survived a series of liquidity crises (and 'panics') both before and after the passing of the Bank Charter Act 1844 – i.e. in 1825, 1836, 1838, 1847, 1859 and 1866 which threatened an essential principle of the system, namely, the convertibility of Bank of England notes and deposits into gold. These crises occurred when 'external drains' of specie (resulting from large overseas lending or trade deficits) coincided with 'internal drains' (excess demand by deposit and note holders for specie currency). The experience of these crises obliged the Bank to accept an obligation to act as a 'lender of last resort' according to the rule enunciated by Walter Bagehot but first fully articulated by Thornton sixty years earlier. The practice of Bagehot's rule helped in central-bank management of the gold standard. Just as important from the point of view of the general acceptance and stability of the system around 1880 were the new gold discoveries in the Rand district of the Transvaal in South Africa, Alaska (the Klondike–Yukon valley), Colorado, and improved lower-cost methods of mining and refining gold. The increased supplies of monetary gold allowed newcomers to the system to build up their gold reserves without subjecting their economies to painful deflationary pressures. In the United States, although the convertibility of deposits into notes was fairly frequently suspended, e.g. in 1882, 1893 and 1907, and the system was a decentralised one without a central bank until 1913, the gold standard was, as in Great Britain, maintained continuously until 1914.

MILL'S SYNTHESIS OF THE TRADITIONAL APPROACH

Marshall was indebted to John Stuart Mill for much of his own monetary theory, including the theory of the international adjustment mechanism. As he did with the barter theory of trade, Mill gave a lucid account of classical theory which was in effect a synthesis of the views of Thornton and Ricardo combined with some elements of Banking School thought. Mill compares the adjustment mechanism under a system of barter with that of a monetary economy and finds that the final outcome is the same in both cases, i.e. domestic and foreign price levels adjust to restore equilibrium. Under barter, relative prices adjust directly, whilst when money is used the adjustment of relative price levels (and consequently the prices of exportables and importables) takes place through changes in the quantity of money induced by gold flows. Mill distinguishes between temporary and permanent disturbances to the balance of payments. A temporary disturbance will be accommodated through a change in the exchange rate within the gold points without the need for bullion movements, whereas a permanent disturbance requires 'the subtraction of actual money from the circulation of one of the countries'.[3]

In an analysis of the difference between real and nominal disturbances (e.g. a remittance or unilateral transfer from one country to another, as against a purely monetary disturbance such as the discovery of a hoard of treasure), Mill discusses the transfer problem and finds that a transfer will be virtually effected in goods (through an export surplus in the paying country) with the paying country also experiencing a deterioration in its terms of trade: 'The paying country will give a higher price for all that it buys from the receiving country, while the latter . . . obtains the exportable produce of the tributary country at a lower price.'[4]

A purely monetary disturbance (under a metallic standard) has no long-run effects; excess domestic money will be diffused throughout the world through a payments deficit which serves merely to raise the world's price level consistent with each country having a real money stock appropriate to its level of real output.

All this is straight early-classical reasoning (derived, it should be noted, in the case of a real disturbance, from Thornton rather than Ricardo, since the latter explicitly denied that gold movements, inflationary/deflationary price movements or shifts in the terms of trade were necessary to the adjustment). But Mill made an important observation concerning the role of short-term capital flows in the adjustment process – a discussion of how Bank Rate could be used as a means of protecting the country's gold reserve by its effect upon the rate of interest on foreign loans. Ricardo's explanation of the adjustment mechanism took no notice of international capital movements; indeed, his formal theory ruled out capital mobility. Gold flows were activated solely by imbalances on current account, and changes in the terms of trade (relative prices) restored equilibrium. Mill was exceptional in recognising the role of capital flows (i.e. the capital account) in the adjustment process:

> It is a fact now beginning to be recognised, that the passage of the precious metals from country to country is determined much more than was formerly supposed by the state of the loan market in different countries and much less by the state of prices.[5]

Gold movements are not necessarily accompanied by shifts in the balance of trade; also, changes in the domestic relative to foreign price level are neither necessary nor sufficient to transmit gold from deficit to surplus countries. Yet by the time of Marshall and Pigou, this important element of overseas investment – international lending and borrowing – was still overlooked in accounts of the equilibrating mechanism. Joan Robinson often criticised them (i.e. Marshall and his followers) for their failure to take notice of such obvious phenomena, and their reliance upon adjustments of relative price levels to keep trade in balance. As she rightly pointed out: 'The operation of the gold standard mechanism was to keep flows of lending in line with income balance.'[6]

MARSHALL

Marshall explains the price-specie flow mechanism and the natural distribution of specie hypothesis in terms of arbitrage in one commodity, gold. The gold standard rule that each country maintains a fixed mint price of its currency in terms of gold ensures uniformity of the price of gold across countries through the process of arbitrage in gold. If gold prices are kept in line, then the natural distribution of specie hypothesis implies that the price levels of all countries are also linked together. Gold flows set in motion by any disturbance affecting one country's price level (by altering relative money supplies) adjust home and foreign price levels until balance of payments equilibrium is restored. Thus, describing the process of arbitrage in gold, Marshall writes: 'trade tends so to adjust the supplies of gold relatively to the demand for gold in the two countries as to bring gold prices at the seaboards of the two countries to equality, allowance being made for carriage'.[7]

This is a restatement of the classical doctrine with regard to the international comparison of the values of moneys. Any deviation from the equilibrium activates the price-specie flow mechanism which restores the equilibrium in the values of moneys in the two countries. He states the law of one price: 'so long as national currencies are effectively based on gold, the wholesale price of each commodity tends to equality everywhere'.[8] Arbitrage in response to payments imbalances takes place not only in gold, but also in any tradeable commodity, e.g. lead, once the 'lead point' is reached. The advantage of gold over other commodities for purposes of arbitrage among countries under the gold standard is that it has 'in each a practically unlimited market'.[9] The integration of markets for standardised commodities makes the adjustment to balance of payments disequilibria less dependent on gold flows; but perhaps more significant in this connection is the integration of national money markets centred in the London discount market:

The growing tendency of intercommunication has shown itself in

> the discount market more than in any other; fluctuations in the price of wheat are being held in check by the growing internationality of the wheat market; but the discount market is becoming international more rapidly than even the wheat market.[10]

Short-term capital movements in response to interest-rate differentials thus equilibrate swings in the balance of payments more speedily than arbitrage in traded goods and obviate the need for gold flows. Here we have an explicit recognition of the role of financial institutions and central banks in the adjustment process.

IRVING FISHER

Fisher's account of the balance of payments adjustment mechanism was inconsistent. On the one hand, he argued that for a small open economy under the international gold standard (e.g. one state within the United States) the price level is ultimately determined by the world price level through commodity arbitrage rather than by the domestic quantity of money – the money supply in such a small open economy is endogenous. Yet in the analysis, he retained the quantity-theory notion of causality between the quantity of money and the price level more appropriate to a closed economy, and indicated that world prices affected domestic prices only indirectly through their influence on the domestic money supply:

> The price level in an outside community is an influence . . . and operates by affecting the money in circulation and not by directly affecting its price level. The price level outside of New York City . . . affects the price level in New York City only via changes in the money in New York City.[11]

The inconsistency is the same as that noticed in Hume's account: how to reconcile strict adherence to the law of one price with the price-specie flow mechanism? However, the inconsistency in Fisher's account is more apparent than real, for in another passage he alludes to the possibility that trade may not in fact bring about uniformity of price levels (i.e. the law of one price does not hold strictly); thus trade will 'produce an adjustment of these levels toward uniformity by regulating . . . the distribution of money'.[12] Where the force of commodity arbitrage is weak, gold will flow, and by affecting the prices of all commodities (not just the prices of traded goods) act more swiftly and powerfully than international commodity arbitrage.

LAUGHLIN

J. Laurence Laughlin, the founder of the *Journal of Political Economy* and first chairman of the Chicago economics department, adopted the Banking School position that the quantity theory was inapplicable to small open economies under fixed exchange rates – only under an inconvertible paper currency does the quantity theory become applicable. According to Laughlin, divergent price levels were not part of the adjustment mechanism under the gold standard; rather, adjustments came about through the rapid workings of commodity arbitrage facilitated by modern methods of communication. He found no statistical evidence of divergent price level adjustments, and concluded that the specie-flow corrective mechanisms no longer worked.[13] Haberler pointed out that far from being a valid objection to classical doctrine (i.e. the criticism that because of quick transport, price differentials cannot exist long enough to produce sufficiently large movements of goods), Laughlin's statement 'calls attention to circumstances which make for a rapid functioning of the mechanism'.[14] But this is precisely the point Laughlin makes:

> The competition between trading countries, as between different parts of the same country, being exceedingly keen, merchants in the leading countries would send the goods themselves to the spot where high prices existed, and by a quick increase of the supply of goods they would reduce prices in the country whose level was artificially high . . . prices would *at once* fall by competition of goods with goods to a normal international level.[15]

The mechanism undoubtedly works, and does so very rapidly; but then Hume's reasoning must be fundamentally defective.

Admittedly, Laughlin was rash in dismissing the price-specie flow mechanism and did not suggest a satisfactory reconciliation of the traditional account of it with the fact of instantaneous international commodity arbitrage; but neither did Haberler and Viner. As Samuelson remarks, 'Haberler and Viner are right to attack Laughlin, but that does not mean Laughlin's critique of the Hume mechanism . . . misses its mark.'[16]

When Laughlin talks about gold movements not being related to price levels (e.g. 'in fact, it has become clear, by the logic of events, that the shipment of gold between commercial countries has little or nothing to do with the level of prices of merchandise in any one country'),[17] he forgets to mention that with positive transport costs, a price differential is needed to induce traders to ship merchandise from one locality to another; and that such price differentials are, however fleetingly, created by gold flows. In addition, Laughlin could have mentioned variations in the exchange rate within the gold points as a mechanism for triggering the arbitraging flow of merchandise between localities. He discusses the workings of arbitrage and the relevance of the traditional adjustment mechanism, but does not sufficiently separate out the implications for real as distinct from purely monetary disturbances.

WICKSELL'S SCEPTICISM

Wicksell was also one who doubted the traditional price-specie flow mechanism. He recognised the role of international capital mobility and the integration of world commodity markets; consequently, prices in different countries were closely related to one another under the gold standard: 'It is . . . clear that international equilibrium of prices is usually restored far more rapidly and far more directly' by changes in the supply and demand for tradeable goods without necessitating divergent movements in general price levels.[18] Wicksell rejected Say's law and suggested that aggregate demand could differ from current aggregate supply; this divergence brings about changes in real income. Therefore, for Wicksell, changes in real income can form part of the adjustment mechanism. He refers to the fact which he says is often forgotten 'that an unfavourable balance of trade or payments undoubtedly *corrects itself automatically* . . . by the steps taken by individual consumers and producers . . . without any serious disturbance of the price or credit structure or, indeed, any influence on the currency other than, at most, a temporary shipment of a part of the gold reserve'.[19] Discussing the adjustment to a disturbance in the balance of payments (due to a capital transfer) in the case of two contiguous countries where transport costs may be assumed to be zero and therefore commodity prices are equalised, Wicksell concludes that the stimulus to increased imports and decreased exports in the borrowing country 'is not to be found in a difference of prices in the two countries, which would be theoretically impossible and practically confined in very narrow limits; the increased demand for commodities in one country, the diminished demand in the other, would in the main be sufficient to call forth the changes alluded to'.[20]

Wicksell is obviously referring to the income-adjustment mechanism. Shifts in the demand curves of both countries consequent upon the desire of people to maintain a balance between their incomes and expenditures normally suffice to transfer the loan by means of goods and restore payments equilibrium. Wicksell admits that a certain quantity of gold may automatically pass from the lending to the borrowing country, not to alter relative price levels but merely to maintain them at their original levels – e.g. the borrowing country, having a larger quantity of goods (on account of the real transfer), requires a greater quantity of gold to circulate it. Wicksell thus highlighted a novel dimension to the adjustment mechanism which subsequently had an influence on Ohlin's view of balance of payments adjustments.

TAUSSIG'S REFORMULATION OF THE THEORY

Frank Taussig objected to Wicksell's denial that relative price changes played the key role in the establishment of balance of payments equilibrium. He referred to the existence of non-traded goods which constituted an exception to the law of one price. There was no mechanism to equalise the prices of these goods in different countries – 'the prices of domestic goods obey laws of their own', he declared.[21] Hence, Taussig believed that balance of payments adjustment comes about through changes in relative prices made possible by the existence of non-traded (domestic) goods. Indeed, Taussig further indicates that the relative price changes referred to are movements in general price levels: 'When specie leaves a country prices tend to fall. Hence that country becomes one in which it is advantageous to buy. Lower prices stimulate exports. Conversely, the country to which specie flows tends to have rising prices. It becomes one in which it is advantageous to sell. Higher prices stimulate imports.'[22] However, no indication is given as to how changes in sectoral relative prices (non-traded goods prices relative to the prices of internationally traded goods) induced by gold flows are related to movements in general price levels.

In general, Taussig interpreted the price-specie flow mechanism in the traditional manner, i.e. in terms of gold flows and relative price changes, be they intersectoral price shifts or changes in the terms of trade.[23]

Taussig and his famous band of students (the Harvard School) are of course well known for their empirical investigations into the adjustment mechanism in connection with the episodes of large capital transfers (or foreign lending) primarily from Great Britain and France in the late nineteenth century up to 1914. Taussig was puzzled by the evidence revealed by these studies: small gold flows and minor relative price changes seemed to be sufficient to restore equilibrium. 'Commodity exports and imports,' reported Taussig,

> [respond] with surprising promptness to the balance of international payments as a whole. The promptness is surprising because each constituent transaction . . . is purely in terms of money . . . Yet the recorded transactions between countries show surprisingly little transfer of the only 'money' that moves from one to the other – gold. It is the goods that move, and they seem to move at once; almost as if there were an automatic connection between these financial operations and the commodity exports and imports . . . What is puzzling is the rapidity, almost simultaneity, of the commodity movements. The presumable intermediate stage of gold flow and price changes is hard to discern, and certainly is extremely short.[24]

EMPIRICAL WORK OF THE HARVARD SCHOOL

The investigations by Viner, Williams, White, Graham and Angell were into the processes and outcomes of real disturbances to the balances of payments (the transfer problem) of countries involved in foreign lending and borrowing – Great Britain, France, Canada, the United States and Argentina – designed to test the traditional tenets of the international adjustment mechanism.

The evidence was mixed, inconclusive and even contradictory. Confronted with the evidence – not always consistent with the simple price-specie flow mechanism – these writers considered gold flows, relative price changes, expenditure shifts and changes within the gold points, with varying degrees of emphasis placed on each in the adjustment process. In general, for the writers of the Harvard School, price changes (intersectoral price shifts or changes in the terms of trade) are the key ingredients in the adjustment outcome; but in tracing the responses to a disequilibrium in the balance of payments they find that specie movements are not essential to adjustment. Disequilibrium in the balance of payments means excess demand for foreign exchange which manifests itself in a change in the domestic money supply with immediate and direct effects on expenditures. These expenditure changes produce the final adjustment, either by directly affecting quantities traded or indirectly via relative price changes (e.g. a change in export prices relative to import prices and/or non-traded commodity prices relative to both import and export prices).[25]

In 1924 Viner tested the classical adjustment mechanism (as expounded by Mill) for Canada during the period 1900–13 when there was a massive inflow of foreign (British) capital into that country.[26] The question was: How was the real transfer effected? The transfer of capital from London to Canada, mediated through the New York money market, increased the reserves of Canadian banks: i.e. rather than importing large sums in gold, Canada built up balances in New York which expanded the Canadian money supply. The gold points between Montreal and New York were narrow, so there was not much scope for adjustments via changes in the exchange rate. Viner expected adjustment to follow from the rise in the Canadian price level and a rise in sectoral price levels, i.e. the prices of domestic goods and perhaps also the prices of exports (for differentiated products and certain export staples in the sale of which Canada possessed some market power). The prices of imports would remain unchanged, since these were determined in world markets. The relative price changes would induce substitution effects, i.e. from domestic goods towards imports. To Viner's satisfaction, the evidence confirmed the price-specie flow mechanism. Thus he found a rise in Canadian imports and fall in exports as well as a rise in export prices relative to import prices. Gold flows generated by Canadian borrowing in London therefore led to increasing prices in Canada, an import surplus and an improvement in the Canadian terms of trade. Reverse effects were experienced in Great Britain, the lending country. Viner concluded: 'This theory has been verified inductively for Canada during the period 1900 to 1913 . . . a corollary of this reasoning is that during a period of international borrowings the terms of international exchange shift in favour of the borrowing country and against the lending country . . . Adequate inductive verification of this proposition is supplied by the demonstration . . . that export prices rose relative to import prices.'[27]

Harry Dexter White reconstructed the French balance-of-payments accounts over the period 1880–1913 and looked for evidence of the price-specie flow mechanism at work, in particular how net capital exports affected the French balance of trade. He concluded that although the price-specie flow mechanism was one of the forces making for adjustment, it was not the only or even the major factor. He wrote:

> The neoclassical theory is not the complete explanation. The theory fails in that it explains what happens only under certain given conditions seldom found . . . the neoclassical exposition exaggerates the effectiveness of gold flows and sectional price changes as a means for establishing equilibrium in international accounts.[28]

The missing link in the classical explanation which puzzled Taussig and the other members of the Harvard School was, of course, the income-adjustment mechanism – direct spending effects induced by a transfer of purchasing power from the lending country to the borrowing country which powerfully affect the balance of payments and short-circuit the conventional intervening sequence of large money flows and relative price-level shifts. As happened so often in the history of economics where theoretical muddles were straightened out on the anvil of urgent policy debates – a process which concentrates minds, exposes hidden assumptions, kindles the spark of intuition, recalls to memory half-forogtten truths and forces the theorist to face obvious facts – so in this case the confusion over what is now known as the 'transfer problem' was sorted out at the end of the 1929 Keynes–Ohlin debate on German reparations.

THE TRANSFER PROBLEM

We proceed now to a statement of the modern version of the transfer problem and a brief review of the antecedents of this account up to the exchange between Keynes and Ohlin. In 1956, Harry Johnson noted: 'The transfer problem bulks large in the literature of international trade theory'; and more recently, in 1974, John Chipman observed that this prominence has not gone along with commensurate understanding and positive results over the issues involved: 'In the century and a half that has gone by since the science of economics began, few topics have been so vigorously and inconclusively debated as the Transfer Problem.'[29]

The transfer problem is concerned with the real or imagined difficulties encountered when one country needs to transfer purchasing power to another (unilateral transfer or gifts, reparations, long-term capital loans, settlement of old debts, etc.) – examples in recent history include US aid for Europe under the Marshall Plan, the recycling of 'petrodollars' in the 1970s and the current debt crisis of Third World countries. The financial transfer is distinct from the real transfer; the real transfer refers to the induced movement of goods between countries. The crucial question is whether the financial transfer results in a movement of an equivalent amount of goods from the transferor to the transferee. Where the financial flows match the trade flows precisely, i.e. the transfer is fully effected, there is no balance of payments problem. The real transfer is effected when the transferor country develops an export surplus and the transferee country an import surplus equal to the transfer.

In terms of the analytical technique of comparative statics, the transfer problem is the inversion of the balance of payments problem. Any actual balance of payments disequilibrium ultimately involves a real transfer in some form from the surplus country to the deficit country: i.e. a deficit country is in fact receiving a transfer of goods and services from the rest of the world on account of spending in the deficit country being in excess of earnings. The correction of the disequilibrium may be viewed as the problem of reversing this transfer – i.e. the problem of generating a real transfer from the deficit country to the rest of the world; although in the short run the payments deficit may be financed by a monetary transfer from the rest of the world to the deficit country.

In classical theory, deprivation of the goods constituting the real transfer was regarded as the 'primary burden'; also there was a strong presumption that the transfer would induce a 'secondary burden' in the form of a deterioration of the paying country's net terms of trade – an international redistribution of income additional to the initial burden of the transfer itself. Effecting a transfer means (1) adjustment of each country's aggregate expenditure, and (2) a change in relative prices, perhaps the terms of trade. Which way do the terms of trade move? According to classical theory (e.g. in the accounts of Mill and Viner, as just mentioned), the presumption was that the terms of trade would move against the paying country on account of the divergent shift in price levels induced by changes in the volume of monetary circulation. In the modern version, the terms of trade can move in either direction or not move at all.

Samuelson showed in two articles (1952, 1954) – investigating the two-country, two-commodity case – that in the absence of transport costs and other impediments to trade there is no presumption as to the movement of the terms of trade.[30] Matters become more complicated when the assumption of zero transport costs and no impediments to trade are relaxed; only in the case of artificial tariff barriers is there a partial vindication of the orthodox view. Later (1971), he demonstrated that the introduction of non-traded goods can give the orthodox result (i.e. in a model where the supply response to a transfer is crucial).[31] In 1952, Samuelson discussed the possibilities in terms of the relative marginal propensities to consume individual tradeables in the two countries (provided dynamic stability holds). For a transfer to worsen the paying country's terms of trade it is necessary and sufficient that the paying country's marginal propensity to consume its export good be greater than the receiving country's marginal propensity to consume the same good. At constant terms of trade, the transfer leads to an excess supply in the world market of the paying country's exportable. Thus if the paying country's marginal propensity to consume is greater than that of the recipient country then the terms of trade of the transferor must deteriorate (given Walrasian stability).

But the argument can equally well be put in terms of the marginal propensities to import. If the two commodities are freely traded with zero transport costs, the terms of trade will be unaffected by the transfer payment when the sum of the two countries' marginal propensities to import is unity – a result guaranteed by the assumption that both countries have identical homothetic preferences which implies that marginal and average propensities to consume are equal. Thus there emerges an export surplus (in the paying country) of just the required magnitude as a result of income effects alone (i.e. the initial change in the two countries' real income, equal in magnitude but opposite in sign, consequent upon the financial transfer). If however, the sum of the two countries' marginal propensities to import falls short of unity (because of non-identical preferences), the surplus generated by income effects alone is inadequate and must be supplemented by an adjustment or movement of the terms of trade, i.e. a change in relative prices induced by gold flows. Finally, according to the transfer criterion, the terms of trade move in favour of the paying country if the sum of import propensities exceeds unity, since the income-generated export surplus will be more than enough to effect the payment.

This is the essence of the modern theory of transfer, but it was not quite the way the problem was conceptualised in the 1920s (except by Ohlin and perhaps Graham) when German reparations brought the matter to the fore. But there was a long minority position, going back to Adam Smith and enlisting the support of Ricardo, Wheatley, Longfield, Lord King, McCulloch, and Bastable and Nicholson as well, for Ohlin's interpretation of the problem, i.e. that shifts in 'purchasing power' or spending make the transfer and restore equilibrium without any large prior movements of gold.[32]

Smith's treatment of the problem was in connection with the financial disbursements necessary in the conduct of a foreign war:

> The commodities most proper for being transported to distant countries, in order to purchase there either the pay and provisions of an army, or some part of the money of the mercantile republic [i.e. bullion] to be employed in purchasing them, seem to be the finer and more improved manufactures . . . A country whose industry produces a great annual surplus of such manufactures . . . may carry on for many years a very expensive foreign war without either exporting any considerable quantity of gold and silver, or even having any such quantity to export.[33]

A writer who, according to Chipman, gave 'probably the first correct formulation of the transfer problem', was Lord King (1803).[34] His contribution arose out of the discussions concerning the causes of the depreciation of the Irish pound at the time of the Bullion controversy. The suggestion was made that it was due to an increase of remittances of rent to Irish absentee landlords; but, argued King, since there was not enough gold bullion in Ireland to settle the debt, the cause of the depreciation must have been due to the excess issue of paper by the Bank of Ireland. He then proceeded to show that the remittances were in fact paid in goods through an Irish export surplus that adjusted to the shift in expenditure flows:

> It must undoubtedly be admitted that very considerable payments arising from Irish property are annually made to residents in England . . . ; but it by no means follows that these payments have been made by an actual transfer of bullion . . . Such continued remittances cannot possibly be made by a nation, like Ireland,

> which has no means of providing a constant supply of the precious metals . . . In the case of Ireland it is evident that the course of trade and the proportion of the exports and imports must adjust themselves to the nature of its connection with Great Britain. In proportion to the increased necessity of remittances to this country the exports of Irish produce and manufactures must be increased, and the imports of English produce and manufactures diminished, till the amount of foreign demands is paid by Irish exports, and the balance of trade restored.[35]

Essentially the same argument was used by J. L. Foster, Sir Henry Parnell and J. R. McCulloch on this question.[36] The argument was a simplified one (some details were neglected – e.g. an initial movement of specie induced by the shifts in levels of expenditure, and considerations of transport costs and taste patterns); but it was nevertheless a correct formulation of the process of adjustment of commodity-trade flows matching the financial flows (or expenditures).

Henry Thornton, an influential member of the Committee which produced the famous Bullion Report (1810), briefly discussed the transfer problem in his remarkable treatise, *An Enquiry into the Nature and Effects of the Paper Credit of Great Britain* (1802).[37] Thornton's view was that both a unilateral transfer (a once-and-for-all subsidy payment to allies) and a bad harvest would depreciate the exchange rate and lead to temporary drains of specie abroad, but a bad harvest would in addition entail a deterioration in the terms of trade. The adverse terms of trade effect in the case of a crop failure presumably follows from the supposition that there would be a fall in the world supply of British importables (food) consequent upon the failure of British production of foodstuffs. Hence the price of importables must rise relative to exportables. But there is no unequivocal statement by Thornton that the terms of trade must deteriorate in the case of a unilateral transfer. J. S. Mill on the other hand stated quite positively, as mentioned previously, that a unilateral transfer of funds from one country to another would worsen the transferor's terms of trade, i.e. create a secondary burden.

When we come to the early neoclassical period, we also find recognition (in Bastable and Nicholson) of the equilibrating effects on the balance of payments of the changes in demand for goods associated with the transfer of purchasing power. Thus Bastable in 1889 presented an argument (in criticism of Mill's reasoning) that the balance of payments tended to adjust itself by means of changes in purchasing power or money incomes in the paying and receiving countries, and therefore denied any significant role in the adjustment of real disturbances to price-level shifts induced by gold movements. Bastable queried 'whether Mill is correct in asserting that the quantity of money will be increased in the creditor and reduced in the debtor country . . . Nor does it follow that the scale of prices will be higher in the creditor than in the debtor country'.[38]

Mill failed to allow for the effect of the transfer on incomes. In Bastable's alternative explanation, a transfer payment would cause a once-and-for-all increase in the receiving country's income (or 'purchasing power') – 'the inhabitants of the [creditor country], having larger money incomes, will purchase more at the same price, and thus bring about the necessary excess of imports over exports'.[39] Nicholson's analysis, a few years later (1897),[40] was even better in that he considered the effects of income changes in both countries. In the case of a tribute,

> the government of the paying country must levy taxes to the amount of the annual tribute, and thereby will diminish the consuming power of the people by so much . . . At the same time the receiving country . . . will have so much more to spend and can take more imports and also consume things formerly exported. In this way an excess of exports from the paying country equivalent to the tribute can be brought about without any change in general prices.[41]

The first formal treatment of the transfer problem was by Pigou (1932)[42] who clarified the barter aspects in the context of a Jevonian model of pure exchange between 'representative' citizens in two countries each having separable (or independent) utility functions for two tradeable commodities – i.e. the marginal utility curves are linear and independent. Pigou derived a condition (expressed in terms of demand elasticities) for a transfer to worsen the transferor's terms of trade.

What all these writers lacked, however, as Metzler observed, was a theory of employment or income determination that would have suggested the extent of income movements and hence the limits to the adjustment process: i.e. they did not have the concept of the multiplier.[43] They all assumed full employment, but Ohlin did not.

He relied on the monetary mechanism to produce secondary (or indirect) changes in expenditure and showed that income-induced quantity adjustments made price changes largely unnecessary. He did not wholly neglect relative price changes; but it was his emphasis on direct-spending effects plus a healthy scepticism regarding the classical presumption on terms-of-trade movements that distinguished him, in the 1920s, from the representatives of orthodox opinion (Taussig, Viner, Pigou – and Keynes who then shared the same conventional classical views).[44]

Ohlin felt that contemporary writers had neglected important income effects of the transfer (i.e. the income-shifting of reciprocal demand curves); and following the lead set by Wicksell, made a distinction between national income and aggregate spending (or 'buying power').[45] In the absence of transport costs and other impediments to trade, i.e. perfect commodity arbitrage, there is no transfer problem, says Ohlin; income shifts are capable of doing all the work.

In his analysis of the problem Ohlin allows for price changes, but they are price changes between non-traded goods and internationally traded commodities. Thus a transfer raises prices of domestic or non-traded goods ('home-market goods', as Ohlin calls them) relative to traded goods in the receiving country and lowers prices of non-traded goods relative to traded goods in the paying country; but with no presumption as to the relative prices of import and export goods. The resultant shift of resources from the production of tradeables to domestic industries (in the receiving country) and from domestic to tradeable-goods industries (in the paying country) will modify the original price changes; but again with no ultimate effect on the terms of trade.[46]

Ohlin admits, however, that in the presence of sizeable domestic (or non-tradeable) industries in both countries, some orthodox price effects may be experienced. These take place if the opposing shift of resources and production in the two countries raises factor costs and therefore export supply prices (in the receiving country), and lowers factor costs and export supply prices (in the paying country). The necessary adjustment of trade balances (import surplus in the receiving country and export surplus in the paying country) may in such cases be accompanied by terms-of-trade changes.

Such was Ohlin's analysis of the transfer problem (as applied to German reparations) which was disputed by Keynes.[47] As is well known, Keynes exaggerated the difficulties faced by Germany in having to pay reparations: (1) Since the Dawes Committee of the Reparations Commission had ruled out any attempt by the Germans to use the expedients of inflation and a devaluation of the mark to accomplish the transfer in a less painful manner, Germany would have to undergo a severe deflation of prices and costs. (2) As a consequence, Germany would have to suffer a massive terms-of-trade deterioration in order to generate the necessary export surplus and effect the transfer. (3) Indeed, Germany would not be able to make the transfer at all because of the low elasticities of demand for her exports and imports (inelastic Marshallian reciprocal demand) – the value of German exports had to be increased by 40 per cent, Keynes estimated. (4) Stemming from (3), Keynes believed that balance of payments adjustments were attended by painful, wrenching movements in relative prices and structural dislocations – for instance, Keynes's remark that adjustments are not as easy 'as shelling peas' and his warning to optimists such as Ohlin and Jacques Rueff not to apply to the transfer problem 'the theory of liquids to what is, if not a solid, at least a sticky mass with strong internal resistances'.[48]

Keynes was, of course, wide off the mark. He was wrong in his assessment of Germany's ability to effectuate the transfer and in the theoretical arguments used to support his pessimistic prognostications. Keynes was confused. Much later, recalling Keynes's arguments, Samuelson notes that Keynes at one stage actually shifts the reciprocal demand curves of both Germany and Britain as a result of income flows, but at another point shifts only Germany's curve.[49] Keynes was resistant to Ohlin's unorthodox interpretation of the adjustment mechanism – in particular, the point that price elasticities of demand have little or nothing to do with the analysis; but Keynes was still firmly in the grip of Mill. As Ellis and Metzler expressed it: 'The paradoxical aspect of the controversy is that Keynes, who later laid the groundwork for the modern theory, adopted an extremely classical view in his discussion of German reparations.'[50]

NEW ISSUES

As we saw previously, major developments in the pure theory of trade occurred during the interwar years; this flowering of new concepts and analytical techniques germinated from ideas internal to the discipline itself. In other words, it was a natural process of growth in response to theoretical needs. The monetary side of international economics was also enormously enriched during this period, but here the stimulus came from practical problems thrown up by the dislocation and monetary instability that characterised the interwar years.

In the previous section we dealt with the clarification of the transfer problem that resulted from the discussion on German reparations, and can now take up three other issues that engaged the attention of economists: (1) the purchasing-power parity (PPP) theory of the determination of equilibrium exchange rates; (2) the possibilities and prospects of international monetary reform; (3) the reconsideration of the balance-of-payments mechanism, i.e. multiplier analysis in an open economy and the elasticities approach. The first was related to an immediate problem – What should be the new parities for countries which because of wartime upheavals had left the gold standard? – but which became a basic assumption of the later monetary approach to the balance of payments. The second concern led, of course, to the work of Keynes and his American opposite number, Harry Dexter White, in the setting-up of the postwar international monetary order institutionalised in the International Monetary Fund (IMF) and the World Bank. The third was an offshoot of Keynes's 1936 closed-economy macroeconomic theory that still contends for recognition as an indispensable framework for balance-of-payments analysis.

Before turning to a consideration of these three areas of concern, it may be helpful to review briefly the monetary experience of the interwar years and the critical discussions on the adjustment mechanism and the gold standard.

THE WORLD ECONOMY, MONEY, AND THE GREAT DEPRESSION

At the outbreak of war in 1914, Great Britain and most other countries suspended the gold standard. The convertibility of paper currency into gold was restricted. International financial transactions, including private gold flows, were terminated, and in many countries governments allowed the fixed relationships between their currencies and gold to lapse (although Great Britain and France pegged their exchange rates to the US dollar at levels quite close to prewar parities). In addition, governments also drew gold coin into official reserve holdings and replaced it with paper currency – the gold withdrawn from circulation formed the basis for wartime inflationary finance. Independent, uncoordinated actions by governments, in effect, served to dismantle the system.

Wartime budgetary deficits were financed by an inflationary expansion of paper money, as already indicated. The monetary legacy of the war was therefore floating exchange rates, large stocks of inconvertible currencies and inflation in all countries, hyper-inflation in others where public finances broke down.[51] In eastern and central Europe, the carving-up of new states out of old empires subjected the balance of payments of those states to enormous strains; but everywhere intolerable strains were exerted by hyper-inflation, inter-Allied debts, reparation payments and rigidities in internal cost structures. These persistent pressures impeded the correction of balance of payments disequilibria, and many countries resorted to exchange depreciation as an alternative to import restrictions – Germany and a few countries in eastern Europe retained import controls set up during the war.

Payments difficulties were intensified by the widespread scarcity of monetary reserves, particularly gold, partly owing to the serious imbalance or maldistribution of world gold stocks – the United States held nearly half, and immobilised much of its bloated share – but also to the European demand for reserves on account of enhanced instability in balances of payments and the slowing-up in the rate of growth of reserves due to the rise in commodity prices relative to gold which made gold production relatively unprofitable. The world price level in terms of dollars and gold roughly doubled since before the war, with the price of gold unchanged at $20.67 an ounce. The lower value of gold in terms of commodity prices and average costs of production resulted in a marked decline in the annual output from the mines.

The shortage of reserves became an international issue when Great Britain and a few other countries determined on a policy of returning to the structure of prewar parities *vis-à-vis* gold and the US dollar. This required in such countries a substantial deflation of internal prices to be brought about by the retirement of excess paper-money stocks. The Genoa International Financial Conference (convened in the spring of 1922 by the British and French governments, but not under the auspices of the League of Nations as in the case of the earlier 1920 Brussels Conference) recommended the adoption of a gold-exchange standard – a system that was supposed to avoid the scramble for gold – and the remedying of the gold shortage by allowing foreign exchange (i.e. dollars and sterling) as well as gold to be used as international reserves.[52] One by one, countries came on to the new gold-exchange standard – Germany in 1924, Great Britain and Holland in 1925, Belgium in 1926, Italy in 1927, France in 1928 – until by 1930 most of the industrialised countries (with the exception of Spain and the USSR) were on it.[53] The United States remained on the gold standard during and after the war, except for a brief interruption during 1917–18.

The restoration of prewar parities combined with reserve stringency and the undervaluation of gold throughout the 1920s contributed to worldwide deflationary pressure in the late 1920s which eventually led into the severe depression of the 1930s. Monetary restraint kept unemployment high everywhere and exercised a depressive influence on primary product prices. Instability and payments disequilibria were exacerbated by flights of capital motivated by fears of bank failures and currency devaluations.

The international payments difficulties of Great Britain resulting from the overvaluation of sterling (and undervaluation of the French franc)[54] were relieved somewhat owing to the fact that, as a reserve centre, Britain was able to finance part of its deficit by accumulating reserve liabilities and also by attracting short-term funds through high interest rates. But London was no longer the world's leading financial centre. That position passed to New York, and countries that were on the gold-exchange standard found themselves increasingly under the influence of US monetary policy. What undermined the attempt to revive the gold standard however was, apart from the misalignment of important parities, the unwillingness of several countries, in particular the United States, to allow changes in gold stocks to exert their full effects on the domestic money supply, and hence employment and prices. In deficit countries, prices did not fall in response to tight monetary policies; instead, such countries suffered deflation and unemployment.

At the onset of the Great Depression the gold-exchange standard was abandoned. In September 1931 sterling was declared inconvertible due to a crisis-of-confidence run on British gold reserves, and the exchange rate depreciated by 30 per cent over the next three months. Twenty-five countries followed Britain and devalued their currencies in terms of gold – Commonwealth countries and dependencies as well as Egypt, the Scandinavian countries and Portugal. The devaluation of the US dollar followed in 1933–4 and the 'gold bloc' currencies in 1936, i.e. the currencies of France, Switzerland, the Netherlands and Belgium. Balance-of-payments restrictions appeared on a massive scale and in a variety of forms. Protectionism and beggar-thy-neighbour policies flourished, as country after country tried to stimulate their domestic economies by exporting unemployment through competitive devaluations, undervalued currencies and import and exchange controls – at least up to the mid-1930s. At that time, of course, Keynes published his *General Theory* which was to have a profound influence on professional (and public) perceptions of the macroeconomic functioning of a modern capitalist economy, hence on the monetary aspects of international economics.

INTERWAR CRITICISMS: EXTERNAL VERSUS INTERNAL STABILITY

The problem of international monetary equilibrium and the kaleidoscopic changes in economic events and policies during the interwar years elicited a critical literature on the traditional interpretation of the adjustment mechanism and the workings of the gold standard.

In contrast to the idealised picture of an automatic monetary mechanism represented by the gold standard – glowingly portrayed by the Cunliffe Report[55] – post-First World War commentators pointed out that the international gold standard was, in fact, a 'sterling standard', managed by Great Britain by virtue of her preponderant role in international trade and investment, aided by the political authority of the *Pax Britannica.*

The system that was restored in the 1920s was a gold standard in name only – it was a 'gold-plated' one; moreover, the hybrid system, unlike its pre-1914 prototype, functioned in a more challenging, unfavourable intellectual and policy environment. Gold coins no longer circulated domestically and citizens could not convert paper money into gold. Internally, the system was a gold bullion rather than a gold specie or coin standard. Externally, as indicated above, it became a gold-exchange standard, since most countries held their international reserves not in the form of gold, but in sterling or dollar balances.[56] In bygone days, the beauty of the gold standard was attributed to the fact that it worked 'without the aid of politicians', as one seventeenth-century writer (Sir Dudley North) put it. That was no longer true after the Great War. Economists, politicians and the public at large increasingly favoured a policy of taking action to obstruct the traditional adjustment mechanism when it threatened the attainment of national economic objectives (i.e. action designed to counteract cyclical swings by monetary measures), even though such action conflicted with the requirements of external equilibrium and the harmonious rhythm of the world economy. The 'rules of the game' were flouted – France (after the stabilisation of the franc) and the United States sterilised the inflow of gold and other reserves in order to block multiple expansions of their money supplies which would have disturbed the stability of prices in their countries.[57] Such actions, however, shifted the burden of adjustment on to the deficit countries; the latter, even if they could temporarily violate the rules, ultimately had to endure severe deflation (i.e. unemployment), given the rigidity of money wages, if the use of import controls (tariffs and quotas) was abjured. The creditor or surplus countries held the trump cards in the altered scenario. Apparently, the new-found freedom was only to be enjoyed by surplus countries.

In general, therefore, in the interwar years, balance of payments adjustment was increasingly seen as a policy problem which was premised on the possible conflict between internal stability and external stability. Initially, the conflict was perceived in terms of exchange-rate stability v. domestic price instability; but later, as the depression deepened and political pressures mounted against large-scale unemployment (resistance to wage and price reductions), the view was taken that the adjustment mechanism had become costlier, since the burden of adjustment fell inordinately on employment and output rather than on prices. The greater concern with the domestic aspects of the gold-standard mechanism reflected a shift in the priorities of the authorities away from external towards domestic goals or targets. Finally, proposals for a better world monetary system that would allow a desirable measure of domestic autonomy were canvassed during this period. The interwar critics included Cassel, Viner, Keynes and Whale. Of course, even before the period under review, the shortcomings of the system were remarked upon by Marshall, Fisher and Wicksell – the first two in fact made proposals for national and international monetary reform.

Cassel observed that the pre-1914 gold standard was not an automatic, non-discretionary system. Gold flows did not always or even normally influence the domestic money supply. Central banks (with the exception of the Bank of England) normally held larger reserves than legally required (out of national pride, undue caution, etc.); but the effect was to weaken the link between reserve changes and price-level movements. The monetary effects of gold flows therefore depended on central-bank policy (discount-rate policy and open-market operations) – 'Thus the currency necessarily became a "managed currency" whose value depended entirely on the policy of the central bank.'[58] Capital flows set in motion by foreign lending and borrowing could help or hinder the adjustment process. A capital exporting country would compensate for a loss of gold due to a deficit on income account (including interest and dividends as well as visible and invisible trade) by a reduction of its overseas lending. It was thus possible to prevent gold exports from having an influence on the domestic price level. Several years later Joan Robinson, an outspoken critic of the conventional version of the gold-standard mechanism, made the same observation. 'The operation of the gold standard mechanism,' she said, 'was to keep flows of lending in line with income balances.'[59] Cassel further observed that because of asymmetrical relationships, i.e. between debtor and creditor countries, gold imports and exports did not 'have any distinct relation to changes in the balance of trade'.[60]

Viner (1932) argued that the prewar gold standard would have proved unworkable were it not for the development of 'a deliberate and centralized mechanism of control of gold movements, using central bank discount policy and credit controls as its chief instruments'. He however supported the restoration of the gold standard despite the fact that it was 'a wretched system' – one associated with bothersome short-term price instability – because a system of flexible exchange rates based on inconvertible paper currencies would be even worse.[61]

Recognition of the potential conflict between internal stability and external equilibrium was particularly noticeable in the work of Keynes, but it was also remarked upon by Cassel, Viner, Hawtrey, Nurkse and others.

In 1923 Keynes argued that altered circumstances suggested that the gold standard was unlikely to be a satisfactory system, then and for the future: 'In truth,' he alleged,

> the gold standard is already a barbarous relic. All of us, from the Governor of the Bank of England downwards, are now primarily interested in preserving the stability of business, prices, and employment, and are not likely, when the choice is forced on us, deliberately to sacrifice these to outworn dogma, which had its value once, of £3 17s. 10½d. per ounce. Advocates of the ancient standard do not observe how remote it now is from the spirit and

> the requirements of the age. A regulated non-metallic standard has slipped in unnoticed. *It exists.*[62]

He wanted to increase the discretion of each national monetary authority over its own rate of interest and the volume of its foreign lending. To achieve these objectives, he suggested (1) government intervention in the foreign exchange market, and (2) direct controls over capital movements.

Referring to the critics who argued that external stability must be sacrificed for the sake of internal stability, Viner remarked in 1932: 'They have really conceded too much to the gold standard when they admitted that it brought external stability, for the only stability guaranteed by even a universal gold standard is a stability in exchange rates, a very different and much more limited thing than stability of external purchasing power.'[63]

P. B. Whale (1937) criticised the Mill–Taussig–Viner gold-standard mechanism. His model of how it worked corresponds remarkably well with the modern monetarist model of a small open economy under fixed exchange rates. Whale holds that specie flows and the money supply are determined by the demand for money which in turn depends on real income and the price level. Like Ohlin and latter-day monetarists, for Whale, the transfer process involves a redistribution of purchasing power, 'the redistribution of spending power itself, . . . apart from any change in the direction of demand and the terms of trade, may require a redistribution of money . . . effected by a movement of gold'.[64]

8.2 The Purchasing-Power Parity Theory (PPP)

THE REVIVAL OF PPP

An old doctrine which came to the fore during and immediately after the First World War was the purchasing-power parity theory of exchange rates.[65] The PPP theory in its simplest form asserts that in the long run, changes in exchange rates among countries will tend to reflect changes in relative price levels. If exchange rates are free to move, i.e. under floating rates, the observed movements can be explained entirely in terms of changes in relative purchasing power. If exchange rates are fixed, equilibrium exchange rates can be determined by comparing relative price levels.

This theory enjoyed considerable popularity among economists during the 1920s, largely due to the writings of the Swedish economists, Gustav Cassel.[66] Cassel and others developed the theory as a method for locating equilibrium exchange rates after the upheavals of the First World War which had produced large discrepancies in the movements of price levels in different countries. Since exchange rates in many countries were uncontrolled, these changes in relative purchasing power exerted a considerable influence on exchange rates. International trade was severely disrupted or distorted by controls and uncertainties which, added to the enormous disparities in prices and costs among countries, produced significant changes in the underlying determinants of comparative advantage and the 'barter' equilibrium in international trade. In the instances of the few countries that still adhered to the gold standard this meant that their fixed exchange rates were hopelessly out of line with the rates that would equilibrate the foreign exchange market. In these circumstances (war-induced inflation) the theory seemed to provide a satisfactory method for (1) explaining the observed movements in exchange rates for countries whose rates were floating, and (2) determining equilibrium parity rates for those countries whose surviving rates were out of line with postwar market conditions. Without the benchmark of PPP it was virtually impossible to discuss sensibly the question whether a particular currency was overvalued or undervalued.

The PPP theory, however, became discredited in the 1930s when attempts were made to apply the theory in markedly different conditions, i.e. the depression years when fluctuations in output and employment combined with large and volatile capital movements were predominant influences on exchange rates and balances of payments.

In 1958, Leland Yeager attempted a rehabilitation of the theory and produced evidence favourable to the predictions of it. A few years later Hendrik Houthakker (1962) applied the theory to determine the degree of overvaluation of the US dollar. These two studies provoked a critical onslaught on the theory and its empirical status from Balassa (1964) and Samuelson (1964) from which it seemed it would never recover.[67]

There was a noticeable absence of any mention of PPP in some popular introductory texts on international economics published at the time. One can only presume that the authors did not consider it worthwhile to bother their readers with what they considered to be a discredited doctrine; or, they themselves were unfamiliar with it. If the former alternative assumption were true, then it is a bit odd that a theory of exchange rates and prices that was accepted by Ricardo, Wheatley, Thornton, Goschen, Marshall and Keynes among others should not rate even a passing mention in the texts.[68] But old doctrines never die – they recede only to rebound later.

In the 1970s there was a revival of interest in PPP together with other old monetarist doctrines which also have had their ups and downs. Certainly, the PPP doctrine has always had its supporters as well as its detractors, but in the 1970s the tide of opinion swung firmly in favour of those who professed belief in the operational plausibility of the doctrine – and that included the opinions of specialists in international economics. As Dornbusch and Krugman remarked at the time (1976): 'Under the skin of any international economist lies a deep-seated belief in some variant of the purchasing-power parity theory of the exchange rate.' Later (1984), Leland Yeager maintained: 'Purchasing-power parity is one of the few dependable generalizations that we have in economics.'[69]

Several factors and events accounted for the revival of interest in PPP, but perhaps the most significant was the generalised 'managed' floating of currencies following the breakdown of the Bretton Woods system in 1971. This occurred at a time of high but uneven inflationary pressures in the world economy. Latterly, we have had the launching of EMS (European Monetary System) by the EEC, the aim of which is to hasten the goal of monetary union by maintaining fixed but jointly floating exchange rates among member countries' currencies. Governments and central banks (whether they are members of currency unions or not) thus need to find methods (1) of assessing the appropriateness of their exchange rates (if floating independently), or (2) for guiding exchange management or intervention policies (if members of a currency union).

These new policy demands were naturally seen by many economists in the context of two key relationships emphasised by the monetarist approach to balance of payments and exchange rate theory:

(1) exchange rate movements do not have permanent effects on relative prices, i.e. the homogeneity postulate of monetary theory;[70]
(2) international price relationships obey the 'law of one price'.[71]

STATEMENT OF THE THEORY AND ITS IMPLICATIONS

There are, in fact, two versions of the PPP hypothesis – the absolute and the relative (the relative is the one frequently used in the empirical literature):

$$S_t = AP_t/P_t^* \ldots \text{absolute version}$$

$$S_t = S_o \cdot \frac{P_t/P_o}{P_t^*/P_o^*} \ldots \text{relative version}$$

where

S_t = the equilibrium spot exchange rate (domestic currency per unit of foreign currency) during period *t*.
S_o = the actual spot exchange rate during a base period.
A = arbitrary constant term.
P = domestic price level in domestic currency.
P^* = foreign price level in foreign currency.
t and *o* subscripts denote the current period and base period respectively.

In empirical work, it is often convenient to state PPP as a proposition about the logarithms of the variables. The estimating equations are then:

$$\log S_t = a + b\,(\log P_t - \log P_t^*)$$

for the absolute version, and

$$\Delta \log S_t = a + b\,(\Delta \log P_t - \Delta \log P_t^*)$$

for the relative version.

The relative version can also be tested in the following alternative form:

$$\Delta X_t = X_t - X_{t-1} = 0$$

where X_t is the logarithm of the ratio of domestic to foreign prices (converted into domestic currency by the appropriate exchange rate) for period *t*.

PPP, as a theory, is very much policy-oriented. As we have seen, it has been used in the past to determine equilibrium exchange rates and the degree of overvaluation or undervaluation of currencies. It can be used to detect and measure divergencies between the actual exchange rate and the long-run equilibrium rate. The OPTICA Report recommended its use as a guideline for exchange-rate intervention policy in the EEC.[72] Indeed, the main reason why PPP has survived despite its abandonment by economists in the 1960s is that it is widely used in practice by money managers, stockbrokers and corporation treasurers as a rule-of-thumb in assessing the anticipated relative strengths and weaknesses of different national currencies in order to make speculative and investment portfolio decisions. International banks and multinational corporations regularly use PPP to forecast the course of floating exchange rates (taking into account anticipated changes in monetary and fiscal policies of the countries concerned). The relative price indices can be forecast from existing econometric models.

The concept of PPP provides the theoretical underpinnings for almost all intercountry comparisons of costs, prices and GDP. It is generally recognised that PPP is preferable to current exchange rates as a conversion factor to transfer data from denomination in one national currency to another.[73] Other uses to which PPP has been put in empirical work include: (1) as a test of the economic rationality of the administered exchange-rate patterns in centrally planned economies; (2) as a method for obtaining independent measures of the extent of inflation in such economies where, as is well known, the officially reported figures are either suspect or unreliable; and (3) the construction of a domestic price index when free-market exchange rates are available (but the former is either non-existent or unreliable) so as to estimate, for example, the demand for money in an economy.

PPP's ascendancy was due to the fact that it was hitched to the rising star of monetarism. No sooner had it reasserted itself, however, there was talk about its 'collapse'. Evidence from the working of the flexible rate period, declared Dornbusch, 'did not allow us to sustain for long a PPP interpretation of exchange rate movement';[74] and by the mid-1980s Haberler observed: 'The theory of purchasing power parity appears to be going out of fashion.'[75]

PPP's new lease of life was short – at least in academic circles it fell from grace together with the other building blocks of global monetarism, i.e. the law of one price and stable demand-for-money functions. During the late 1970s and early 1980s there were large and persistent deviations from PPP, i.e. changes in real exchange rates. Nominal exchange rates typically changed by more than was justified by relative price differentials. Deviations of the real exchange rate from trend were found to be serially correlated, i.e. deviations from PPP were persistent.

PPP is a deceptively simple hypothesis. As a generalisation about relative price levels and equilibrium exchange rates it is liable to be interpreted in a variety of ways, ranging from trivial truisms (e.g. spatial arbitrage in homogeneous commodities without transport costs and trade impediments) to more sophisticated theories of exchange rate determination (e.g. open-economy monetarist models which supplement PPP with an adjustment mechanism).

Some writers interpret the hypothesis in so exaggerated and rigid a manner that it manifestly lacks credibility. Additionally, they use it for predicting exchange-rate behaviour rather than for the purpose of appraising that behaviour, i.e. accounting for the range within which a floating exchange rate tends to fluctuate. Some theorists hold what Cassel called the PPP 'dogma', the parameters of which they then proceed to estimate by means of elaborate testing procedures. Cassel himself would have joined those who criticise much of the current work on PPP. Even with the benefit of vastly improved econometric techniques, the contemporary debate on the relevance of PPP is really a rehearsal of the arguments used in Cassel's time.

CASSEL'S STATEMENT AND USE OF THE DOCTRINE

When Cassel wrote, the German inflation controversy (1916–23) raged between adherents of the balance of payments school and the monetarists. During the hyperinflation episode of the early 1920s (when the German mark depreciated from an average value of 4.70 marks to the dollar in 1919 to 26 202 marks in June 1923, and the inflation rate peaked at 619 per cent in mid-November 1923) the balance of payments school attributed the massive exchange depreciation to external real shocks to the balance of payments (e.g. reparations, the huge import bill incurred on account of the need to restock the country's factories and shops with raw materials, capital equipment and foodstuffs). Depreciation led to domestic inflation through the rise in import prices. The Reichsbank was forced to expand the money supply; failure to do so would have meant a disastrous contraction of the real money stock, and hence massive unemployment.

The monetarists detected a quite different order in the chain of causation. For them, the extraordinary exchange depreciation was caused by overissue of currency and the monetisation of government debt. The consequent rise in the price level led to the adverse balance of payments and exchange rate depreciation. It was in this context and with reference to other similar monetary episodes that Cassel developed his PPP hypothesis. He agreed with the monetarists and criticised the balance of payments school for failure to see that the payments deficit and exchange depreciation were determined by an excess supply of domestic money relative to monetary developments abroad.

Fritz Machlup recalled that in a book he wrote at the time he had 'a running battle with what was generally called the balance-of-payments theory of currency depreciation', and that, 'Against this benightedness I had to quote authorities on the purchasing-power parity theory, not just in the form in which it was expouded by Gustav Cassel, but also in its earlier versions advanced by Ricardo, George J. Goschen, Ludwig Bamberger and others.'[76]

Cassel used his PPP hypothesis to define (and estimate) equilibrium exchange rates both during and after the First World War. For Cassel, the exchange rate is in equilibrium between two currencies only when those currencies can be used to buy the same bundles of goods and services: 'a certain representative quantity of commodities must cost the same in both countries, if the exchange rate . . . stands at its equilibrium'.[77] So defined, the value of one country's currency relative to the other's is the short-run equilibrium exchange rate:

> The purchasing power parities represent the true equilibrium of the exchanges, and it is of great practical value to know those parities. It is in fact to them we have to refer when we wish to get an idea of the real value of currencies whose exchanges are subject to arbitrary and sometimes wild fluctuations.[78]

For the conditions of the time – where inflation and the resulting price-level differences played such a dominant part in the determination of nominal exchange rates – Cassel's theory offered a simple but sensible guide to exchange-rate policy, infinitely better than the ill-considered advice of some economists and bankers for a return to prewar mint parities. A greater reliance on PPP calculations might have led to more sensible exchange rates in the various stabilisation exercises of the 1920s.[79]

However, Cassel was aware of the rough and ready nature of PPP calculations or inflation differentials as indicators of equilibrium exchange rates in the short and medium run. PPP, concerned as it was only with changes in nominal prices, could never pretend to be a general theory of exchange-rate determination. Cassel criticised the PPP 'dogma' already referred to, and in his later writings introduced various qualifications to his original doctrine – ironically, the very list that still forms the basis for critical attacks on the doctrine. Cassel's list of qualifications includes: (1) tariffs and quantitative restrictions on exports and imports which alter relative commodity prices in and between countries may introduce a divergence between PPP and the exchange rate; (2) autonomous capital movements; (3) speculation in the foreign exchange market and expectations about future monetary conditions – e.g. expectations about continuing inflation generate systematic movements in velocity that break the one-to-one link between money and prices, hence the relationship with the exchange rate; (4) official intervention in the foreign exchange market; and (5) random real disturbances to the balance of payments. Cassel fully recognised the role of these non-monetary factors in exchange-rate movements. Only when monetary changes dominate real changes would PPP provide a reliable indicator of short run exchange-rate movements; although Cassel further believed that monetary factors were the most important determinants of the exchange rate in the long run – in the sense that when the monetary disturbances have subsided, the cumulative changes in money, prices and the exchange rate will tend to be the same.

Cassel, however, did not naively believe in the simple quantity theory of money, and he rejected the neutrality-of-money concept applied to the short run. It is clear that for Cassel the PPP hypothesis specifies an equilibrium condition between relative price level and the exchange rate, and that in a weak sense it also specifies a causal relationship between the two variables. Most economists would accept that PPP holds in some sufficiently long run as an equilibrium tendency between the endogenous variables in question, or merely as a result of the operation of international commodity arbitrage. There seems to be no historical record of a case in which one country's price level rose (fell) significantly relative to another's over a substantial period of time, and the price of the second country's currency fell (rose) in terms of the first country's. In addition, large changes in exchange rates over substantial periods of time have taken place only when there have been equally substantial changes in relative price levels.

It seemed clear to Cassel that the direction of causation ran from price levels to the exchange rate, with the further implication that it was from money to price levels and then to the exchange rate. But as indicated above, he was careful enough to point out that whilst prices change was the primary determinant of the exchange rate in the long run, secondary factors (transport costs, tariffs and other trade impediments, capital flows, and expectations of inflation or deflation which exert real effects) were also important influences. PPP can be expected to hold when disturbances are purely monetary in origin. When they are not, then we can expect exchange-rate movements that deviate from the PPP relationship. According to Cassel, then, his PPP doctrine can be used to define the long-run response of the exchange rate to a purely monetary shock but not to describe actual exchange-rate behaviour during the course of a disturbance. Who can rightly quarrel with this?

Cassel developed his theory over a number of years against a background of dramatic changes in inflation and exchange rates among countries, and it was never conveniently and precisely set down in any one piece of writing. Inevitably, some exaggeration crept into the exposition. Perhaps because of this, Cassel's hypothesis has been caricatured, distorted, misrepresented and misunderstood even by such eminent practitioners as Viner, Metzler, Samuelson and Balassa. Nevertheless, Samuelson at any rate did sense Cassel's true position correctly when, in his 1964 article, he judged that a pragmatic case could be made for Cassel's hypothesis when applied to the dislocated exchange-rate situation of the immediate post-First World War period and the depressed 1930s;[80] and later, in 1982, when Samuelson declared that 'the correct grain of truth in the purchasing-power-parity dogma hinges on the hypothesis that in the longest run the money supply is neutral as far as real magnitudes and nominal ratios are concerned'.[81] Samuelson added that this was a good-sense relation, poorly perceived in the standard literature.

8.3 Keynes and International Monetary Arrangements

INTERNATIONAL MONETARY PLANS – POST-FIRST WORLD WAR

Keynes is associated in everyone's mind with Second World War plans for international monetary reform. But before that time there were various schemes for the creation of a supranational monetary agency designed to ensure the harmonisation of national economic policies.

Even as early as 1850, Michel Chevalier, the French negotiator of the Anglo-French Treaty of Commerce 1860, was prepared to think along those lines. He wrote: 'One does not see why the progress of commercial and political relations among the peoples of Europe should not lead to the creation of an international bank, which would have at least one seat in each of the great States.'[82]

At the International Financial Conference held in Brussels (24 September to 8 October 1920) Léon Delacroix, the former Belgian Prime Minister, proposed the establishment of an International Institute (or Bank) of Issue empowered to issue short-term interest-bearing 'gold bonds' acceptable to creditors in exchange for genuine securities of European states. The guarantees for such securities included joint liabilities of the country's banks, earmarked tax revenues, customs revenues, agricultural yields, etc. Since the bonds would correspond to the actual requirements of international trade, representing real values in terms of gold, they were presumed to create no inflationary potential. A recycling process in the use of bonds was envisaged in order to assist the Bank in intermediating between investors and the borrowing states.[83]

A year earlier, Bertrand Nogaro, a French economist at the University of Caen called for an international bank to issue a new international currency. The issue of notes equivalent to the world stock of monetary gold could be used by debtor countries to settle their international accounts. It called for a willingness of the creditor countries to grant the notes legal tender and thus make them acceptable to the public.[84]

In 1921 Frank Vanderlip, a former New York banker, proposed a central bank for Europe (the Gold Reserve Bank) authorised to issue notes convertible into gold and backed by an initial capital of $1 billion (20 per cent of which was to be in gold). Vanderlip's plan was designed to channel American capital to Europe and also to provide a productive use for that country's excess gold stock.[85]

In 1930 Keynes outlined a scheme for a modified gold standard managed by a supranational bank acting as a lender of last resort. The aim was to secure long-run price stability and the revival of trade activity. The supranational bank's liabilities would be deposits by national central banks. The bank would use discount-rate policy and open-market operations to vary its deposit liabilities to maintain price stability. The assent of a country's central bank would be required only in the case of purchases, not sales. No provisions were made for the adjustment of exchange rates.[86]

No government was interested in considering, let alone backing, any of these proposals. The spirit of cooperation was lacking to hasten the reconstruction of an international monetary system. The plans were generally regarded as crackpot or utopian ideas contrary to traditional canons of 'sound finance'. In the 1920s governments looked for solutions in the direction of a return to the gold standard, sound finance and balanced budgets. in the 1930s the remedies took nationalistic, non-cooperative forms – except for the Tripartite Monetary Agreement, 25 September 1936. This was a feeble attempt at international monetary cooperation, but it did allow the devaluation of the French franc to take place under orderly conditions, i.e. without inviting American and British retaliation. However, amidst the monetary disintegration of the 1930s it was seen as a token of what could be accomplished by cooperation.

Effective international cooperation came with the outbreak of the Second World War – e.g. Lend–Lease. In the monetary sphere, it manifested itself in the search for a new international monetary standard or order to replace the monetary disintegration of prewar days. The time was propitious for such an endeavour. Apart from close inter-Allied cooperation, other elements in the situation favoured a successful outcome: nearly all foreign exchange markets were closed; trade and private capital movements were virtually at a standstill and whatever foreign-exchange transactions took place were channelled through central banks. Thus there was every chance that discussions on monetary reform could proceed without producing disruptive effects on foreign exchange markets and exchange rates.

Keynes influenced the direction of the quest both by this copious interwar writings and by his leadership as head of the British delegation in the round of talks leading up to Bretton Woods.

KEYNES'S PRINCIPLES AND BRETTON WOODS

Former US President Richard Nixon referred to the December 1971 Smithsonian Institution agreement on the realignment of exchange rates after the dollar crisis of that year as 'the greatest monetary agreement in history'. But the agreement lasted only fourteen months. With greater justification this title might be claimed for the monetary arrangements set up at Bretton Woods, New Hampshire, in the summer of 1944. Certainly, the 1000 delegates from forty-four countries who attended this UN Monetary and Financial Conference at the Mount Washington Hotel felt they were engaged in a momentous undertaking. The job to be done was to devise an international monetary system that would rid the new postwar business and financial world community of the chronic monetary instability, currency disorders, excessive trade barriers, exchange restrictions, barter deals and widespread 'beggar-thy-neighbour' policies that paralysed the interwar world economy.

Much has been written (by scholars, politicians, journalists and bankers) about Keynes's role in the wartime negotiations – the story is fairly well told in the texts. A few comments may, however, be offered about Keynes's imprint on the postwar international monetary order.

Although the Bretton Woods agreement included few of the specific proposals advocated by Keynes, yet it reflected the intellectual consensus fostered by his work in the interwar period – the consensus later known as Keynesian economics. Indeed, the wartime economies were run on Keynesian principles. Keynes was the one who had offered the most convincing interpretation of the interwar experience and it was in the light of his testimony that the Conference participants faced the task of constructing postwar monetary arrangements.

What, then, were the principles for which he stood? Keynes stood for a Domestic Standard supplemented or supported by improved international monetary cooperation. If a Domestic Standard was not possible, then a Gold Standard managed on behalf of all (deficit and surplus countries alike) was his goal. He wanted to see a world where every nation would enjoy monetary independence so that each could achieve internal balance. He had earlier conceived of internal balance in terms of long-run price stability, but later defined it in terms of the short-run stabilisation of aggregate demand, i.e. the achievement of a full employment target.

To ensure monetary independence for Great Britain in the early 1920s Keynes had advocated the following: (1) the maintenance of adequate gold reserves; (2) widening of the gold points so as to permit fluctuations of the rates within a range of 2 per cent; (3) changes in the gold parity or exchange depreciation; and (4) revenue tariffs and bounties on export.[87] In the 1930s he added to the list, control of capital movements. Capital flows often led to disequilibrium because the foreign balance (the current account) responded sluggishly to flights of capital.

Keynes inveighed against what he called the 'deflationary bias' of the gold standard, particularly as the system functioned in the last decade before the war, i.e. the period following the collapse of sterling in 1931 and the Great Depression. Most of the pressure to restore equilibrium in the balance of payments fell on the deficit countries. Threatened with a loss of foreign exchange reserves, deficit countries were forced to deflate and slow down economic activity. To insulate the British economy from the pressures of interdependence and remedy the inadequacies of the classical adjustment mechanism, some control over the balance of payments was required. Such control was necessary to ease the pressure for higher Bank rates.

Flexible exchange rates were not the answer, however. As the experience of the 1930s showed, such a system was liable to be abused;[88] moreover, despite all the large changes, exchange rates settled down by 1939 at levels not very different from those ruling in 1930. Keynes opted for stable exchange rates in the short run with mechanisms for adjustment in the long run. He revolted against permanently fixed exchange rates (i.e. he argued for a managed exchange rate rather than either a free-floating or a rigidly fixed exchange rate), the automatic gold standard and the loss of domestic monetary autonomy. The ideal of domestic monetary independence (in aid of full employment) meant for Keynes nothing less than independence in wages policy, i.e. he favoured a wage standard. If wages got out of line then the resulting balance-of-payments problem could be rectified by an appropriate adjustment of the exchange rate. But throughout the 1930s he opposed any attempt to combat unemployment through a policy of reducing the nominal wage rate; this he defended both on theoretical and practical grounds. To buttress the independence for which he sought Keynes also pleaded that a country should be free to choose the interest rate appropriate to its needs. Such was the essence of Keynes's call for a domestic standard – a standard described more fully in his *General Theory*.

On this point it is of interest to note the recent comments of Sir John Hicks. Keynes's domestic standard is, says Hicks, a Labour Standard – given Keynes's assumption in the *General Theory* of rigid money wages, the recognition of the influence of social forces in wages policy, the formal expression of all real variables in terms of wage-units, etc. Under such a Labour Standard, the domestic monetary system adjusts itself to the level of money wages.[89] Thirty years earlier, Hicks gave an interpretation of Keynes's Labour Standard.[90] In the recent paper he looks at its operation in historical perspective. The weakness of the Labour Standard in an open-economy context is that it has no reserves; it has an inherently inflationary bias. When subjected to external shocks (e.g. the oil-price increases in the 1970s) it shows no resilience, and crumbles, leaving only depression and unemployment among the ruins.

Hicks's historical analysis is insightful and no doubt correct in regard to the shattering of the Keynesian dream. Nevertheless, to Keynes's satisfaction and in tribute to his teaching, independence in wages policies was provided for in the final Bretton Woods agreements. The agreements also permitted the use of capital controls. The International Monetary Fund system was intended to provide an escape from the conflict between internal and external stability and to give primacy to internal stability by allowing agreed exchange rate changes in cases of 'fundamental disequilibrium'.

Things did not work out quite the way they were intended, however; and perhaps Keynes knew that there were going to be problems, for despite his eloquence in favour of a domestic Labour Standard, he had agreed (at Bretton Woods) to an International Standard. But why did he agree to an International Standard? Historians and biographers give various answers: Keynes simply changed his mind; he yielded to American pressure; his plan for a sensible world economic order was thwarted by the hegemonic ambitions of the United States; he felt he had achieved his prime objective, i.e. the national right to follow an internal economic policy consistent with full employment; and finally, Keynes simply did not realise the extent to which his proposals were being rejected.[91] There is no way to unravel the puzzle, and different interpretations of Keynes's action (or reaction) will continue to be offered.

Certain relevant facts need to be considered. Lend–lease aid to Britain was abruptly stopped after the surrender of Japan in August 1945. On behalf of the British government Keynes asked the Americans for a gift of \$6 billion; instead, he was offered a loan of \$3 billion. Keynes had to accept as a condition for the loan section 8 of the Financial Agreement (December 1945), whereby Britain had to agree to (1) introduce current account convertibility within one year and (2) ratify the Bretton Woods Agreements.

Keynes publicly defended the Bretton Woods arrangements, but privately was extremely irritated by the Savannah decisions (i.e. the first meeting of the IMF and World Bank at Savannah, Georgia in March 1946) and threatened to advise the British government to withdraw from the Fund and Bank. However, in his posthumous article 'The Balance of Payments of the United States', June 1946, Keynes declared that he had helped to draft the blueprints for a world economic order designed 'not to defeat, but to implement the wisdom of Adam Smith'.[92]

Adam Smith referred to the international monetary system as the 'Great Wheel' – a system of orderly recycling. Perhaps Keynes thought that something like it could be restored for the postwar period, even under the compromise agreements. Did he still hold his optimistic conviction (expressed fifteen years earlier)?: 'It is plain that one can ensure nothing by the terms of a paper constitution. The desirable objectives can only be attained through the exercise of daily wisdom by the monetary authorities of the world.'[93]

8.4 Keynesian and Contemporary Balance of Payments Models

KEYNESIAN MODELS

Keynesian balance of payments adjustment analysis predominated in postwar writings on international monetary and financial economics up to the late 1960s, against an isolated rearguard defence of the traditional theory of international monetary equilibrium by Robert Mundell and Jacques Polak.

Keynes's *General Theory* is, of course, a sketchy but nevertheless penetrating analysis of the macroeconomic failures of a decentralised (capitalist) closed economy, notably a failure to achieve the full employment of all resources – failure resulting from disequilibrium prices when 'effective demand' is deficient, uncertainty of expectations and the volatility of private investment. But the immediate reaction to Keynes's work was one which regarded it as a macroeconomic theory concerned with the determination of income and employment when prices (in particular, the money wage-rate and the interest rate) do not adjust to clear markets.

An early analytical development was the application of Keynesian multiplier theory to the mechanism of international adjustment by Metzler, Harrod and Machlup and the criterion for exchange stability developed by Joan Robinson and Abba Lerner. This development embraced (1) a theory of automatic balance of payments adjustments under fixed exchange rates, and (2) a theory of flexible exchange rates – or, more accurately, a theory about official manipulation of a pegged exchange rate to preserve balanced trade (the so-called 'elasticities approach'). In the second theory, exchange stability is analysed in terms of elasticities of demand for and supply of imports and exports, with a scepticism concerning exchange-rate adjustments in correcting payments imbalances in the short run. Both theories deal with the mechanism by which a country can adjust to a shift in its current account balance. The multiplier or income-adjustment analysis describes what happens when income changes, with prices constant; whilst the elasticities approach investigates the adjustment process when prices change, with income constant.

The first theory was an outgrowth of the Keynesian revolution which undermined the traditional price-specie flow theory and emphasised in the adjustment process the role of output and employment changes induced by payments disturbances. The assumptions are: (1) that prices, including the exchange rate, are fixed; (2) the normal situation is one of less than full employment, so output changes in response to demand variations without price changes – real income and money income move in a completely parallel manner; (3) money supply adjusts passively to money demand due to the maintenance by the central bank of a constant interest rate – the central bank also stabilises reserve flows; and (4) capital is internationally immobile, i.e. the capital account can be ignored, hence the balance of payments is equal to the trade balance (in some versions, to the current account plus unilateral transfers).

The analysis starts with the income identity in an open-economy Keynesian model (where government expenditure, investment and exports are treated as exogenous) and simple behavioural relationships connecting a country's income with its demands for home and foreign goods, and then proceeds with the derivation of various foreign-trade multipliers. These relate to the effects of changes in the exogeneous variables (i.e. I, G and X) on the level of income and on the trade balance. Multiplier analysis shows that when trade equilibrium is disturbed by an autonomous change in exports or imports there is a mechanism of adjustment that works automatically to restore equilibrium. The restoration of trade balance equilibrium through induced variations in income and employment both at home and abroad will not be complete, however, in the normal case of a positive marginal propensity to save in both countries. In such cases, where adjustment is incomplete through income effects alone, price changes may also be required. If wages and commodity prices are sticky, the necessary price adjustments may be effected through exchange-rate changes, e.g. devaluation for a deficit country. The analysis also indicates how income fluctuations or business cycles are transmitted from country to country via changes in exports and imports – exports are exogenous to the home country, but they are endogenous with respect to the level of income in the foreign trading partner.

THE ELASTICITIES APPROACH

Around the same time, the elasticities approach was developed by some of the people responsible for the extension of Keynesian theory to income determination in open economies, and others, who partly in response to the interwar experience of fluctuating exchange rates, worked on the theory of exchange rates. It resulted from the joining of two strands of theoretical work: (1) the development of the theory of exchange rates in terms of the demand and supply of foreign exchange, and (2) the statement of the criterion for exchange stability. The theory sought to determine the response of a country's balance of trade (or current account) to parametric changes in its rate of exchange.

Haberler introduced the concept of supply and demand curves for foreign exchange in 1933 which was soon afterwards more fully developed by Bresciani-Turroni (1934), Joan Robinson (1937) and Machlup in his classic 1939–40 two-part article.[94] The criterion for exchange stability was discovered independently by Bickerdike, Joan Robinson, Brown and Metzler, and is an arrangement of partial-equilibrium elasticities that emerges from the differentiation of the balance of trade equation with respect to an exogenous parameter, i.e. the exchange rate – on the assumption that export and import prices adjust to equate the demand and supply of exports and imports. It is sometimes referred to as the 'Bickerdike–Robinson–Metzler condition'[95] (although Robinson and Metzler were only the early expositors of it), but is more commonly known as the Marshall–Lerner condition – a term first employed by Albert Hirschmann which stuck (e.g. in all textbook expositions of the elasticities approach).[96]

As is perhaps well known by now, the M–L appellation is unfortunately misplaced. Alfred Marshall and Abba Lerner never wrote anything together – when Marshall died (1924), Lerner was just twenty-one years old. Partly to avoid this misnomer, Machlup (always a great stickler for precision in definitions) referred to the elasticities condition in a neutral manner as 'the theorem of the critical value of the sum of the demand elasticities in international trade'.[97] But the attribution is inappropriate in a more fundamental sense. Marshall was concerned with the stability properties of a pure (barter) trade model, whereas Lerner's inerest was with the foreign exchange market – specifically in the sense of a condition for a positive effect of a devaluation on the trade balance in a monetary economy with infinite supply elasticities. Thus Lerner's interest was not at all in disequilibrium dynamics. The so-called Marshall–Lerner condition (for a change in the exchange rate to improve the trade balance) is different from what Mundell calls Marshall's 'barter theory pseudostability condition' in terms of the elasticities of the offer curves.[98] Marshall made no mention of devaluation or of the balance of payments; nor did he equate the exchange rate with the terms of trade. The Marshallian stability condition (in terms of the elasticities of excess demand in both countries) requires that the sum of the two countries' elasticities of demand for imports, in absolute terms, be greater than zero – in terms of the offer curve, a sufficient condition is that one country's offer curve is upward-sloping around the equilibrium point. However, the 'Marshall–Lerner condition', the Bickerdike–Robinson–Metzler formulas and the Marshallian condition come to the same thing, i.e. they are formally identical in the case of infinite supply elasticities of exports in both countries and zero cross-elasticities of demand functions. The common condition (expressed in terms of the demand elasticities for imports of the two countries, A and B) becomes $e_A + e_B < -1$ (which is a necessary and sufficient condition for local stability). Since both demand elasticities are generally negative, the condition requires that the sum of the elasticities of demand for imports be greater than unity.

The offer curve analysis used by Marshall and Lerner are not really suitable for dealing with the effects of exchange rate changes – these necessarily involve money-price elasticities. The elasticities of Marshall's offer curves, by contrast, relate to the total quantities traded, and are general-equilibrium elasticities derived from changes in the real terms of trade within the context of a barter model. Furthermore, the M–L condition is not really a stability condition, but a comparative-static condition, i.e. for a devaluation to improve the trade balance under an adjustable-peg exchange rate system, as indicated above.

The elasticities approach focuses on commodity markets and analyses the impact on the balance of trade (or more generally, the current account balance) of the changes in relative prices induced by a devaluation of the exchange rate. The general level of internal prices in both countries is constant, and on account of this price inflexibility (in particular, the prices of domestic or non-traded goods) it was natural to look for price adjustments (i.e. changes in relative prices) as resulting from changes in the nominal exchange rate (the price of foreign currency in terms of domestic currency). A change in the nominal exchange rate altered the real exchange rate (the price of foreign output in terms of domestic output, or the terms of trade). In some versions, it was implied that terms-of-trade changes were the only initial effect of devaluation – the earlier view being that the terms of trade would deteriorate; but that the increase in exports sold abroad and the reduction in imports bought by domestic residents would more than compensate for the terms-of-trade loss. But, as in the monetary approach, changes in the terms of trade are not an essential aspect of devaluation according to the elasticities approach, but rather changes between non-traded goods and internationally traded goods in both countries, i.e. changes in the sectoral composition of output.

Initially, empirical studies suggested low elasticities and this raised doubts about the efficacy of devaluation as a remedy for payments disequilibria – 'elasticity pessimism'. The case of infinite supply elasticities is regarded as an assumption consistent with unemployment; but this assumption is also not necessary to the elasticities approach, since whatever the supply elasticities may be, provided they are non-negative, the Bickerdike–Robinson–Metzler condition still applies, i.e. if the demand elasticities dominate the supply elasticities. In that event, a devaluation of the domestic currency can improve the current-account balance even though the demand elasticities are not high enough to satisfy the usual condition.

Since the 1950s, opinion has veered towards 'elasticity optimism', i.e. toward the view that if the proper adjustment period is chosen, allowing for *J*-curve effects, devaluation is likely to improve the balance of payments on current account. This was influenced by three factors: (1) revised empirical estimates, which allowed for lengthy lags in the response of trade flows to price changes, indicated higher demand elasticities well within the range specified in the M–L condition; (2) the observation that countries with overvalued real exchange rates during the 1960s experienced payments crises rather than ever-growing surpluses; and (3) increased recognition of the practical certainty that a 'small' country facing given world market prices encounters no elasticity constraints – i.e. the trade balance cannot deteriorate following devaluation. But elasticity optimism was not enough to dispel doubts about devaluation as a 'sure-fire' remedy for payments deficits. The outcome of several devaluations during the 1960s (an inflationary period associated with full employment policies) suggested that when underlying economic policies and problems that led to a devaluation were not corrected, devaluation offered only a temporary respite.

Proponents of the elasticities approach were on the defensive in the 1960s. The model did not square with reality and it did not comply with the requirements of the fashionable general-equilibrium theorising. On the latter count, it was accused of being cast in a partial-equilibrium mould, e.g. the assumption of infinite supply elasticities or the implicit assumption of the existence of unemployed resources, which abstracted from limitations on total output. On the first count, it was alleged to be at variance with the contemporary economic environment characterised by full employment of resources, rapid changes of money stocks, high international capital mobility and worldwide inflationary pressures. The main weakness here was no explicit recognition of money and the monetary effects of exchange-rate changes. Those who are persuaded by these charges against the elasticities approach would do well to study and consider Chipman's important 1978 reconstruction of the elasticities approach which re-establishes its relevance and validity, and shows how it can be reconciled with the neoclassical model of general equilibrium.[99] He concludes with a point-by-point rebuttal of the (six) charges made by critics of the approach.

It is also instructive to refer back to what those who helped to develop the elasticities approach had to say on some matters brought into focus by the rival monetary approach, but ignored until then. Long before the monetary approach became fashionable, these writers stressed the importance of monetary equilibrium in balance of payments adjustments, recognised the roles of non-traded goods and income effects, described shifts of the supply and demand curves for foreign exchange and hence recognised the general-equilibrium nature of the curves. In 1949 Haberler wrote: 'The second reason why domestic demand and supply curves may shift in consequence of a depreciation is much more important and is monetary in nature. A depreciation of the currency is likely to result in an increase in total expenditures, in *MV*, implying a shift to the right of demand and supply curves; in other words, it is likely to have an inflationary or expansionary effect.'[100] Fritz Machlup's famous article on the theory of foreign exchange distinguished between movements along the curves (in terms of elasticities) from shifts of the curves (caused by monetary factors). Many years later (1980), commenting on his early work, he repeated what he said then: 'an excess supply of domestic money, caused by a rise in the stock of money or a decline in the demand for it, would shift the demand curve for foreign exchange to the right, and perhaps also the supply curve to the left. Hence, the curve analysis which I proposed may also be used in an exposition of the monetary approach to exchange-rate and balance-of-payments analysis.'[101]

THE ABSORPTION APPROACH

Monetary wisdom did not descend like an angel of enlightenment in 1973 or thereabouts. The fact is that both Keynesian and monetarist theorists in the 1940s and 1950s accepted what Ronald McKinnon calls the model of 'an insular economy', i.e. an economy where both commodity and financial arbitrage with the outsie world is limited, but which still engages in some foreign trade.[102] In such an economy – typical of the early postwar years – the purchasing power of domestic money is independently established and the domestic monetary system is insulated from the foreign exchanges. Internal balance is maintained through government control over aggregate demand so that income repercussions from changes in exchange rates and the trade balance can be ignored. The plausibility of the elasticities approach thus reflected the prevailing economic situation, and for such an insular economy the elasticities model was logically consistent and afforded a fairly reliable guide to policy-making. Thus Machlup was only stating what was the older consensus when he declared in 1980: 'I submit that the elasticity approach is relevant as long as the assumption of unchanged incomes is pertinent, but loses some of its relevance when monetary changes lead to significant changes in income.'[103]

When in 1952 Sidney Alexander, then at the IMF, proposed his absorption approach to devaluation as an alternative to the relative prices or elasticities approach,[104] the world was beginning to change. The world economy was in boom, and the doors of national economies were opening more widely – to international trade and financial flows. The later phenomenal growth of Eurocurrency trading (international financial intermediation) was an obvious indication of the increased integration of national financial markets. This change in the world economic environment altered economists' and policy-makers' perceptions of the adjustment process. The monetary nature of a payments imbalance could no longer be ignored, and the notion of an insular economy became less credible as a theoretical and practical framework. However, the new models fashioned at that time – Alexander's absorption approach and James Meade's policy-objectives approach – failed to incorporate essential elements in that internationalisation process. The extant models were still cast in the mould of the insular economy, the prototype of an autonomous nation state. Nevertheless, on the positive side, these models did reveal that adjustment to payments disequilibria (whether discretionary or automatic) was a macroeconomic problem. This recognition made it relatively easy for monetarist critics to shift the discussion to a level they judged more in touch with reality. As a result of various developments and refinements we now have the monetary and portfolio-balance approaches to balance of payments and exchange rate theory.

Alexander viewed the trade deficit as the excess of national expenditure (or absorption) over income – thus making it a macroeconomic problem. He considered production and spending in the economy as a whole which would have the effect of shifting the supply and demand curves for exports and imports, a result overlooked by the elasticities approach. Devaluation is analysed in terms of how it affects the relative levels of total expenditure and income: that is, to the extent that it reduces expenditure relative to output, devaluation may improve the trade balance. However, with a current-account deficit in a situation of domestic full employment (no unused capacity, no scope for additional output through increased production), a devaluation must be followed by discretionary policy (deflationary monetary and fiscal policy) to reduce aggregate demand so as to make room for improvement in the balance of trade, i.e. by releasing goods for export.

Although there was no precise monetary significance in Alexander's treatment, Harry Johnson highlighted this particular point as being 'the fundamental contribution of the absorption approach'. He further claimed that the national-income identity used in the approach, together with the macroeconomic implications of a deficit, illuminated 'the monetary aspects of balance-of-payments disequilibrium and emphasizes its essentially monetary nature'.[105] Harry Johnson, the great synthesiser and guide who erected signposts for theorists, did much to encourage others to explore the path that led to global monetarism.

MEADE'S APPROACH AND THE MUNDELL–FLEMING MODEL

Meade's work on the policy conflicts between internal and external equilibrium initiated another fruitful line of development which culminated in the Mundell–Fleming model and other variants such as the contemporary portfolio balance theory. Although the potential conflict between internal stability (full employment combined with long-run price stability) and external stability (balance of payments equilibrium) was long recognised, Meade was the first to work out a systematic theory to deal with this problem, at about the same time that Jan Tinbergen developed the idea that became known as 'the theory of economic policy' – the rule that the achievement of *n* policy targets requires the use of *n* independent policy instruments.[106] Meade's theory ran in terms of interacting price and income (or expenditure) effects, i.e. price elasticities as well as income propensities; and he showed that in order to achieve internal and external balance simultaneously, it was necessary to have one policy to influence the level of expenditure and another to work on the composition of demand. Johnson later characterised these policy responses in the case of a deficit as (a) expenditure-reducing policies and (b) expenditure-switching policies (e.g. devaluation),[107] since both policies influence output as well as absorption. With respect to a fully employed economy in external deficit, Meade's conclusion was therefore very similar to the policy implications of Alexander's approach – although it must be noted that in his formal analysis Meade gave more prominence to price elasticities and less to the possibility of endogenous changes in absorption.[108] His work was, of course, an attempt to synthesise Keynesian expenditure theory with neoclassical price theory. The macroeconomic analysis of open economies initiated by Meade came into prominence a decade later with the diagrammatic and formal extensions of Mundell and Fleming (for the world of currency convertibility, especially capital-account convertibility).

Meade lumped monetary and fiscal policies in one category – expenditure policy – which, through its operation on income adjustments (i.e. its regulation of aggregate demand), he regarded as the instrument for the attainment of internal balance.[109] External balance was essentially a matter of price adjustments, and these could be appropriately engineered by exchange-rate changes and/or import restrictions. However, for two so-called 'dilemma cases' that Meade identified, policy conflicts between the two objectives of internal and external balance could arise when a country was committed to a fixed exchange rate and the use of trade restrictions was ruled out – there would be one instrument short and therefore the two objectives could not be attained simultaneously. The apparent dilemma can be resolved in a world of capital mobility if one re-defines external balance to include both the current account and the capital account (short-term capital flows). The current account then responds negatively to increases in the level of income and employment and capital flows (in the capital account) become responsive to changes in international interest-rate differentials. Monetary and fiscal policies will now have differential impacts on the level of income on the one hand, and the balance of payments on the other; and for the purposes of achieving external and internal balance can be regarded as two separate instruments according to their sensitivity to interest-rate changes. An appropriate combination or assignment of monetary and fiscal instruments (known as the optimal policy mix) can achieve both targets inclusive of dilemma cases; for example, a country suffering unemployment and a balance of payments deficit under fixed exchange rates can successfully correct both disequilibria by an expansionary fiscal policy (to stimulate the level of activity and employment) combined with a restrictive monetary policy (to induce a capital inflow).

The foregoing was the extension of Meade's model developed by Robert Mundell and John Marcus Fleming in the early 1960s.[110] In a pathbreaking series of articles Mundell explored the anatomy of disequilibrium under alternative exchange-rate systems and showed that the direction of policy adjustment to disequilibrium depended upon what he called the 'principle of effective market classification', i.e. the assignment of each policy instrument to the target variable upon which it has the stronger relative effect. With proper assignment the model is stable, i.e. the policy path converges to optimal equilibrium; but an opposite pairing of instruments and targets results in dynamic instability. With perfect capital mobility (infinite interest elasticity or perfect substitutability between domestic and foreign bonds) Mundell's analysis indicates that monetary policy has a strong effect on income and internal stability, whilst fiscal policy has no effect at all under flexible exchange rates. The opposite is the case under fixed exchange rates. Fleming makes the same basic assumptions as Mundell, except that he defines monetary policy as changes in the money stock – in Mundell, it is defined as interest-rate policy – and finds (like Mundell) that monetary policy is more effective under flexible exchange rates, but the corresponding result with respect to fiscal policy is uncertain. This analysis is now known as the basic Mundell–Fleming model. The model was influential, not only in academic circles but also among policy-makers (including officials of the IMF), since it seemed to offer simple stabilisation rules or strategies for optimal macroeconomic equilibrium in the new environment of freer trade and integrated financial markets. The authorities may not be omniscient. They may be unsure about the underlying parameters and responses of the system. They may know neither the exact slopes nor the positions of the internal and external balance curves (*IS*, *LM*, *BP* and *Y* curves), but provided they can recognise an incipient payments deficit or internal imbalance (incipient unemployment or incipient inflation) these qualitative indicators or signals will be sufficient to enable them to pull the correct levers according to the prearranged assignment rule. The smooth adjustment of policy instruments will then lead the economy toward internal and external balance at the stable equilibrium point.

The model has several weaknesses, however. The basic framework is a Keynesian-type *IS/LM/BP* model. There is a constant domestic price level (reflecting underemployment equilibrium). The 'small country' assumption is made, which means that world interest rates and prices are taken as given. There are no lags – the economy moves smoothly and rapidly to its new equilibrium. Real income is demand-determined, i.e. it is a function of monetary and fiscal policies, increasing with increases in government expenditure and decreasing with the interest rate. It is a short-run equilibrium analysis. It neglects the debt-service payments (and also the 'crowding out' of domestic investment) associated with short-term capital inflows induced by tighter monetary policy. Unless the current-account balance is restored to some sort of sustainable equilibrium, mounting foreign debt (or interest-income payments to foreigners) will aggravate future imbalances on current account. Reliance on the manipulation of the capital account to maintain balance is therefore not a viable long-term solution. Moreover, under flexible exchange rates, capital mobility increases the risk of dynamic instability. With monetary policy targeted on internal balance there will be large fluctuations in the exchange rate. If the assignment rule is followed strictly (i.e. the authorities take no account of the exchange-rate changes resulting from their monetary policy) there can be uncontrollable (or explosive) oscillations in domestic income and the exchange rate. The theory does not address the longer-run problem of how national price levels are to be aligned so as to avoid the need to rely on short-term foreign borrowings under a system of fixed exchange rates. The treatment of capital flows is unsatisfactory in another respect. It adopts a flow theory of the capital account (i.e. the specification of the capital account as a function of international interest-rate levels); but modern asset-market theory suggests that capital flows are the consequences of portfolio adjustments to desired stock positions. Thus, once balance in wealth owners' portfolios is restored, the flow will tend to dry up and can only be sustained by a widening or continuous change in interest-rate differentials – because only a changing interest-rate differential will create further portfolio disequilibrium that leads to a continuous shifting of stocks of capital from foreign to domestic bonds, i.e. a continuing flow. In general, then, equilibrium under the Mundell–Fleming model can be achieved only by the proper rates of change in the policy instruments rather than by the proper levels. What was lacking in the model was an analysis of stock equilibrium in international asset markets.

Nevertheless, by highlighting capital-account transactions, the Mundell–Fleming model did serve a useful purpose in directing attention to the overall balance of payments rather than just the current account. In this sense, the model prepared the way for both the monetary approach and the portfolio-balance model of exchange rate and balance-of-payments theory. After being overshadowed in the 1970s by the monetary approach, the Mundell–Fleming model made a rapid recovery as the main frame of reference for exchange-rate questions, and directly inspired asset-market approaches to exchange-rate determination, in particular the portfolio-balance framework. The latter was developed to overcome the inadequacies of the initial Mundell–Fleming model, but still retains the model's open-economy macroeconomic framework. Recent theories of exchange rate determination will be reviewed in the next section. It is now time to consider the monetary approach to the balance of payments, which until recently 'crowded out' rival approaches in academic journals and other forums where such matters were discussed.

MONETARIST MODELS

The intellectual antecedents of the modern monetary approach are, of course, of venerable vintage; indeed, its roots can be traced to the very dawn of economics as a discipline; but it was a minority tradition represented by Ricardo and Wheatley, somewhat at variance with the more orthodox price-specie flow mechanism associated with Hume.

Monetary modes of analysis of balance of payments disequilibrium surfaced as early as the late 1950s and early 1960s in the work of the Dutch economist Jacques Polak and others at the International Monetary Fund.[111] This work provided comfort to those who harboured doubts about the conventional wisdom on three points: (1) the failure of devaluations to bring about lasting improvements in deficit countries; (2) the allegation that existing theories could not explain the relatively high growth rates and external surpluses of some countries (e.g. Germany, Switzerland and Japan); and (3) their inability to explain the convergence of inflation rates during the Bretton Woods era. On the second point, it may be noted that higher growth rates generate high growth rates of demand for real money balances which lead to an increase in the stock of international reserves as reflected in a balance of payments surplus; however, the monetarists themselves could not explain why the authorities in those countries did not increase commensurately the credit bases of their monetary systems. In the elasticities and absorption approaches the monetary effects of payments imbalances are 'sterilised' – a sterilisation policy, if successful, totally separates the link between a country's money supply and its balance of payments. Changes in the price level consequent upon changes in the exchange rate alters real money balances and thus real aggregate demand. Through this temporary real-balance effect, devaluation is then equivalent to a policy of contracting the domestic money supply – i.e. a devaluation results in an increase in the domestic price level which induces individuals to reduce their real expenditures to restore their initial real cash balances. The pre-1971 fixed-exchange-rate system was called the 'disequilibrium system' on account of the common practice of sterilisation, and Johnson was perhaps right, after all, when he claimed that the absorption approach illuminated and explained the essentially monetary nature of balance of payments disequilibrium. It directs attention to two important aspects of a deficit, he said – its monetary implications and its relation to aggregate supply and aggregate demand. 'I would hazard the conjecture,' writes Dietrich Fausten in 1979, 'that a selective picking through the elasticity-multiplier-absorption-policy approach literature would yield an ample basket of *obiter dicta* referring in one way or another to monetary aspects of balance of payments analysis.'[112] The fully developed monetary approach to the balance of payments stresses this proposition – that the balance of payments is essentially a monetary phenomenon; it puts money at the centre. In this connection, it considers not just the current account but the overall balance of payments – the 'money account' or the change in international reserves, known in the Bretton Woods system as 'the official settlements balance'.

Polak's model assumed no capital mobility and took domestic credit expansion as a policy variable, and therefore exogenous.[113] A payments deficit under fixed exchange rates implies a loss of reserves which can only occur if credit creation or dishoarding (a fall in domestic money holdings) takes place. Since dishoarding is a disequilibrium phenomenon and can only be temporary, a payments deficit can persist only when domestic credit creation is positive, i.e. the authorities sterilise reserve losses.[114] A payments deficit (the excess of the value of goods, services and assets imported over the value exported) is then the means whereby residents rid themselves of an excess supply of money – any additional credit creation beyond that required for monetary equilibrium will ultimately leak out abroad. A payments deficit fuelled by credit creation cannot persist indefinitely since reserves will ultimately be exhausted. The moral of Polak's analysis was not lost on officials of the IMF charged with making recommendations for stabilisation programmes for countries in payments difficulties in the late 1960s – control over the balance of payments requires placing limits on the growth of the domestic component of the money supply.

After a while, work on open-economy monetary models was resumed in earnest at the University of Chicago under the intellectual leadership of Robert Mundell and Harry Johnson; and, in the early 1970s, in the UK – both at the London School of Economics (i.e. the International Monetary Economics Research Programme under Johnson and Alexander Swoboda) and at Manchester University (i.e. the Inflation Workshop under David Laidler and Michael Parkin).

Versions of the basic model were published in the early 1970s.[115] Coinciding with the rise of monetarism as a social and economic doctrine, the monetary approach enjoyed worldwide popularity in the decade of the 1970s. It recognised the monetary stock-flow adjustment process of the balance of payments under fixed exchange rates and made use of various well-known monetarist assumptions and relations to reach the conclusion that the automatic operation of the international adjustment mechanism eventually corrects balance of payments surpluses and deficits.

An extreme version of the theory, christened 'global monetarism' by Marina Whitman,[116] posits that the world economy is one integrated market wherein the law of one price (for both goods and securities) prevails, with a consequent endogeneity of the domestic (nominal) money supply (since the price level, real income and the domestic interest rate in the demand for money function are all exogenously determined) – a version which breaks sharply with the competing classical price-specie flow mechanism. In the modern approach, the relation between money demand and money supply affects spending and the balance of payments directly, without the need for relative price shifts. The model assumes full employment and perfect competition in all markets with full price and wage flexibility. A critical assumption is that the authorities cannot or do not sterilise (or offset) reserve flows. The 'small country' assumption and the PPP condition hold, so that the fixed exchange rate determines the domestic price level. Given the exogenously determined price level (via the exchange rate and internationally equalised prices) the demand for money is fixed. The demand for money in conjunction with the money supply determine the rate of money-stock adjustment. This adjustment determines spending, trade balances, and the direction and volume of international money flows. If monetary equilibrium is momentarily disturbed, say through an excess supply of money, reserves decrease and the excess money 'leaks out' to other countries through a balance of payments deficit. When stock-flow equilibrium is restored, initially held balances are at their desired levels, the change in reserves is zero and the balance of payments is in equilibrium. The basic premise is that any balance of payments disequilibrium must be understood in terms of monetary disequilibrium – an application of Walras's law, since a deficit implies that the economy has excess demands in its goods and securities markets taken together and therefore must have excess supply in its money market. A payments deficit is identified with the process of getting rid of an excess supply of money and a surplus with the process of satisfying an excess demand for money. No real effects are implied by the model; it embodies the classical 'neutrality' postulate – the proposition that real variables are invariant to monetary disturbances in the long run – an extension to the open economy of the theory of real-balance adjustments.

The monetarist model yielded some fresh insights: e.g. (1) the prediction about the international convergence of inflation rates towards the end of the Bretton Woods period; (2) the plausible explanation for the co-existence of high growth rates and external surpluses in some countries; and (3) the theoretical demonstration (under the assumptions of the model) of the transitory effects of devaluation on the balance of payments and the level of domestic output, summarised in Dornbusch's assertion that 'an exchange rate change in and of itself will exert no real effects'.[117] Real effects will be produced by a devaluation, for instance, only if the nominal price of one good is held constant or if the authorities hold the nominal money supply constant following devaluation.

However, the model makes use of several generalisations that have been interpreted in so exaggerated and rigid a manner that they are not strictly true – e.g. instantaneous and successful arbitrage in goods and securities, the exogeneity of real income. John Williamson observes: 'The hypothesis that arbitrage quickly equates goods prices internationally has probably been rejected more decisively by empirical evidence than any other hypothesis in the history of economics.'[118] Even when joined with the rational expectations hypothesis, the monetarist position on the exogeneity of real income (apart from deviations caused by random factors) amounts to a suspension of disbelief in the face of a trebling of United Kingdom unemployment in 1977–81 and similar trends elsewhere. Moreover, critics have always held that the market-clearing assumption is a travesty of the facts. The monetarist model gives a long-run equilibrium or steady-state solution, but this may not be relevant for short-run stabilisation policy, i.e. the assumptions may not hold over any realistic current policy-making horizon. John Williamson notes, however, that the monetary approach should not be summarily dismissed on this score since it may be quite indispensable 'as a tool for short-term forecasting of payments flows in countries with a high degree of capital mobility'.[119]

EXCHANGE-RATE THEORIES

Leading proponents of the monetary approach were also ardent advocates of flexible exchange rates (notable exceptions being Robert Mundell and Arthur Laffer), and when, amidst disrupted foreign exchange markets (and divergent movement in national price levels), the world moved to floating rates in 1973 following the collapse of the Bretton Woods system, they had no difficulty in applying the model to the determination of exchange rates.[120] In the meantime, an alternative model based on financial portfolio-balance analysis was being developed, commonly known as the asset market or portfolio-balance model (so named because investors hold diversified portfolios). An extended Mundell–Fleming model was the basic frame of reference for this alternative approach. The extension was made by McKinnon and Oates in the late 1960s.[121] They replaced the Mundell–Fleming formulation in which the capital account was treated as a flow related to the level of the interest differential between home and abroad, by a new, more realistic specification in terms of a stock-adjustment response of the capital account (capital flows) to a change in interest-rate differentials. The amendment recognises that capital flows are consequences of adaptations to desired stock positions – i.e. that available stocks of national moneys and other financial asserts must equal stock demands for these assets, as a necessary condition for equilibrium. This was the decisive breakthrough for the new approach. Theoretical progress was subsequently marked by the recognition of the central role of wealth variables in the framework; money demand depends not only on income, but also on wealth and interest rates – i.e. the notion that individuals allocate their wealth among alternative assets, including domestic and foreign moneys and domestic and foreign securities. Shifts in the international redistribution of wealth induced by current account imbalances create monetary imbalance (price-level expectations) and hence lead to exchange-rate movements. The exchange rate then performs the role of balancing asset demands and supplies (financial-market equilibrium), given domestic money supplies and assets. The exchange rate so determined, in turn influences the trade balance and the current account. The portfolio-balance model thus describes a dynamic feedback mechanism in foreign assets and exchange rates.

The initial monetarist model of exchange-rate determination suggested a one-way causation from money to exchange rates via PPP, just as basic monetarism argued for uni-directional causality from money supply to nominal income. By contrast, portfolio balance models view the exchange rate as being proximately determined by financial-market equilibrium conditions, i.e. it behaves like an asset price in the short run. Nevertheless, there is a relationship over time between current account balances (the net rate of accumulation of foreign assets) and the exchange rate because of the two-way interaction between goods and asset markets. Thus, current account surpluses are associated with domestic currency appreciation that tends to eliminate the surpluses, and deficits with domestic currency depreciation that tends to eliminate the deficits. In this manner, the exchange rate approaches its long-run equilibrium value. Portfolio-balance models usually incorporate expectations and imperfect asset substitution in the modelling of exchange-rate dynamics, and this feature of the model brings out most clearly the fact that exchange-rate determination in the long run is a macroeconomic problem involving the interaction of goods and asset markets.

Part of the appeal of the portfolio-balance approach over the monetary model is that it is more general, can more readily incorporate significant phenomena and conforms somewhat more closely to reality than the latter. Krueger observes that these theoretical advantages 'renders the portfolio-balance model more tempting' in view of 'the fact that some of the assumptions underpinning the monetary approach are violated by empirical reality'.[122] She points to one empirically valid insight of the portfolio-balance model – namely, the recognition that the exchange rate in the short run reflects conditions of equilibrium in the asset market, since the existing stocks of domestic and foreign financial assets must be willingly held and their volume far outweighs (at least for major countries) the current account at any given moment. The monetary approach is also criticised by Rudiger Dornbusch – an open-economy monetarist who now takes up a much more eclectic position. Anchored as it is in 'two outrageous simplifications of the economic scene', he wrote in 1986, 'there are, I believe, no more serious claims for the empirical relevance of this model'.[123]

However, at the onset of generalised floating of currencies in 1973, the monetary approach was the most popular model of exchange rate determination. But it soon suffered major setbacks. Theoretical predictions were inconsistent with empirical reality in several notable incidents: (1) dollar depreciation during the period 1973–9 when US inflation was averaging 1 per cent less than in other major industrial countries; (2) the sharp real appreciation of sterling in 1979–81; (3) the fact that at times, countries with strong and appreciating currencies have had huge trade deficits; (4) the breakdown of demand-for-money functions. Monetarists were led to invoke *ad hoc* hypotheses (unrelated to the model's structure) to explain these and other problematic currency episodes.

Dornbusch (1976) originated an important popular modification of the monetarist approach with his exchange-rate 'overshooting' model which replaced the assumption of instantaneous adjustment in all markets with the more realistic hypothesis that some markets adjust sluggishly.[124] In response to monetary and other shocks, the spot exchange rate may 'overshoot' its new long-run equilibrium value (determined by interest parity and PPP) even with perfect foresight, because asset markets clear instantaneously whereas goods and labour markets do not. The exchange rate reacts instantaneously to maintain continuous (uncovered) interest parity, but adjusts more slowly to maintain PPP in the long run. This analysis suggests that in the short run, monetary policy can have effects on real variables – that short-run change in the real exchange rate affects the net trade balance and domestic output. It also offers a convincing explanation for the volatility of major exchange rates. Like Friedmanite monetarism, the monetary approach sustained a gradual loss of corroborative empirical content. To restore credibility for the approach, theorists working within the monetarist tradition extended and modified the original model, starting with the 1975 Frenkel–Rodriguez treatment of asset accumulation and current-account determination which brought the approach close to the portfolio-balance model espoused by Branson, Kenen, Dooley, Isard and others. Krueger, writing in 1981, observed 'at the present time it is difficult to distinguish an adherent of the monetary approach from an author of a portfolio-balance model'.[125] The convergence has led to renewed interest in the extended Mundell–Fleming model as a framework for the general modelling of exchange rates – witness Dornbusch's remark that 'the traditional Mundell–Fleming model . . . remains, with some adaptations, the backbone of macroeconomic models of the exchange rate'.[126]

SUMMARY APPRAISAL OF EXCHANGE-RATE THEORIES

We have now reviewed the three basic theories of exchange-rate determination developed during the years since the last war and may now summarise them, offering critical comments on each. Exchange-rate determination theory under flexible rates is, of course, the counterpart to balance of payments theory under fixed rates. With the institutional change to floating exchange rates, emphasis has shifted from asking how quantities change under fixed rates to how prices change under flexible rates; but the two questions are very closely related – the former is the 'primal' problem and the latter is its 'dual'. The three basic models are: (1) the balance of payments (or current-account) theory of exchange rates – the exchange rate is viewed as the relative price of goods; (2) the monetary theory – the exchange rate is the relative price of moneys; and (3) the portfolio-balance (or asset-market) approach to exchange-rate theory – the exchange rate is the relative price of bonds.

The first, popular in the 1950s and 1960s, is a Keynesian-type model developed by Joan Robinson, Machlup and Haberler. It analyses exchange-rate stability in terms of the elasticities of demand for and supply of imports and exports – the Marshall–Lerner condition – and was commonly used in the analysis of devaluation or revaluation in the Bretton Woods fixed exchange-rate system. This model focuses on commodity trade (usually the current account or trade balance). In defining the 'equilibrium' exchange rate, balanced trade, rather than internationally aligned price levels or interest rates, held the centre stage. The current account was taken as the independent variable, and the depreciation (or appreciation) of the currency in the foreign exchange market as the dependent variable. Limitations of this model include: (a) It is logically consistent for economies that are somewhat insulated from each other with respect to commodity and financial arbitrage – as indeed they probably were in the 1950s. (b) The equations describing the model are often written without directly specifying levels of real income, real expenditures or money stocks in each country. (c) The general purchasing power of money (at home and abroad) are assumed invariant to exchange-rate changes, although both the domestic supply of exports and the demand for imports are simple functions of their domestic money prices. The Marshall–Lerner condition relates to the effect of a change in the real exchange rate – i.e. a change in the nominal exchange rate can affect the current-account balance only by changing the real exchange rate. Since, in the Keynesian framework, price levels in each country remain constant, any change in the nominal exchange rate is roughly equivalent to a change in the real exchange rate. But price levels might not be constant, so that a devaluation or revaluation may be offset by opposite-signed movements in domestic and foreign prices that prevent the real exchange rate from changing (e.g. this arises when real wage-rates are completely rigid). (d) The capital account is ignored – private portfolio adjustments (capital movements) are insufficient to finance, automatically, current-account deficits or surpluses. This is clearly an untenable position. The integration of world financial markets has increased enormously the international mobility of capital. Syndicated international bank lending was less than $7 billion in 1971, but totalled $90 billion in 1981. It is no longer true that a country's large trade deficit weakens its currency in foreign exchange markets or that the exchange rate adjusts over any short time-period to eliminate current account imbalances. The behaviour of the US dollar in the 1980s is a case in point. Despite huge current-account deficits, the US dollar strengthened in foreign exchange markets. (e) The national monetary sector is insulated from the foreign exchanges – reserve flows are 'sterilised' (through open-market operations) so as to offset their impact on the domestic monetary base.

The monetary approach was developed in the 1970s when PPP was on everyone's mind. The model relies on the PPP equilibrium condition, or in an extreme version, the 'law of one price' enforced through international commodity arbitrage. There is an integrated capital market as well, with the domestic interest rate determined by the international rate (for small open economies). Domestic and foreign bonds can be treated as a single asset (justified by the composite-commodity theorem). In this connection, use is made of the interest-parity theory, i.e. the link between the spot and forward exchange rates, and therefore between interest rates in the home country and the rest of the world. The presence of risk-neutral asset holders ensures that uncovered interest parity is also maintained: i.e. the domestic interest rate equals the foreign interest rate plus the expected rate of change of the spot exchange rate. The monetary approach can be called the 'inflation theory' of changes in exchange rates: the exchange rate depreciates because of domestic inflation higher than world inflation. The model assumes a fully employed economy; perfect competition prevails in all markets, and markets clear with full price and wage flexibility. With given demand functions for money in two countries, the exchange rate is determined by the relative demand and supply of the two currencies, i.e. it is the relative price of two moneys, determined in money markets. The exchange rate is determined jointly with the alignment of foreign and domestic price levels without any explicit reference to the net trade balance, as in the old elasticities (or balance of payments) model.

The third model provides an alternative explanation of exchange-rate behaviour, particularly the observed volatility in exchange rates. According to this approach, the exchange rate is not a purely monetary phenomenon, since non-monetary assets and the goods market play significant roles in its determination. Changes in the exchange rate which occur to maintain asset-market equilibrium (and thus the valuation of foreign assets) may induce disequilibrium in the goods market. Changes in exchange rates can have real effects (or vice versa) – a point made by the first model. The monetary model, by assuming perfect substitution between domestic and foreign bonds, focuses on the single remaining asset – money. By contrast, the portfolio-balance approach emphasises aspects of individuals' choices between holding domestic and foreign currency-denominated assets. It also analyses behaviour in labour, product and bond markets. The model by Kenen and Allen has, in addition to three goods, three assets – money, a government bond, and a foreign bond denominated in foreign currency.[127] Investors are risk-averse and hold all three assets. The strategic stock-flow relationship in the model is the double link between saving and wealth. Saving adds to wealth, but an increase in wealth reduces saving. A change in the exchange rate affects wealth, too, because it confers a capital gain or loss on holders of the foreign bond. Expectations and exchange-rate dynamics (including 'overshooting' and 'undershooting') are also analysed in these models. Short-run exchange rate movements can be dominated by the frequent shifts of wealth between alternative financial assets, although long-run trends in the exchange rate may reflect changes in the relative prices of goods and services. However, one shortcoming of this model is that it does not equally emphasise current account and capital account disturbances. Either causes a balance of payments disequilibrium that must be accommodated by spot exchange-rate changes (assuming, that is, no official intervention). The time-path of real exchange rates obviously depends on the elasticity of trade flows (as in the traditional elasticities approach) as well as on the substitutability of assets in portfolios. The anticipated spot exchange rate must be one which reflects future relative commodity price changes (movements in domestic and foreign inflation rates) as the goods market clears. The justification for the relative neglect of the current account (the role of trade in goods) in the determination of the exchange rate is made by reference to the fact that today's foreign exchange markets are dominated by transactions in financial assets. The daily volume of such transactions far outweighs transactions related to trade in goods across national boundaries. Recent estimates suggest that trade-related transactions account for no more than 5 to 30 per cent of the daily turnover on foreign exchange markets. For theorists of the old elasticities approach this would have appeared as a case of the tail wagging the dog.

The most striking feature of the years of floating has been the exchange rate's short-run volatility and its persistent departures from the maintenance of purchasing-power parity (deviations between nominal exchange rates and real or price-level adjusted exchange rates) and trade balance. We witnessed large real exchange-rate movements (i.e. large and persistent misalignments), for the most part unrelated to the 'fundamentals' highlighted by exchange-rate theories. Observed exchange-rate dynamics seem to approximate closely to a random walk. The observed fluctuations in major exchange rates appear to be dominated by speculative 'bubbles' triggered by 'follow-the-leader' and bandwagon behaviour, safe-haven effects (a shift in portfolio preferences from foreign to domestic assets), immediate over-reactions, and sometimes inertia, on the part of market participants when faced with unanticipated news of exogenous and policy-induced happenings, and responses to inappropriate national monetary-fiscal policy mixes. This experience suggested to Dornbusch 'that modern exchange rate theories have failed across the board to account for exchange rate behaviour'.[128] Any one of the three theories identified above may not be totally enlightening about observed phenomena, but that does not imply that each may not be relevant for the understanding of particular phases of reality. An all-encompassing model may equally be empty of empirical content in tracking the forces that move markets at any given juncture. Dornbusch supports this when he states: 'I regard any one of these views [the three models discussed above] as a partial picture of exchange rate determination; although each may be especially important in explaining a particular historical episode.'[129]

Floating rates and capital mobility have not relaxed the constraints of international interdependence even for such a large economy as the United States. The extensive discussions and anlyses of the causes and consequences of the 1980–85 real appreciation of the US dollar (despite huge budgetary and current-account deficits) have brought to the surface the relevance of the extended Mundell–Fleming model in an understanding of the policy choices under the current regime.[130] Whilst one school of thought holds the view that the regime renders the use of national monetary policy obsolete, and therefore points in the direction of a return to some form of fixed exchange rates, another view faces the dilemma posed by capital mobility and flexible exchange rates with a call for monetary policy coordination, or else for some effective measures to interfere with capital flows so as to allow scope for the pursuit of national macroeconomic objectives. At any rate, in response to matters of considerable policy interest in the 1980s – the effects of uncoordinated national monetary and fiscal policies on national output, the real exchange rate and the current account of the balance of payments – exchange-rate economics has returned to the Mundell–Fleming model, particularly its use in the analysis of fiscal policy in open economies. Finally, recognition of the short-run costs associated with exchange-rate misalignments has stimulated interesting research on the microeconomic effects of exchange-rate movements.

Notes and References

Note: The term 'loc. cit.' is used when a text has just been mentioned and the term 'op. cit.' is used when a text has been referenced some distance back.

1 The Classical Legacy

1. For a recent critical survey of classical trade theory, including the debate on the Corn Laws and the Bullionist and Banking/Currency school controversies, see Leonard Gomes, *Foreign Trade and the National Economy: Mercantilist and Classical Perspectives* (London: Macmillan, 1987) part II. Part I of the same book surveys the foreign trade doctrines of the mercantilists.
2. Joan Robinson, 'Reflections on the Theory of International Trade', in her *Collected Economic Papers*, vol. 5 (Oxford: Blackwell, 1979) p. 130.

2 Early Neoclassical Contributions

1. A. A. Cournot, *Recherches sur les Principes Mathématiques de la Théorie des Richesses* (Paris: Hachette, 1838). Translated by Nathaniel T. Bacon as *Researches into the Mathematical Principles of the Theory of Wealth* (London: Macmillan, 1897) p. 117.
2. Cournot's arithmetical example is in *Principes*, pp. 314–15.
3. See Edgeworth, 'The Theory of International Values', *Economic Journal*, 1894, p. 627.
4. *Researches*, p. 157.
5. *Researches*, p. 156.
6. Ibid. pp. 162–3.
7. The 1844 criticism was by Carl Heinrich Hagen, in his book, *Die Nothwendigkeit der Handelsfreiheit für das Nationaleinkommen, mathematisch nachgewiesen* (Königsberg, 1844) pp. 30–1. Samuelson praises Cournot's treatment of interspatial price equilibrium as being 'marvellously modern and fruitful', but adds, 'his analysis of tariff protection appears to be ambiguous and of doubtful validity'. P. A. Samuelson, 'The Way of An Economist', in Paul Samuelson (ed.), *International Economic Relations* (London: Macmillan, 1969) p. 5.
8. See Edgeworth, 'The Theory of International Values', loc. cit. p. 628 and p. 630; A. Landry, *Manuel d'Économie Politique* (Paris: 1908) p. 839; J. Bertrand's review article, 'Recherches sur les Principes Mathématiques de la Théorie des Richesses, par Augustin Cournot', *Journal des Savants* (1883) p. 504.
9. On these points of criticism, see the review by R. de Fontenay, 'Principes de la Théorie des Richesses', *Journal des Economistes*, vol. 43 (August 1864) p. 239; also Hagen, op. cit. p. 30, and C. F. Bastable, *The Theory*

of International Trade (Dublin, 1887) appendix C, pp. 172–4. Edgeworth thought that Bastable exaggerated the difficulties with Cournot's use of money prices, and claimed that such a procedure was acceptable since Cournot 'means to restrict his theory to small disturbances of trade, the effects of which on the level of money may be neglected'. See Edgeworth, op. cit. p. 629.

10. J. Viner, *Studies in the Theory of International Trade* (London: Allen & Unwin, 1955) p. 586. Reghinos Theocaris writes that Viner 'appears to have misunderstood Cournot's reasoning' in regard to income changes resulting from free trade in the importing country. See Reghinos D. Theocaris, *Early Developments in Mathematical Economics*, 2nd edn (London: Macmillan, 1983) p. 229. What most critics failed to realise was that Cournot used a 'first order approximation' rather than a full equilibrium system in his study of the benefits of the opening-up of trade.
11. Viner, op. cit. p. 589.
12. Viner, op. cit. p. 587, n. 7.
13. J. W. Angell, *The Theory of International Prices: History, Criticism and Restatement*, Harvard Economic Studies, vol. XXVIII (Cambridge, Mass.: Harvard Univ. Press, 1926) p. 244.
14. For Cournot's reply, see *Principes*, pp. 329–30.
15. *Researches*, p. 151.
16. Theocaris, op. cit. p. 198.
17. Theocaris, op. cit. p. 199.
18. Citing a passage from Cournot stressing the need for the development of productive powers, Theocaris notes: 'The influence of List is obvious.' Theocaris, op. cit. p. 234, n. 363. According to Cournot, an extensive industrial sector and a skilled labour force were the objectives of a programme geared to the development of 'productive powers'. A country so equipped would be an exporter of manufactured goods and an importer of agricultural products and raw materials.
19. Cournot, *Principes de la théorie des richesses* (Paris: Hachette, 1863) p. 456.
20. Ibid. p. 456.
21. Ibid. p. 493.
22. Ibid. p. 458.
23. Ibid. p. 461, p. 462. Cournot judged free trade a desirable objective in the long run when productive forces have been built up – again a position similar to that of List's. Thus 'new products can indefinitely be exchanged one against another, provided that a suitable direction is given to the various branches of production', *Principes*, p. 287. Towards the end of his life Cournot became conservative-minded on account of his fear of socialism. Thus in the book published in the year of his death, *Revue sommaire des doctrines économiques* (1877), Cournot departed from his early interventionist views and espoused the tenets of economic liberalism.
24. Ibid. book III, ch. 6, pp. 338 *et seq.*
25. Ibid. p. 341.
26. On this point, see the exchange between D. R. Appleyard, J. C. Ingram and J. Chipman in *History of Political Economy*, vol. 11, no. 4 (Winter

1979); also the summary in Gomes, op. cit. pp. 164–6.
27. *Principes*, p. 345.
28. Ibid. p. 346.
29. F. Y. Edgeworth, 'Antoine Augustin Cournot', in *Palgrave's Dictionary of Political Economy* (London: Macmillan, 1925) vol. I, p. 446. But Jevons also wrote that Cournot's treatise, 'apart from its economic importance . . . presents a beautiful example of mathematical reasoning, in which knowledge is apparently evolved out of ignorance'. W. S. Jevons, *The Theory of Political Economy* (1871) 2nd edn (London: Macmillan, 1879) p. xxxiii.
30. In the identity, B_i denotes the balance of international transactions of the ith country. The surpluses and deficits of all the individual countries will cancel out, leaving the algebraic sum, zero.
31. Theocaris, op. cit. p. 187. Theocaris continues, 'the *Recherches* was, as Walras says, one of the first books which he read as an undergraduate', quoting a passage from Walras's article on Cournot in the *Gazette de Lausanne*, 13 July 1905. Here, Walras writes: 'My father . . . was Cournot's friend at the École Normale de Paris . . . and had no doubt received a gift of this monograph [*Recherches*] which I found in his library and read in 1853–54 during my third year of mathematics.' See Theocaris, op. cit. p. 226. Cournot's analysis in mathematical form of various microeconomic problems led him to believe that 'for a complete and rigorous solution of the problems relative to some parts of the economic system, it is indispensable to take the entire system into consideration'. Cournot, *Researches*, p. 127. The first (1781) mathematical formulation of a general-equilibrium system of exchange was, however, the work of Achille Nicolas Isnard. He expressed the interdependence between equilibrium commodity prices by means of a system of simultaneous equations. See A. N. Isnard, *Traité des richesses* (London and Lausanne: F. Grasset, 1781).
32. Johann H. von Thünen, *Der Isolierte Staat in Beziehung auf Landwirtschaft und Nationalökonomie*, 3rd edn, Heinrich Waentig (ed.) (Jena: Gustav Fischer, 1930). Abridged translations are Peter Hall (ed.), *Von Thünen's Isolated State* (London: Pergamon Press, 1966); and Bernard W. Dempsey, *The Frontier Wage: With the Text of the Second Part of the Isolated State* (Chicago: Loyola Univ. Press, 1960). For a recent analysis of Thünen's system, see Paul A. Samuelson, 'Thünen at Two Hundred', in Kate Crowley (ed.), *The Collected Scientific Papers of Paul A. Samuelson*, vol. V (Cambridge, Mass.: The MIT Press, 1986) pp. 575–95. Samuelson noted that Thünen elaborated one of the first models of general equilibrium, and that Thünen's system included among other things, elements of the Ricardian theory of comparative advantage and the 'Heckscher–Ohlin and Stolper–Samuelson theory of factors-and-goods pricing', p. 588.
33. For a biographical sketch of Mangoldt, see Mark Blaug, *Great Economists Before Keynes* (Brighton: Wheatsheaf Books, 1986) pp. 147–9. K. H. Hennings, 'The Transition from Classical to Neoclassical Economic Theory: Hans von Mangoldt', *Kyklos*, vol. 33, no. 4, 1980, considers Mangoldt's role in the development of neoclassical theory.

34. Mangoldt's contribution to trade theory is contained in appendix II, entitled 'Von der Gleichung der internationalen Nachfrage' ('On the Equation of International Demand') of his major work, *Grundriss der Volkswirtschaftslehre* (Outline of Political Economy), (Stuttgart: Verlag von J. Engelhorn, 1863).

    Misleading statements by Schumpeter (unintentionally done, of course), concerning the contents of the second (posthumous) edition of the *Grundriss* edited by Friedrich Kleinwächer (1871), were corrected by John S. Chipman in 'A Survey of the Theory of International Trade: Part 1, The Classical Theory', *Econometrica*, vol. 33, no. 3 (July 1965) pp. 501–2, note 20. A translation of appendix II with an introductory note by Chipman appeared in *Journal of International Economics*, vol. 5 (1975) pp. 55–97. This is most welcome and meets a long-felt need, since English-language readers come to Mangoldt's trade analysis at second hand, mainly through the expositions of Edgeworth and Viner – F. Y. Edgeworth, *Papers Relating to Political Economy*, vol. II (London: Macmillan, 1925) pp. 52–8; J. Viner, *Studies*, op. cit. pp. 458–62. See also Gottfried von Haberler, *The Theory of International Trade* (London: William Hodge & Co. Ltd., 1936) pp. 136–9. The issues raised by Mangoldt have been discussed and analysed by Chipman in his trade survey, op. cit. pp. 501–4.
35. Mangoldt, *Grundriss*, op. cit. p. 188.
36. Edgeworth, op. cit. pp. 52–8. Referring to his 1894 article on the pure theory of international values, Edgeworth wrote in 1925: 'Of all the writers, classical or mathematical, who are passed in review in the article of 1894, Mangoldt is the one who emerges unscathed from the critical examination.' Ibid. p. 4.
37. Ibid. pp. 53–4.
38. Ibid. p. 55. Edgeworth mentions the impossibility of obtaining precision as regards multi-commodity and multi-country trade, and says that when these cases are considered, the conclusions are best left to 'the intelligence of the reader'. Ibid. p. 46.
39. Viner, op. cit. pp. 465–7.
40. T. M. Whitin, 'Classical Theory, Graham's Theory and Linear Programming in International Trade', *Quarterly Journal of Economics*, vol. 67 (November 1953) pp. 520–44; Lionel W. McKenzie, 'Specialisation and Efficiency in World production', *Review of Economic Studies*, vol. 21 (June 1954) pp. 165–80.
41. Chipman, op. cit. p. 507, writes: 'I have not been able to find a single example in the classical literature of the use of bilateral comparison in the analysis of multilateral trade.'
42. R. W. Jones, 'Comparative Advantage and the Theory of Tariffs: A Multi-Country, Multi-Commodity Model', *Review of Economic Studies*, vol. 28 (June 1961) pp. 161–75, reprinted in R. W. Jones, *International Trade: Essays in Theory* (Amsterdam: North-Holland, 1979).
43. Jones, *International Trade: Essays in Theory*, op. cit. p. 296. As Caves and Jones point out in their well-known textbook, *World Trade and Payments*, 3rd edn (Boston: Little Brown, 1981) p. 88, a major feature of Ricardian models is the demonstration of how 'trade forces an extremely

high degree of specialization in production' on account of their assumptions of constant costs and perfect mobility of labour among occupations.

44. R. Dornbusch, S. Fischer and P. A. Samuelson, 'Comparative Advantage, Trade, and Payments in a Ricardian Model with a Continuum of Goods', *American Economic Review*, vol. 67, no. 5 (Dec. 1977) pp. 823–39.

3 Trade Theory in the Age of Marshall

1. Marshall declares that the terms of international trade can properly be said to be governed by the relations of international demand; 'but, with equal correctness they can be said to be governed by the relations of international supply. It seems best to speak of them as governed by international demand and supply.' Alfred Marshall, *Money, Credit and Commerce* (1923) (New York: Augustus M. Kelley, 1965) p. 160.
2. For Marshall, 'real costs' are the supply prices of productive factors, e.g. wages (the reward of labour's efforts), the supply price of 'waiting'. 'Land' has no supply price, but from the perspective of the individual farmer or firm, land rent is a cost of production which must be paid, just as labour and capital costs must be paid. Therefore, 'the efforts and sacrifices which are the real cost of production of a thing, underlie the expenses which are money cost'. *Marshall, Principles of Economics*, 8th edn (London: Macmillan, 1930) p. 352.
3. Marshall, *Money, Credit and Commerce*, op. cit. p. 157.
4. Marian Bowley was not happy about this device, however. She wrote: 'Marshall in dealing with several commodities just evaded the issue by introducing the device of "bales"'. Marian Bowley, *Nassau Senior and Classical Economics* (1937), (London: Allen & Unwin, 1967) p. 201.
5. Marshall, *Money, Credit and Commerce*, op. cit. appendix J, pp. 330–60.
6. Ibid. p. 178.
7. The disputed points in the controversy are clearly set forth by Bhagwati and Johnson, in 'Notes on Some Controversies in the Theory of International Trade', *Economic Journal*, vol. 70 (March 1960) pp. 74–93, reprinted in Jagdish N. Bhagwati, *Trade, Tariffs and Growth* (London: Weidenfeld & Nicolson, 1972) pp. 124–9. See also, Murray C. Kemp, *The Pure Theory of International Trade* (Englewood Cliffs, N.J.: Prentice-Hall, 1964) pp. 75–9; Richard E. Caves, *Trade and Economic Structure: Models and Methods* (Cambridge, Mass.: Harvard Univ. Press, 1960) pp. 200–4.
8. J. S. Mill, *Principles of Political Economy*, 3rd edn (1852), Ashley edition (London: Longmans, Green & Co., 1929) p. 163.
9. Marshall, *Money, Credit and Commerce*, op. cit. p. 169.
10. Ibid. p. 167.
11. Ibid. pp. 161–3. The gain is therefore the amount of the export commodity of which the country could be deprived, and still be as well off as in a 'no-trade' situation.

12. The graphical technique is set out and described in ibid. appendix J, sec. 3, pp. 338–40.
13. Viner, *Studies*, op. cit. p. 571.
14. Viner, ibid. pp. 571–5. Again, for an excellent treatment of the matter, see Bhagwati and Johnson, op. cit. pp. 135–41; also Caves, op. cit. pp. 226–9.
15. F. Y. Edgeworth, *Papers Relating to Political Economy*, vol. II, op. cit. pp. 31–47; also, see the earlier paper by Edgeworth, 'On the Application of Mathematics to Political Economy', *Journal of the Royal Statistical Society*, vol. 52 (1889) pp. 555–60.
16. Bhagwati and Johnson, op. cit. pp. 136–41. Hicks's article is 'The Rehabilitation of Consumer's Surplus', *Review of Economic Studies*, vol. 8 (1941) pp. 108–16.
17. John M. Currie, John A. Murphy and Andrew Schmitz, 'The Concept of Economic Surplus and its Use in Economic Analysis', *Economic Journal*, vol. 81 (Dec. 1971) p. 779.
18. Murray C. Kemp, op. cit. p. 66.
19. John S. Chipman, 'A Survey of the Theory of International Trade: Part 2, The Neo-classical Theory', *Econometrica*, vol. 33, no. 4 (October 1965) p. 721.
20. Alfred Marshall, *The Pure Theory of Foreign Trade* (privately printed, 1879). Reprinted London School of Economics, 1930, p. 12; or the reprint in J. K. Whitaker (ed.), *The Early Economic Writings of Alfred Marshall 1867–1890*, vol. II (London: Macmillan for the Royal Economic Society, 1975) p. 143.
21. Marshall, loc. cit., in J. K. Whitaker (ed.), op. cit. p. 149. The diagram referred to is Marshall's well-known offer curve figure (also reproduced in *Money, Credit and Commerce*, op. cit. p. 353) which shows that unstable equilibrium is always framed by stable ones, i.e. that equilibria are in all cases alternatively stable and unstable.
22. In J. K. Whitaker (ed.), op. cit. p. 150.
23. Marshall, *The Pure Theory of Foreign Trade*, LSE reprint (1930) op. cit. p. 19 n. Marshall studiously avoided the temptation to put the dynamic system underlying his adjustment process into mathematical form, saying: 'Such calculations might afford considerable scope to the ingenuity of those who devise mathematical problems, but . . . they would afford no aid to the Economist', loc. cit. p. 19 n.
24. Samuelson also presented a mathematical model of the Marshallian dynamic adjustment mechanism. See Paul A. Samuelson, *Foundations of Economic Analysis* (Cambridge, Mass.: Harvard Univ. Press, 1947). Marshall had overlooked the possibility of oscillatory paths spiralling around the equilibrium point (like damped sine waves) in the case of unstable equilibrium. With elastic offer curves (which Marshall called 'the Normal class') the approach to equilibrium is direct, not oscillatory, i.e. where the path to equilibrium can at most cross only one offer curve. For good analyses of Marshallian and other stability conditions in trade theory, see Chipman (1965) op. cit. pp. 721–36, and Kemp, op. cit. pp. 59–71.
25. Chipman, op. cit. pp. 722–3.

26. Marshall, *Pure Theory of Foreign Trade*, in Whitaker (ed.), op. cit. p. 164; also LSE reprint (1930) op. cit. p. 26.
27. Chipman, op. cit. p. 723.
28. Marshall, op. cit. p. 164.
29. Akihiro Amano, 'Stability Conditions in the Pure Theory of International Trade: A Rehabilitation of the Marshallian Approach', *Quarterly Journal of Economics*, vol. 82 (1968) p. 329. Amano considers the stability of both temporary and long-run equilibria. In temporary equilibrium (given fixed output levels), producers may not be maximising profits. Over time, however, producers will adjust output to achieve profit maximisation. Long-run adjustment is therefore a succession of locally stable temporary equilibria.
30. Amano, op. cit. pp. 336–7.
31. Harvey Gram, 'Offer Curve or Reciprocal Demand Curve', in J. Eatwell, M. Milgate and P. Newman (eds), *The New Palgrave: A Dictionary of Economics* (London: Macmillan, 1987) p. 697.
32. Marshall, *Money, Credit and Commerce*, op. cit. pp. 177–90; Marshall, in Whitaker (ed.), op. cit. pp. 62–89. Marshall's systematic reflections on tariffs, free trade and protection began as early as 1872. The manuscript containing these writings (held in the Marshall Library, Cambridge) was published by Professor J. K. Whitaker, vol. II, op. cit. pp. 3–111. Whitaker also reproduces surviving portions of a volume on foreign trade which Marshall wrote beween 1874 and 1877, but never published. This includes the chapters privately printed and circulated by Henry Sidgwick in 1879 – *The Pure Theory of Foreign Trade and The Pure Theory of Domestic Values.*
33. Marshall, *Money, Credit and Commerce*, op. cit. p. 212, n. 1.
34. Ibid. p. 192. As noted earlier in the text, Marshall fully recognises the *theoretical* possibility – indeed, in his words, 'the almost universal rule' – that an import tax can turn the terms of trade in favour of the tariff-imposing country. But he notes two exceptions to this rule: (1) if the government spends the tariff revenue on imported goods and if import demand is inelastic, and (2) if the imported commodity is a 'Giffen good' (e.g. wheat). See Alfred Marshall, *Memorandum on the Fiscal Policy of International Trade*, House of Commons No. 321, 1908. Reprinted in J. M. Keynes (ed.), *Official Papers by Alfred Marshall* (London: Macmillan for the Royal Economic Society, 1926) pp. 374, 382–3. Murray Kemp examines the validity of Marshall's two conjectures concerning the perverse effects. He agrees with the first (also confirmed by Abba Lerner (1936)) but concludes that 'the "Giffen effect" is neither necessary nor sufficient to ensure that the terms of trade move against the tariff-imposing country'. See Murray C. Kemp, 'Note on a Marshallian Conjecture', *Quarterly Journal of Economics*, vol. 80 (1966) pp. 481–4.
35. Marshall, *Money, Credit and Commerce*, op. cit. p. 198.
36. Marshall, in Whitaker (ed.), op. cit. pp. 67, 70.
37. Marshall, 'An Export Duty on Coal', letter to *The Times*, 19 April 1901, reprinted in *Economic Journal*, vol. 11 (June 1901) p. 265; also

A. C. Pigou (ed.), *Memorials of Alfred Marshall* (London: Macmillan, 1925) p. 322.

38. Marshall, *Money, Credit and Commerce*, op. cit. pp. 217, 219. Marshall criticises British economists for not taking the infant-industry argument seriously, saying, their 'treatment of this question generally has been timid and weak'; but he credits J. S. Mill for giving a clear statement of the case. See Marshall, in Whitaker (ed.), op. cit. p. 56. For Marshall's further views on this matter, see *Memorials*, Pigou (ed.), pp. 258–60. Here Marshall writes, 'when John Stuart Mill ventured to tell the English people that some arguments for Protection in new countries were scientifically valid, his friends spoke of it in anger . . . as his one sad departure from the sound principles of economic rectitude'. Ibid. p. 259.
39. Marshall, in Whitaker (ed.), op. cit. p. 87; also Marshall, *Memorandum*, loc. cit.
40. *Memorials*, Pigou (ed.), p. 263.
41. Narmadeshwar Jha, *The Age of Mashall: Aspects of British Economic Thought 1890–1915*, 2nd edn (London: Frank Cass, 1973) p. 31. This book (pp. 31–79) provides a very useful review of the contributions and controversies of the early British neoclassical economists in the area of trade theory and policy.
42. The concepts of internal and external economies of scale are extensively discussed in Marshall's *Principles* (1920), book IV, chs 9–11. In his trade theory he discussed the relationship between economies of scale and the terms of trade. If Germany imports cloth from England in exchange for linen, and cloth is produced under conditions of increasing returns to scale, then by expanding her demand for English cloth Germany can improve her barter terms of trade: 'an increase in Germany's demand for English cloth may cause each yard of linen to be sold here on such terms as to give command over a larger amount of cloth than before; it is possible that the increase in Germany's demand for English cloth may cause her to obtain an import of English cloth increased *in a greater ratio* than is her export of linen to England'. Marshall, 'The Pure Theory of Foreign Trade', in Whitaker (ed.), op. cit. p. 145.
43. Ibid. pp. 145, 164.
44. Jha, op. cit. p. 31.
45. *Memorials*, op. cit. p. 263.
46. Marshall, *Money, Credit and Commerce*, op. cit. p. 220. The remark about Free Trade being the absence of a device or policy was good rhetoric, but a trifle disingenuous; of course, for nineteenth-century Britain free trade was itself a policy, and some historians write about 'the imperialism of free trade'. Elsewhere, Marshall himself wrote that 'because it was clearly to the interests of England that her manufactures should be admitted free by other countries', any Englishman who questioned such a policy was denounced as unpatriotic. See *Memorials*, Pigou (ed.), op. cit. pp. 258–9.
47. Marshall, *Money, Credit and Commerce*, op. cit. p. 222.

48. Ibid. p. 222. The *Zollverein* was in the forefront in the negotiation of commercial treaties incorporating the 'most-favoured-nation clause' during 1860–70. Much of the impetus and momentum came from Rudolf von Delbrück. In a handsome tribute to Friedrich List, Marshall referred to 'the brilliant genius and national enthusiasm of List stands in contrast to the insular narrowness and self-confidence of the Ricardian school . . . he showed that in Germany and still more in America, many of its [Free Trade's] indirect effects were evils . . . Many of his arguments were invalid, but many were not.' *Marshall, Principles*, 9th (Variorum) edn, vol. I (1961) p. 767.
49. G. J. Stigler, *Production and Distribution Theories* (New York: Macmillan, 1941) p. 62. Stigler thought, however, that this characteristic plus his veneration for the classical economists tend to diminish Marshall's contribution to theoretical economics.
50. Quoted by Ronald Findlay, in Ronald W. Jones and Peter B. Kenen (eds), *Handbook of International Economics*, vol. I (Amsterdam: North-Holland, 1984) p. 186.
51. Marshall, *Principles of Economics*, 5th edn (London: Macmillan, 1907) p. 674. As early as 1903 (two years before the Battle of Tsushima Strait, May 1905, when the Japanese sunk the Russian Baltic Fleet) Marshall wrote about the industrial potential of the Japanese and was prophetic about their industrial and technological challenge to the Western industrialised countries. He noted that Britain was losing its trading advantage to 'people like the Japanese, who can assimilate every part of the work of an advanced factory'; and 'they [the Japanese] are so alert, so closely in touch with western thought, and so full of independent enterprise, that her manufactures for export are growing rapidly'. *Memorandum*, op. cit. p. 404, and *Money, Credit and Commerce*, p. 173.
52. Marshall, *Memorandum*, loc. cit. p. 404. Marshall, of course, did not integrate these insights on innovation and the international transfer of technology into his trade theory, but his observations foreshadowed the work of modern theorists on 'product-cycle' and technological trade.
53. Marshall, *Industry and Trade* (London: Macmillan, 1919) p. 118.
54. Ibid. pp. 174–5.
55. Ibid. pp. 132–3.
56. Arthur I. Bloomfield, 'The Impact of Growth and Technology on Trade in Nineteenth-Century British Thought', *History of Political Economy*, vol. 10, no. 4 (1978) p. 617; Marshall, *Memorandum*, loc. cit. p. 406.
57. Hutchison suspects, however, that the type of diagram used by Edgeworth 'may have been suggested by Marshall's privately printed diagrammatic studies of the Pure Theory of Domestic Values and of Foreign Trade'. T. W. Hutchison, *A Review of Economic Doctrines 1870–1929* (Oxford: Clarendon Press, 1953) p. 114.
58. F. Y. Edgeworth, *Mathematical Psychics: An Essay on the Application of Mathematics to the Moral Sciences* (London: Kegan Paul, 1881) p. 113. W. E. Johnson, one of Marshall's pupils, was apparently the first to use the name *offer curve*. W. E. Johnson, 'The Pure Theory of Utility Curves', *Economic Journal*, vol. 23 (1913) pp. 483–513. Edgeworth did

not care much for the new term, since it did not convey the essential symmetry between supply and demand implied by the older expression 'reciprocal demand'.

59. Edgeworth, *Mathematical Psychics*, op. cit. pp. 20–28.
60. These works are cited later in the present text (7.1).
61. This is the way Meade's diagram is described in Jürg Niehans, *International Monetary Economics* (Oxford: Philip Allan, 1984) p. 17.
62. Edgeworth, *Papers* (1925), op. cit. p. 295. The reference is to the work of the two Austrians, Rudolf Auspitz and Richard Lieben, *Untersuchungen über die theorie des preises* (1889). Auspitz and Lieben must therefore be considered as independent discoverers of the concept of the indifference curve. Edgeworth was less insular than the run of British economists of the time and used his linguistic skill to familiarise himself with the works of other European economists. Samuelson observed: 'He made it a point to know the literature in every language, and he went out of his way to give credit where credit was due.' Paul A. Samuelson, 'On Complementarity', *Journal of Economic Literature*, vol. 12, no. 4 (Dec. 1974) p. 1279, n. 19. Referring to the fact, often remarked upon, that very few foreign economists managed to get their articles published in the *Economic Journal* whilst Edgeworth was editor, John Creedy suggests that this was due to 'the dominance of Marshall' and a desire not to burden the pages of the *Journal* with abstract, theoretical debates. See John Creedy, *Edgeworth and the Development of Neoclassical Economics* (Oxford: Blackwell, 1986) pp. 130–31.
63. C. F. Bickerdike's 'Theory of Incipient Taxes' (1906), referred to below.
64. F. Y. Edgeworth, 'Appreciations of Mathematical Theories, III', *Economic Journal*, vol. 18 (Sept. 1908) p. 392; also Edgeworth, *Papers*, op. cit. pp. 344, 365–6. N. Jha comments: 'It is not clear what Edgeworth really meant by calling Bickerdike's discovery "poison". But it appears that, as with poison, he would have sanctioned medicinal applications of Bickerdike's analysis.' N. Jha, *The Age of Marshall*, op. cit. p. 49.

    Modern game theory as applied to duopoly provides additional support for the Edgeworth–Bickerdike optimum tariff argument – e.g. the Edgeworth–Stackelberg solution. If everyone in the world is avoiding trade restrictions, it can be shown that it is always possible for a country that is not insignificantly small to deviate and gain by imposing trade restrictions. Alternatively, if our rogue country's action prompts others to follow suit and depart from free trade, the appropriate solution is the Nash–Cournot one which postulates a more symmetric response from rivals. One consequence of the Nash–Cournot solution (where every country seeks an optimal interventionist policy), however, is that countries find themselves in the classic position of the Prisoners' Dilemma: all are likely to lose because of the positive deadweight loss for the world as a whole.
65. Edgeworth, *Papers*, op. cit. p. 17, no. 5. Just to illustrate that opinion has not changed on this matter, here is Samuelson's end-piece in a 1985

article on general trade issues: 'I have tried in the present paper to frame the exposition so that readers may persuade themselves that protectionism, like war, is a game in actuality that is not worth the candle'. P. A. Samuelson, 'Analytics of Free-Trade or Protectionist Response by America to Japan's Growth Spurt' (1985), in *The Collected Scientific Papers of Paul A. Samuelson*, vol. 5 (1986), op. cit. p. 492. Similarly, reviewing modern arguments for trade intervention, Deardorff and Stern declare, 'the only conclusion we can draw from the optimal tariff literature is that although the optimal tariff argument is valid, it would be best if no country were to try to take advantage of it'. Alan V. Deardorff and Robert M. Stern, 'Current Issues in Trade Policy: An Overview', in Robert M. Stern (ed.), *US Trade Policies in a Changing World Economy* (Cambridge, Mass.: MIT Press, 1987) p. 38.

66. J. S. Mill, *Principles of Political Economy*, book III, ch. 18, § 5.
67. Edgeworth, 'The Theory of International Values', op. cit. p. 40.
68. J. S. Nicholson, *Principles of Political Economy*, vol. II (London: Macmillan, 1897) p. 311 *et seq.*
69. Edgeworth, 'On a Point in the Pure Theory of International trade', *Economic Journal*, vol. i (1899) pp. 125–8.
70. C. F. Bastable, *The Theory of International Trade*, 4th edn revised (London: Macmillan, 1903) pp. 186–7.
71. Bertil Ohlin, *Interregional and International Trade*, Harvard Economic Studies, vol. XXXIX (Cambridge, Mass.: Harvard Univ. Press, 1933) pp. 517–18.
72. W. M. Corden, 'Harry Johnson's Contributions to International Trade Theory', *Journal of Political Economy*, vol. 92, no. 4 (1984) p. 571.
73. See two articles by Johnson, 'Economic Expansion and International Trade' and 'Equilibrium Growth in an International Economy', reprinted in H. G. Johnson, *International Trade and Economic Growth* (London: Allen & Unwin, 1958). J. Bhagwati, 'Immiserizing Growth: A Geometrical Note', *Review of Economic Studies*, vol. 25 (June 1958) pp. 201–5.
74. See reference in note 7 (above) to Bhagwati and Johnson, 'Notes on Some Controversies . . .' (1960). For a brief sketch of the history of thought on this topic, see Murray C. Kemp, 'Technological Change. The Terms of Trade and Welfare', *Economic Journal*, vol. 65, no. 3 (Sept. 1955) pp. 467–8.
75. Bo Södersten, *A Study of Economic Growth and International Trade* (Stockholm: Almqvist & Wiksell, 1964) p. 53.
76. For a useful summary of the arguments in this controversy, see N. Jha, op. cit. pp. 39–41.
77. J. Shield Nicholson, *Principles of Political Economy*, op. cit. pp. 317–18. Caves notes that Nicholson's argument betrays some confusion, 'for he seems to presume that the introduction of trade can lower the exchange value of exports and imports simultaneously'. R. E. Caves, op. cit. p. 63.
78. Achille Loria, 'Notes on the Theory of International Trade', *Economic Journal*, vol. 11 (March 1901) pp. 85–9.
79. C. F. Bastable, 'On Some Disputed Points in the Theory of Internation-

al Trade', *Economic Journal*, vol. 11 (1901) pp. 227–8.
80. Bastable, *The Theory of International Trade*, op. cit. p. 102.
81. Edgeworth, 'On Some Disputed Points in the Theory of International Trade', loc. cit. p. 582.
82. Bastable, in *Economic Journal*, vol. 11, p. 229.
83. A. C. Pigou, *Protective and Preferential Import Duties* (London: Macmillan, 1906) pp. 58–9.
84. Pigou, ibid. p. 59.
85. Chipman writes, 'an analysis which came very close to anticipating the Stolper–Samuelson treatment was provided by Nicholson . . . but the required analytical apparatus was missing'. John S. Chipman, 'A Survey of the Theory of International Trade: Part 3, The Modern Theory', *Econometrica*, vol. 34, no. 1 (Jan. 1966) p. 36. For Nicholson's analysis, see J. Shield Nicholson, op. cit. pp. 317–18.
86. Pigou, ibid. pp. 59–60.
87. C. F. Bickerdike, 'The Theory of Incipient Taxes', *Economic Journal*, vol. 16 (Dec. 1906) p. 529.
88. Bickerdike, ibid. p. 529.
89. Pigou, *Protective and Preferential Import Duties*, p. 13. In an introductory text published many years later, Pigou again supported List's infant-industry argument in these words: 'by putting obstacles in the way of foreign trade, a country, though it would sacrifice income-getting power at the moment, would gain on the whole, because it would be building up income-getting power in the future'. A. C. Pigou, *Income: An Introduction to Economics* (1946) (London: Macmillan, 1966) p. 42.
90. This is in Bickerdike's famous 1907 review of Pigou's book. See C. F. Bickerdike, 'Review of *Protective and Preferential Import Duties* by A. C. Pigou', *Economic Journal*, vol. 17 (March 1907) p. 99. A seventeenth-century mercantilist could not have put the question any better. The justification for chartered trading companies (as distinct from the competition by individual merchants) was that they enabled such national gains to be secured.
91. In a recent short review of Bickerdike's life and work, Bruce Larson comments: 'Bickerdike's 1907 review is an example of a substantial contribution made in a footnote of a book review!' Bruce Larson, 'Bickerdike's Life and Work', *History of Political Economy*, vol. 19, no. 1 (1987) p. 7. Larson summarises Bickerdike's algebraic model and gives a brief account of the exchange between Pigou and Bickerdike, pp. 7–9. See also N. Jha, op. cit. pp. 45–8. Bickerdike ignored the possibility that the tariff-imposing country's trading partners might retaliate against the raising of duties.
92. A. C. Pigou, 'The Incidence of Import Duties', *Economic Journal*, vol. 17 (June 1907) p. 90. Marshall introduced the device of a 'particular expenses curve' in relation to the long-period supply curve to indicate the 'rent' or surplus accruing to scarce factors as output varies.
93. N. Jha, op. cit. p. 47.
94. Bickerdike, 'Relation of the General Supply Curve to a "Particular Expenses" Curve', *Economic Journal*, vol. 17 (Dec. 1907) pp. 583–5.
95. F. Y. Edgeworth, 'Appreciations of Mathematical Theories, IV',

Economic Journal, vol. 18 (Dec. 1908) p. 544. Edgeworth indicated that from the conditions for a stable equilibrium, it followed that the denominator of Bickerdike's expression for the benefit from a tariff must have a positive sign.

96. C. F. Bickerdike, 'The Instability of Foreign Exchange', *Economic Journal*, vol. 30 (March 1920) pp. 118–22. Bickerdike's important contribution to the theory of foreign exchange was overlooked until noticed by Lloyd Metzler in 1948. Metzler wrote: 'the correct conditions of exchange stability appeared first in the *Economic Journal* of 1920, in a brief and unfortunately neglected note by C. F. Bickerdike'. Lloyd A. Metzler, 'The Theory of International Trade', in Howard S. Ellis (ed.), *A Survey of Contemporary Economics*, vol. 1 (Philadelphia: The Blakiston Co. 1948) p. 228.
97. In a review of the 1930s debate over economic calculation under socialism, Karen Vaughan writes: 'Enrico Barone developed the most complete exploration into the economics of socialism applying neoclassical tools to the problem of a centrally directed economy in an article written in 1908.' Karen I. Vaughan, 'Economic Calculation Under Socialism: The Austrian Contribution', *Economic Inquiry*, vol. 18 (Oct. 1980) p. 538.
98. N. Kaldor, 'Welfare Propositions of Economics and Interpersonal Comparisons of Utility', *Economic Journal*, vol. 49 (September 1939) pp. 549–52; J. R. Hicks, 'The Foundations of Welfare Economics', *Economic Journal*, vol. 49 (1939) pp. 696–712.
99. E. Barone, 'The Ministry of Production in the Collectivist State', in *Collectivist Economic Planning: Critical Studies on the Possibilities of Socialism by N. G. Pierson, Ludwig von Mises, George Hahn and Enrico Barone*, F. A. von Hayek (ed.) (London: Routledge & Kegan Paul, 1935). Originally published as 'Il Ministro della Produzione nello Stato Collettivista', *Giornale degli Economisti* (Sept./Oct. 1908) pp. 267–93.
100. Sir Henry Cunynghame, *A Geometrical Political Economy* (Oxford: Oxford Univ. Press, 1904) p. 98, figure 51.
101. E. Barone, *Grundzüge der Theoretischen Nationalökonomie*, trans. by Hans Staehle (Bonn: K. Schroeder Verlag, 1927) fig. 30, p. 102, and fig. 32, p. 105. This German translation of the 1913 edition of Barone's 1908 work, *Principi di Economia Politica* (Rome: Tipografia Nazionale di G. Bertero), is the source almost exclusively relied upon by English-language writers. However, the 1913 edition on which it is based is a slightly abridged version of the first edition and does not contain the famous footnote on international equilibrium and the gains from trade referred to later in the present survey of Barone. This, plus the fact that Barone's 1908 book is a rare item, has resulted in a rather partial appreciation of Barone's contribution to neoclassical trade theory.
102. For a review and critical comments on Barone's technique, see Viner, *Studies*, op. cit. pp. 589–91.
103. Stephen Enke, 'The Monopsony Case for Tariffs', *Quarterly Journal of Economics*, vol. 58 (Feb. 1944) p. 230.
104. W. M. Corden, 'The Calculation of the Cost of Protection', *Economic*

Record, vol. 33 (May 1957).

105. Andrea Maneschi and William O. Thweatt, 'Barone's 1908 Representation of an Economy's Trade Equilibrium and the Gains from Trade', *Journal of International Economics*, vol. 22 (1987) pp. 375–82. A translation of Barone's footnote is here provided by Andrea Maneschi. The authors discuss the misunderstandings, translation problems and editorial oversights which account for the neglect of Barone's diagrams and analysis for so long. Barone draws his transformation or production-possibility curve on the basis of non-constant costs, but it is not the usual uniform increasing-costs variety, since he allows for increasing as well as decreasing costs. It is remarkably similar to a diagram constructed by Jan Tinbergen (1945) to illustrate the case where one commodity is produced under decreasing costs and the other under increasing costs. See J. Tinbergen, *International Economic Cooperation* (Amsterdam: Elsevier, 1945) p. 182. As Chipman noted (reported by Maneschi and Thweatt, p. 376, n. 1), Barone does not, however, explain the reasons for the non-convex shape of his production-possibility set. Nor does he relate the trading equilibrium to two countries, as Lerner later did. But Barone's exposition anticipated in all other respects the 1930s development, including the emphasis on the demand side (preferences) in the trading equilibrium, i.e. the increase in utility which individuals derive from trading, in addition to the resource-allocation or cost-saving benefit.
106. R. Auspitz and R. Lieben, *Untersuchungen über die theorie des preises* (Leipzig: Duncker & Humblot, 1889). There is a French translation by Louis Suret, *Recherches sur la Théorie des Prix* (Paris: M. Giard & E. Brière, 1914), but apparently no English one.
107. Marshall wrote in 1923: 'In 1889 also appeared Auspitz and Lieben's powerful *Theorie des Preises*, in which use is made of diagrams similar to mine, which they had constructed independently.' Marshall, *Money, Credit and Commerce* (1923) p. 330, n. 1. In the same year (1889), Maffeo Pantaleoni (1857–1924) – with Marshall's consent – published a textbook which reproduced Marshall's privately circulated foreign-trade diagrams (offer curves). Pantaleoni, a friend of Barone, Walras and Pareto, was one of Italy's leading neoclassical economists. See, M. Pantaleoni, *Principii di economia pura* (Florence: Barbera, 1889). There is an English translation by T. Boston Bruce, *Pure Economics*, published by Macmillan, London and New York, 1898; reprinted by Kelley and Millman, New York, 1957.
108. Auspitz and Lieben, *Untersuchungen*, op. cit. pp. 408–29.
109. Viner, *Studies*, op. cit. p. 593.
110. The term 'Pareto optimality' was apparently coined by Ian Little in 1950. I. M. D. Little, *A Critique of Welfare Economics* (Oxford: Clarendon Press, 1950). For an excellent modern review of Pareto's attempt to relate competitive equilibrium to welfare optimality, see John Chipman, 'The Paretian Heritage', *Revue Européenne des Sciences Sociales et Cahiers Vilfredo Pareto*, vol. 14, no. 37 (1976) pp. 65–171.
111. Note, however, Samuelson's warning that 'the Pareto-optimality prop-

erty of competitive equilibrium is no theoretical argument for laissez-faire'. Paul A. Samuelson, 'Bergsonian Welfare Economics' (1981), in Kate Crowley (ed.), *The Scientific Papers of Paul A. Samuelson*, vol. 5 (1986), op. cit. p. 6.

112. Vilfredo Pareto, *Manual of Political Economy*, Ann S. Schwier and Alfred N. Page (eds) (London: Macmillan, 1972) p. 106. French edition, *Manuel d'économie politique* (Paris: M. Giard et E. Brière, 1909). Original Italian edition, *Manuale di economia politica, con una introduzione alla scienza sociale* (Milan: Società Editrice, 1906).
113. Pareto, *Manual of Political Economy*, op. cit. pp. 369–73.
114. Viner, *Studies*, op. cit. pp. 451–3; also Richard E. Caves, *Trade and Economic Structure*, op. cit. p. 22, who writes that since there is nothing in the comparative cost model which requires that *all* countries specialise completely, 'Pareto's point simply constitutes a clarification'. Pareto's demonstration that complete specialisation under free trade may be unprofitable appears to have convinced other writers – e.g. Arthur Burns and James Angell. Angell even goes so far as to state that, therefore, the principle of comparative costs is 'not universal in its application, and may involve a *non sequitur*'. James W. Angell, *The Theory of International Prices*, op. cit. p. 256; also Arthur F. Burns, 'A Note on Comparative Costs', *Quarterly Journal of Economics*, vol. 42 (May 1928) pp. 495–500.
115. Book III, ch. 18, of Mill's *Principles*.
116. See John S. Chipman, 'A Survey of the Theory of International Trade: Part 1, The Classical Theory' (1965), op. cit. pp. 488–9; also Akira Takayama, *International Trade* (New York: Holt, Rinehart & Winston, 1972) pp. 142–4.
117. Gottfried Haberler, *A Survey of International Trade Theory* (revised and enlarged edition) (Princeton: Princeton Univ. Press, 1961) p. 15.

    For Pareto's model, see V. Pareto, 'Teoria matematica del commercio internazionale', *Giornale degli Economisti*, vol. 8 (April 1895) pp. 476–98; also in Pareto, *Cours d'économie politique*, vol. II, para. 862–78.
118. T. O. Yntema, *A Mathematical Reformulation of the General Theory of International Trade* (Chicago: Chicago Univ. Press, 1931); J. L. Mosak, *General Equilibrium Theory in International Trade* (Bloomington, Ind.: Principia Press, 1944).
119. V. Pareto, *Cours d'économie politique*, vol. II (Lausanne: F. Rougé, 1896–7) pp. 210–12.
120. Caves, *Trade and Economic Structure*, op. cit. p. 220.
121. Pareto, *Manual of Political Economy*, op. cit. p. 374.
122. Pareto, ibid. p. 375.
123. Noticed by Samuelson in connection with Pareto's writings on demand theory, 'as is so often the case with him [Pareto], his writings contain confusions. (A lone scholar, Pareto had no students or colleagues; like Diderot, God gave him every gift but the gift of dialogue.)' P. A. Samuelson, 'Oh Complementarity' (1974) loc. cit. p. 1280.
124. Pareto, *Manual*, op. cit. pp. 376–7.
125. Ibid. p. 377, note 43.

126. T. W. Hutchison, *A Review of Economic Doctrines* (1953), op. cit. p. 216.
127. See, *Manual*, op. cit. pp. 377–83.
128. C. F. Bastable, *The Theory of International Trade*, 4th edn (1903) op. cit. ch. 6.

4 The Tariff Reform Debate (1903)

1. Quoted from Theodore Martin, *The Life of His Royal Highness The Prince Consort*, vol. II, p. 451, by Sir John Clapham, *An Economic History of Modern Britain*, vol. II (Cambridge: Cambridge Univ. Press, 1967) p. 1. Professor A. W. Coats kindly read a draft of this chapter and I am grateful to him for several helpful comments.
2. J. S. Mill, *Principles of Political Economy*, W. J. Ashley (ed.) (London: Longmans Green & Co., 1909) p. 384; W. S. Jevons, *The Coal Question: An Enquiry Concerning the Progress of the Nation and the Probable Exhaustion of Our Coal Mines* (1865), 3rd edn (London: Macmillan, 1906) p. 241. James Wilson, founder and editor of *The Economist*, also held the same opinion. Some modern historians question the causal link between free trade and British economic growth; indeed, it is even suggested that free trade lowered the rate of growth of British national income during the period 1841–81. For a brief discussion, see Leonard Gomes, *Foreign Trade and the National Economy: Mercantilist and Classical Perspectives*, op. cit. pp. 207–9. Douglas Irwin has kindly pointed out to me that the main econometric work in this area says nothing about free trade having reduced the *rate* of economic growth in Britain. Both his own work and that of Donald McCloskey are concerned with a comparative static proposition concerning *levels* of income. This approach does not deal with the dynamic path taken by national income consequent upon tariff reduction. It is conceivable, though, that free trade might reduce income without altering its growth rate. Irwin's recent work suggests that introducing foreign tariff reductions into the analysis makes it quite possible that Britain did, in fact, benefit from free trade. See Douglas A. Irwin, 'Welfare Effects of British Free Trade: Debate and Evidence from the 1840s', *Journal of Political Economy*, vol. 96, no. 6 (1988) pp. 1142–64.
3. The Morrill Act (1861) inaugurated the high tariff policy. Tariff rates were raised again in 1862 and 1864. Of the 1864 Act, Taussig wrote: 'It established protective duties more extreme than had been ventured on in any previous tariff act in our country's history.' F. W. Taussig, *The Tariff History of the United States* (New York: Putnam, 1892) p. 167. The McKinley Tariff raised average duties to 49.5 per cent, and by the Dingley Tariff (which remained in force for twelve years) the average level increased to 57 per cent. C. and M. Beard wrote in 1930 that the American protectionists were able 'to fasten their system upon the nation so tightly that it was not even shaken for nearly half a century'. Charles A. Beard and Mary R. Beard, *The Rise of American Civilization*, vol. 2 (New York: Macmillan, 1930) p. 108.

4. Bismarck introduced his new tariff policy with the personal declaration: 'I had the impression that under free trade we were gradually bleeding to death.' Speech, 2 May 1879, quoted in Louis L. Snyder, *Roots of German Nationalism* (Bloomington, Ind.: Indiana Univ. Press, 1978) p. 93. After 1873, Bismarck became more receptive to the anti-free trade complaints of his confidential assistant, Lothar Bucher. Bucher 'considered the Manchester free-trade movement the most colossal and the most audacious campaign of political and economic deception which the world had ever seen'. Snyder, op. cit. n. 1, p. 93. Bismarck's protectionist policy also led to friction between Germany and the United States over American exports of livestock and pork.
5. Germany's output of pig-iron increased more than sixfold between 1850 and 1869 – from 212 000 to 1 413 000 tonnes. Britain's output doubled from 2.25 million to 5.5 million tonnes. The British steel industry declined in competitiveness because firms lagged behind foreign rivals in the adoption of new mass-production methods. See B. Elbaum and W. Lazonick, *The Decline of the British Economy* (Oxford: Clarendon Press, 1986) pp. 52–5.
6. J. G. Williamson, 'What Do We Know About Skill Accumulation in 19th Century Britain', Discussion paper in Economic History, University of Wisconsin-Madison, 1981, p. 28. Quoted in Crafts and Thomas (see below) p. 641.
7. N.F.R. Crafts and Mark Thomas, 'Comparative Advantage in UK Manufacturing Trade, 1910–1935', *Economic Journal*, vol. 96 (Sept. 1986) pp. 629–45.
8. Marshall, *Industry and Trade* (London: Macmillan, 1919) p. 3. The inference is, of course, valid only if we make the assumptions of identical homothetic preferences and international equalisation of factor prices.
9. Crafts and Thomas, op. cit. pp. 629, 637, and 643.
10. Quoted in Hans Rosenberg, *Grosse Depression und Bismarckzeit: Wirtschaftsablauf, Gesellschaft und Politik in Mitteleuropa* (Berlin: Walter de Gruyter, 1967) p. 170. Schmoller supported Bismarck's new protectionist policy when the matter was debated before the Verein für Sozialpolitik in 1879; so did most of the other leading German political economists. The ideas of Friedrich List became popular in academic circles at that time. Lujo Brentano, professor of political economy at Munich University from 1892, although a prominent member of the historical school, remained a free-trader. He was a friend and correspondent of Marshall's during the tariff controversy.
11. W. Farrer Ecroyd, 'Fair Trade', *The Nineteenth Century*, vol. 10 (1881) p. 589. See also idem. *Self-Help: Suggestions Towards the Consolidation of the Empire and the Defence of its Industries and Commerce* (London: Hamilton, Adams & Co., 1879).
12. Leopold Amery, later a prominent Conservative minister, wrote in his memoirs: 'The Birmingham speech was a challenge to free trade as direct and provocative as the theses which Luther nailed to the church door at Wittenberg.' See L. S. Amery, *My Political Life* (London: Hutchinson, 1953) vol. I, p. 236. Quoted in Robert Blake, *The Conservative Party – From Peel to Thatcher*, rev. edn (London: Methuen, 1985) p. 179. E. E.

William's book, *Made in Germany* (London: Heinemann, 1896), carried stories which confirmed the fears of many about German competition in key areas of manufacturing.

13. Bernard Porter, *Britain, Europe and the World 1850–1986: Delusions of Grandeur*, 2nd edn (London: Allen & Unwin, 1987) p. 64. Chamberlain attracted support from the industrialists in the metal-working trades of the West Midlands – Chamberlain was a Birmingham manufacturer of screws – and the iron and steel magnates who complained about foreign 'dumping'. Press support came from J. L. Garvin of *The Observer* and Leo Maxse, the imperialist editor and owner of the right-wing *National Review*. Against Chamberlain, there was a formidable array of interests, including the Treasury, the TUC, cotton manufacturers, colliery owners, shipbuilders, shipowners, dealers in commodities, export–import merchants and international bankers (e.g. Sir Ernest Cassell, Albert Beit). Working-class voters were particularly influenced by the Liberal poster which showed a big 'free-trade loaf' side by side with a little 'tariff loaf'.
14. It was Chamberlain's son, Neville, who realised his father's dream when, as Chancellor of the Exchequer in the National Government, he introduced the Import Duties Bill (1932) into Parliament.
15. Jevons, *The Coal Question*, op. cit. p. 11.
16. Jevons, *The Coal Question*, 2nd edn (London: Macmillan, 1866) p. 346.
17. John Cunningham Wood, *British Economists and the Empire* (London: Croom Helm, 1983) p. 105.
18. Jevons, *The Coal Question*, 3rd edn, op. cit. p. 447.
19. Jevons, *Methods of Social Reform* (London: Macmillan, 1883) pp. 181–2. Jevons's solution was a proposal to pay off the National Debt.
20. Kenneth Young, *Arthur James Balfour* (London: 1963) p. 213. Quoted in A. W. Coats, 'Political Economy and the Tariff Reform Campaign of 1903', *Journal of Law and Economics*, vol. 2 (April 1968) p. 181.
21. Hewins collaborated with Chamberlain from the time they first met in June 1903 until the end of the year. Chamberlain asked Hewins 'to supply the economic arguments'. See W. A. S. Hewins, *The Apologia of an Imperialist* (London: Constable, 1929) note 11, p. 68. Later in the year Hewins became secretary of the Tariff Commission – a body set up by Chamberlain and his supporters to investigate the probable consequences of the proposals for tariff reform sponsored by the group.
22. W. A. S. Hewins, 'Papers and Correspondence', in the *Hewins Papers*, Sheffield University Library, Box Mss. 160, p. 182.
23. *Hewins Papers*, Box Mss. 160, pp. 183–4. A summary of Hewins's argument was published in *Economic Journal* (Sept. 1903) p. 445.
24. 'Professors of Economics and the Tariff Question', *The Times*, 15 August 1903, p. 4. Those who signed the letter were: Bastable, Bowley, Cannan, Courtney, Edgeworth, Gonner, Marshall, Nicholson, Phelps, Pigou, Sanger, Scott, Smart, Armitage Smith. The manifesto was later reprinted in *Economic Journal* (Sept. 1903) pp. 446–8. All the critical points made by the economists were used by the Liberals in their attack on the government. Pigou spoke on public platforms in support of free-trade candidates.
25. N. Jha, *The Age of Marshall*, op. cit. p. 57. It is not clear how many

practising economists were asked to sign. There were not many professors about at the time, and a number of the signatories were very young, e.g. Pigou was only 26.

26. By signing his articles, 'An Economist', Hewins deliberately gave the impression that he was speaking for the profession. Indeed, he further maintained that 'the whole trend of economic method and investigation in recent times is in the direction indicated by Mr Chamberlain'. *The Times*, 'The Fiscal Policy of the Empire', 20 August 1903.
27. *The Times*, 15 August 1903, p. 4, cols. 2–3. Price's call for a Royal Commission to investigate the matter received support from a variety of quarters, including the King. In a letter written at Marienbad to Balfour, Edward VII asked: 'Would it not be possible to refer the whole matter to a Royal Commission which has been suggested by Mr Price of Oxford?' Sir Sidney Lee, *King Edward VII – A Biography* (London: Macmillan, 1927) vol. II, pp. 173–4, quoted in Coats, op. cit. p. 202. Price was chairman of the Oxford University Tariff Reform League.
28. W. J. Ashley, *Political Economy and the Tariff problem* (London: Macmillan, 1905) p. 256.
29. L. L. Price, 'The Fiscal Question: Retrospect and Prospect', *Economic Review*, vol. 16 (Jan. 1906) p. 137.

    After the economists' manifesto, Price became disenchanted with what he regarded as the abstract, *laissez-faire* theory of the Marshallian school: 'For the conclusion, to which abstract theory conducted the signers of that pronouncement on a political problem of great delicacy and vital moment, appeared to me but a barren negation.' Price, 'Economic Theory and Fiscal Policy', *Economic Journal*, vol. 14 (Sept. 1904) p. 375. For more on Price's views, see L. L. Price, 'The Economic Possibilities of an Imperial Fiscal Reform', *Economic Journal*, vol. 13 (1903) p. 486 *et seq*.
30. W. Cunningham, *The Progress of Capitalism in England* (Cambridge: Cambridge Univ. Press, 1916) p. 13.
31. Ashley, *The Progress of the German Working Classes in the Last Quarter of the Century* (London: Longmans, Green & Co., 1904) pp. 140–41.
32. Cunningham, *The Rise and Decline of the Free Trade Movement* (Cambridge: Cambridge Univ. Press, 1912 edn) p. 144. Cunningham protested that the signatories 'take for granted that an economic principle [i.e. Free Trade] which is framed on the assumption that all political considerations are neglected also holds good in all political considerations alike'. W. Cunningham, 'The Failure of the Free Traders to Attain their Ideals', *Report of the Proceedings of the British Association for the Advancement of Science, Section F* (London: 1904) p. 751.
33. Charles Booth, 'Fiscal Reform', *National Review*, no. 42 (Jan. 1904) p. 699. According to Coats, op. cit. p. 192, n. 24, 'Booth subsequently became a member of Chamberlain's Tariff Commission and was regarded by its opponents as the only reputable figure on it.'
34. See the extracts from Balfour's *Notes*, in W. H. B. Court, *British Economic History 1870–1914: Commentary and Documents* (Cambridge: Cambridge Univ. Press, 1965) pp. 452–9. Balfour's proposals were a compromise. This would place tariffs only on manufactured goods from

countries whose own tariffs kept out British products, and would continue the policy of duty-free import of foodstuffs.

35. J. S. Mill, *Collected Works* (Toronto: Univ. Press, 1965) vol. IV, p. 251. Even earlier, support for a policy of retaliation came from none other than Adam Smith. He argued that retaliation against trade taxes imposed by foreign competitors was perfectly justified if such action had the effect of ensuring the 'repeal of the high duties or prohibitions complained of. The recovery of a great foreign market will generally more than compensate the transitory inconvenience of paying dearer during a short time for some sorts of goods.' A. Smith, *The Wealth of Nations* (1776): Glasgow edn, R. H. Campbell and A. S. Skinner (eds) (Oxford: Oxford Univ. Press, 1976) book IV, ch. ii, para. 39.

36. Earlier, in the mercantilist past, Britain's economic interests were well served by cleverly designed commercial treaties (e.g. the Methuen Treaty, 1703); and the almost universal acceptance of free trade in the 1860s – except for the United States – was due to the spread of MFN treaties. But just as the world was being subjected to strong protectionist pressures, Gladstone's abandonment of any tariff negotiations based on reciprocal concessions meant that Britain found itself in a defenceless position. In the words of Lord Curzon (1895), the country entered keen world competition with one hand tied behind its back 'without anything to give, to promise, or to threaten'. Viscount Curzon's speech to the House of Commons, 36 *Parliamentary Debates*, 4s. 1272 (30 August 1895), quoted in D. C. M. Platt, *Finance, Trade and Politics: British Foreign Policy 1815–1914* (Oxford: Clarendon Press, 1968) p. 145. Gladstone and the Liberals were not persuaded; for Gladstone, adopting a retaliationist policy was tantamount to following 'the protectionist precept: if somebody smites you on the one cheek, you should smite yourself on the other'. Gladstone speech at Leeds, 1881. See Platt, op. cit. p. 145.

Free-traders often use such metaphors to suggest the foolishness of autarky or retaliation: e.g. 'To say that our government must depart from free trade because other governments are not free traders is like saying that because other countries have rocky coasts, we must block up our own harbours.' Paul R. Krugman, 'Introduction: New Thinking about Trade Policy', in Paul R. Krugman (ed.), *Strategic Trade Policy and the New International Economics* (Cambridge, Mass.: MIT Press, 1986) p. 11. In general, it is foolish to add to one harm caused by foreign tariffs a second, self-inflicted harm. If, however, our retaliation has the desired effect and both countries' tariffs are then removed, the net result could be an increase in our welfare above what it would have been in the absence of our retaliatory tariff.

37. See H. G. Johnson, 'An Economic Theory of Protectionism, Tariff Bargaining, and the Formation of Customs Unions', *Journal of Political Economy*, vol. 73 (June 1965) pp. 256–83.

38. T. W. Hutchison, *On Revolutions and Progress in Economic Knowledge* (Cambridge: Cambridge Univ. Press, 1978) p. 114; Wood, op. cit. p. 124. A reprint of Marshall's 1908 *Memorandum on the Fiscal Policy of International Trade* is in J. M. Keynes (ed.), *Official Papers by Alfred*

Marshall (1926), op. cit. pp. 367–420. Extracts appear in Court, op. cit. pp. 459–68. References are to these extracts. On matters relating to the origin and revision of Marshall's memorandum and also for further discussion of his opinions, see John C. Wood, 'Alfred Marshall and the Tariff-reform Campaign of 1903', *Journal of Law and Economics*, vol. 22, no. 2 (Oct. 1980) pp. 481–95.

39. Marshall, *Memorandum*, in Court, op. cit. p. 466.
40. Ibid. p. 468.
41. Ibid. p. 464.
42. Marshall, in *Economic Journal*, vol. 11 (1901) p. 265; also A. C. Pigou (ed.), *Memorials of Alfred Marshall*, op. cit. p. 67.
43. Quoted by Price in his review of Balfour's *Notes: Economic Journal*, vol. 13, p. 567; also see Jha, op. cit. p. 60.
44. See Wood, *British Economists and the Empire*, op. cit. p. 167; R. Giffen, *The Recent Rate of Material Progress in England* (London: George Bell, 1887) p. 26. Giffen was a champion of the free-trade cause during the earlier Fair Trade controversy. He argued then against any move to aid British sugar producers and refiners by the imposition of countervailing duties against the sale of foreign bounty-fed sugar in the British market. When, however, in 1902, the British government was driven by circumstances to adhere to the Brussels Sugar Convention, Giffen altered his position. He admitted that the state could not ignore a threat to the very livelihood of a section of the community, despite theoretical arguments which showed that consumers as a whole gained from foreign bounties. See, Minutes of Evidence, *Report of the Select Committee on Steamship Subsidies*, Parliamentary Papers 1902 (385) IX, Q. 180; also Platt, op. cit. p. 145. In 1903, the Sugar Convention Act was passed in response to the dumping of subsidised beet sugar in Britain. Marshall himself admitted that 'in fact foreign bounties have never done any considerable harm to any British industry with the exception of the sugar industry'; but felt that the harm done was much exaggerated. See H. W. McCready, 'Alfred Marshall and Tariff Reform, 1903: Some Unpublished Letters', *Journal of Political Economy*, vol. LXIII (1955) p. 264.
45. Giffen, 'Protection and Manufactures in New Countries', *Economic Journal*, vol. 8 (1898). Reprinted in Giffen, *Economic Inquiries and Studies*, vol. II (London: G. Bell & Sons, 1904) p. 159.
46. R. Giffen, *The Growth of Capital* (1887) (New York: A. M. Kelley, 1970) p. 113.
47. A. L. Bowley, 'Statistical Methods and the Fiscal Controversy', *Economic Journal*, vol. 13 (Sept. 1903) p. 311; see also Jha, op. cit. p. 66, and Bowley, *England's Foreign Trade in the Nineteenth Century* (London: Swan, Sonneschein & Co., 1893).
48. Jha, op. cit. p. 66.
49. See C. F. Bastable, 'An Imperial Zollverein with Preferential Tariffs', *Economic Journal*, vol. 12 (Dec. 1902) pp. 507–13.
50. Peter Cain, 'Political Economy in Edwardian England: The Tariff Reform Controversy', in Alan O'Day (ed.), *The Edwardian Age: Conflict and Stability 1900–1914* (London: Macmillan, 1979) p. 51. For another historical analysis of the political aspects of tariff reform, see

Alan Sykes, *Tariff Reform in British Politics, 1903–1913* (Oxford: Clarendon Press, 1979).

51. Alan Sked, *Britain's Decline: Problems and Perspectives* (Oxford: Blackwell, 1987) p. 20.
52. Jim Tomlinson, *Problems of British Economic Policy 1870–1945* (London: Methuen, 1981) p. 55.
53. Michael Barrett Brown, *After Imperialism* (London: Heinemann, 1970) rev. edn, p. 106. J. A. Hobson, for instance, discussed the tariff reform debate in terms of his analysis of financial capitalism and imperialism. See J. A. Hobson, 'The Inner Meaning of Protectionism', *Contemporary Review*, no. 84 (1903) pp. 366–7.
54. Crafts and Thomas, op. cit. p. 643.

5 Two Arguments for Protection

1. Richard Schüller, *Schutzzoll und Freihandel: Die Voraussetzungen und Grenzen ihrer Berechtigung* (Vienna: Tempsky, 1905). A summary translation is in F. W. Taussig (ed.), *Selected Readings in International Trade and Tariff Problems* (Boston: Ginn & Co., 1921) pp. 371–91.
2. Gottfried Haberler, *The Theory of International Trade* (1936), op. cit. p. 253. For Haberler's summary and critique of Schüller's argument, see pp. 187–9; 253–9. See also, Haberler, 'The Theory of Comparative Costs and its Use in the Defense of Free Trade' (1930), reprinted in Anthony Y. C. Koo, *Selected Essays of Gottfried Haberler* (Cambridge, Mass.: MIT Press, 1985) esp. pp. 14–16.
3. Schüller, op. cit. p. 136.
4. Ibid. p. 78.
5. See G. Mackenroth, 'Zollpolitik und Produktionsmittelversorgung', *Weltwirtschaftliches Archiv*, vol. 29, Heft 1 (1929) pp. 77–105. Bickerdike reviewed Schüller's book in 1905 and commented: 'This book is an ambitious attempt to find a theoretical basis for genuine protection . . . Dr Schüller makes the best of his case and impresses the reader favourably . . . There is less of that vagueness that so frequently characterizes works written in defence of protection.' Bickerdike was, however, dissatisfied with Schüller's treatment. It did not provide a satisfactory basis for a general theory of permanent protection and would not convince the English free-traders, particularly Schüller's claim that competitive imports cause greater loss to producers than gain to consumers. N. Jha notes that Bickerdike was 'keenly exercised' by the book and suggests that it was Schüller's 'half-finished task that Bickerdike attempted to complete in his "Theory of Incipient Taxes"'. See C. F. Bickerdike, 'Dr R. Schüller "Schutzzoll und Freihandel"', *Economic Journal*, vol. 15 (1905) p. 529; and N. Jha, *The Age of Marshall*, op. cit. pp. 44–5.
6. Haberler, *The Theory of International Trade*, op. cit. p. 187.
7. Mihail Manoilescu, *Théorie du protectionnisme et de l'échange international* (Paris: Librairies Techniques, 1929) (original French edition); *The*

Theory of Protection and International Trade (English edition) (London: P. S. King, 1931).

Manoilescu restated his views in 'Die theoretische Problematik des Aussenhandels: Synthese-Beweisführung-Polemik', *Weltwirtschaftliches Archiv*, vol. 51, Heft 1 (1940) pp. 1–82. Nicholas Georgescu-Roegen, then a student, had occasion to meet Manoilescu in the 1920s and described him as 'the renowned advocate of industrial protectionism'. See N. Georgescu-Roegen, 'An Emigrant from a Developing Country: Autobiographical Notes – I', *Banca Nazionale del Lavoro Quarterly Review*, no. 164 (March 1988) p. 11. For an informative sketch of Manoilescu's life and work, see N. Georgescu-Roegen, 'Mihail Manoilescu', in *The New Palgrave: A Dictionary of Economics*, op. cit. vol. 3, pp. 299–300.

8. See Jacob Viner, 'Mihail Manoilesco on the Theory of Protection', *Journal of Political Economy*, vol. 40, no. 1 (Feb. 1932) pp. 121–5, reprinted in Viner, *International Economics* (Glencoe, Ill.: The Free Press, 1951) pp. 119–22. For Manoilescu's reply to Viner's review, see M. Manoilescu, 'Arbeitsproductivität und Aussenhandel', *Weltwirtschaftliches Archiv* (June 1935).
9. Gottfried Haberler, *The Theory of International Trade* (1936), op. cit. p. 197. In modern terminology, the economy will not operate on the efficient transformation frontier and the feasible production-possibility set may cease to be convex.
10. Viner, *International Economics*, op. cit. p. 122. Viner did not, however, address himself to the central issue in Manoilescu's argument which (although initially expressed in static terms of inter-sectoral productivity differences) ultimately turned on the possibility of transforming (through industrial tariff protection) an agrarian and overpopulated country into an industrialised economy – one with a higher level of productivity. At this level, Manoilescu's argument was similar to the case made in the 1950s for the industrialisation of Latin American countries by ECLA (Economic Commission for Latin America).
11. Viner, ibid. p. 122; and Viner, *Studies*, op. cit. p. 500.
12. B. Ohlin, 'Protection and Non-Competing Groups', *Weltwirtschaftliches Archiv*, vol. 33, Heft 1 (1931) p. 44. For other reviews of Manoilescu's argument, see L. Pasvolsky, in *American Economic Review*, vol. 22, no. 3 (Sept. 1932) pp. 477–8; J. Condliffe, in *Economic Journal*, vol. 43 (March 1933) pp. 143–5.
13. Haberler, *The Theory of International Trade*, op. cit. p. 198, n. 1, and p. 284.
14. In one passage (p. 59) of his book, Manoilescu criticises List for having put forward a doctrine of protection 'more or less unconnected with strictly economic factors', and on p. 19 (of the original French edition) he wrote: 'Industries are like women, they always want to appear young.'

Georgescu-Roegen, in his recent review of Manoilescu's life and work deals sympathetically with Manoilescu's thesis, maintaining that most prewar critics failed to come to grips with the argument. The argument was not based on the 'static model of an economy which just strives toward its best comparative advantage compatible with *given, immutable* possibilities', but was concerned instead with the advantages of industrialisation for agrarian and overpopulated countries and with the benefits an industrialised country enjoys of being 'able to purchase food for less labour than that of its exports'. Georgescu-Roegen points out that no economist today would deny that 'industrialization was responsible for economic development from the Tennessee Valley to Korea'. See N. Georgescu-Roegen, 'Mihail Manoilescu', op. cit. p. 300.

15. W. M. Corden, 'The Normative Theory of International Trade', in Ronald Jones and Peter Kenen (eds), *Handbook of International Economics*, vol. 1 (New York: North-Holland, 1984) pp. 89–91, provides a critical review of the literature mentioned in the text.

    The Manoilescu tradition (industrial nationalism) evidently dies hard in Romania. For most of the postwar years, Romania was at loggerheads with its trading partners in COMECON – the East European common market – over 'agreed specialisation' within the economic bloc. Romania insisted upon having a full range of modern industrial capacity (steel mills, engineering and automotive works, etc.) despite the lack of appropriate resource endowments and comparative advantages *vis-à-vis* the more advanced members of COMECON.

6 Graham's Critique

1. In his Graham Memorial Lecture at Princeton University, 1967, Professor Jagdish Bhagwati referred to Graham's influence: 'There is scarcely a major economist writing in the area of international economics today who has not come under the influence of Graham's writings.' Jagdish Bhagwati, 'The Theory and Practice of Commercial Policy: Departures from Unified Exchange Rates', *Special Papers in International Economics*, no. 8, January 1968 (Princeton: Princeton Univ. Press, 1968). Preface, p. iii.
2. Graham's critique is contained in two articles and a book: Frank D. Graham, 'The Theory of International Values Re-examined', *Quarterly Journal of Economics*, vol. 38 (Nov. 1923) pp. 54–86, reprinted in H. S. Ellis and L. A. Metzler (eds), *Readings in the Theory of International Trade* (London: Allen & Unwin, 1950) pp. 301–30; 'The Theory of International Values', *Quarterly Journal of Economics*, vol. 46 (Aug. 1932) pp. 581–616; *The Theory of International Values* (Princeton, N.J.: Princeton Univ. Press, 1948). In the book published shortly before his death, Graham restated and elaborated his basic ideas.
3. Published as 'Two-ness in Trade Theory: Costs and Benefits' (Princeton University, 1976); reprinted in Ronald W. Jones, *International Trade: Essays in Theory* (Amsterdam: North-Holland, 1979) p. 291.
4. Lloyd A. Metzler, 'Graham's Theory of International Values', *American Economic Review*, vol. 40 (June 1950) p. 305; reprinted in Metzler, *Collected Papers* (Cambridge, Mass.: Harvard Univ. Press, 1973) p. 237. Metzler's 1950 evaluation of Graham's theory is still the best in the literature.
5. Graham exaggerated the volatility of world demand. Later empirical

studies suggested stability. A plausible mechanism for Graham's conclusion about the exceptional nature of 'limbo' price ratios has been suggested by James Melvin. Melvin showed that with Graham's specific demand assumption (commodities always consumed in fixed proportions) the global instability of the terms of trade (at the intersection of two offer curves) would cause them to rest at one country's cost ratio. Such instability it was suggested could support Graham's thesis. See J. R. Melvin, 'On a Demand Assumption made by Graham', *Southern Economic Journal*, vol. 36 (July 1969). However, Takayama doubts whether such a mechanism is sufficient to establish Graham's result. See A. Takayama, *International Trade* (1972), op. cit. pp. 148–50.

6. Graham, *Theory of International Values* (1948), op. cit. p. 154. With cost structures of the various countries locked together, international adjustment takes place through shifts in outputs as long as the the same commodities continue to be produced by the same countries. In this book, Graham illustrated his hypothesis with a model containing as many as ten commodities and ten countries.
7. See Senior's anonymous article, 'Free Trade and Retaliation', in *Edinburgh Review*, vol. LXXVIII (July 1843) pp. 1–47. On the use of this approach by Senior in his controversy with Torrens on the terms of trade, see L. Gomes, *Foreign Trade and the National Economy* (1987), op. cit. pp. 199–201.
8. E.g. in the works of Elliott (1950), Whitin (1953) and McKenzie (1954) which were strongly influenced by Graham's analysis (Whitin and McKenzie were students of Graham's). Whitin, for instance, showed that there exists a close similarity between Graham's analysis of the multi-country, multi-commodity case and the maximisation procedure of linear programming or activity analysis. In fact, wrote Whitin, Graham's work 'anticipated linear programming models by many years'. In his attempt to prove the existence of a solution in Graham's model, McKenzie derived important results concerning the existence of a competitive equilibrium and showed that a unique solution exists for Grahamesque demand functions. See T. M. Whitin, 'Classical Theory, Graham's Theory, and Linear Programming in International Trade', *Quarterly Journal of Economics*, vol. 67 (Nov. 1953) pp. 520–44; L. W. McKenzie, 'On Equilibrium in Graham's Model of World Trade and Other Competitive Systems', *Econometrica*, vol. 22 (April 1954) pp. 147–61. These studies also further developed the concept of a world production-possibilities set (or surface) originally depicted by Abba Lerner. Incidentally, one can use this analytical construction (combined with a set of smoothly bowed-in indifference curves) to provide counter-examples to those suggested by Graham, i.e. to reject Graham's presumption that 'limbo' prices were improbable.
9. F. Y. Edgeworth, *Papers Relating to Political Economy*, vol. II, op. cit. p. 32.
10. E.g. in *Theory of International Values* (1948), op. cit. pp. 79–82. Commodities are consumed in fixed proportions with identical and homothetic utility functions in every country. Given constant costs and

two commodities, for instance, these identical utility functions imply that countries allocate labour between industries in the same proportion. This type of demand function is still frequently used in modern trade theory.

11. Chipman (1965), op. cit. pp. 493–4.
12. Commenting (1937) on Graham's contention, Haberler admitted that the terms of trade would be stable when the number of commodities exported and imported was large; 'but,' said Haberler, 'to conclude from this that the nature of the demand schedules does not affect the exchange ratio is about as logical as to deny that demand, in the usual sense, influences price, on the ground that when there are numerous actual and potential sources of supply, every increase in price will call forth a greater supply'. Haberler, *Theory of International Trade*, op. cit. p. 150. Haberler later described Graham's theory as 'ultra classical' rather than 'anti-classical', presumably on the supposition that it harked back to a pre-Millian cost-of-production theory of relative prices. Haberler, *A Survey of International Trade Theory* (1961), op. cit. p. 10.
13. R. W. Jones, 'Two-ness in Trade Theory', loc. cit. p. 292.
14. On this, see Metzler, 'Graham's Theory of International Values', in idem. *Collected Papers*, op. cit. pp. 255–6.
15. For a resolution of the problem, see Murray C. Kemp, *The Pure Theory of International Trade*, op. cit. pp. 75–9, and 'The Relation Between Changes in International Demand and the Terms of Trade', *Econometrica*, vol. 24, no. 1 (Jan. 1956) pp. 41–6. Good surveys and analyses are also in Bhagwati and Johnson, 'Notes on Some Controversies in the Theory of International Trade', in Bhagwati, *Trade, Tariffs and Growth*, op. cit. pp. 124–9; R. E. Caves, *Trade and Economic Structure*, op. cit. pp. 200–4.
16. Marshall, *Principles of Economics*, 8th edn, op. cit. p. 97.
17. Graham, *Theory of International Values* (1948), op. cit. pp. 157, 158–9.
18. In other words, Graham implicitly recognised an 'identification problem' here. Jones referred to this in connection with the market stability criterion (Marshall–Lerner). See R. W. Jones, op. cit. p. 307.
19. Graham, *Theory of International Values*, op. cit. p. 178.
20. Frank D. Graham, 'Some Aspects of Protection Further Considered', *Quarterly Journal of Economics*, vol. 37 (Feb. 1923) pp. 199–227; idem. 'Some Fallacies in the Interpretation of Social Cost. A Reply', ibid. vol. 39 (Feb. 1925) pp. 324–30.

    It must be noted here that Graham was not a protectionist; nor was he a doctrinaire free-trader. In *Protective Tariffs* (1934) he accepted various well-known neoclassical exceptions to the case for free trade – the traditional infant-industry argument, the terms-of-trade argument, the temporary adoption of a tariff as a bargaining counter in tariff negotiations; but stressed the benefits of specialisation according to comparative advantage. He added: 'The presumption is always in favour of free trade . . . This presumption is rebuttable but it is ever present; and, in this sense, the classical economists were right in insisting that free trade is a ubiquitous and timeless principle.' See Frank D. Graham, *Protective Tariffs* (New York: Harper & Bros, 1934) p. 59. Graham, however, retained the argument for permanent protection of decreasing-cost industries – despite the sharp criticisms of it – and included a chapter on 'Rational Protection'.

21. See Haberler, *The Theory of International Trade*, op. cit. pp. 198–208; Viner, *Studies*, op. cit. pp. 475–82; F. H. Knight, 'Some Fallacies in the Interpretation of Social Cost', *Quarterly Journal of Economics*, vol. 38 (August 1924) pp. 582–606, reprinted in Kenneth J. Arrow and Tibor Scitovsky (eds), *Readings in Welfare Economics* (London: Allen & Unwin, 1969) pp. 213–27. The controversy is reviewed in Caves, *Trade and Economic Structure*, op. cit. pp. 169–74.
22. For instance, Knight's position was that competitive conditions were incompatible with internally decreasing costs (internal economies of scale) – a proof of which was given by Piero Sraffa in 1926. Hence, Graham's conjecture about possible losses from free trade could only apply where the economies of scale were external to the firm and internal to the industry. Knight, however, objected to the concept (and even the reality) of external economies, saying, 'I have never succeeded in picturing them in my mind'; and 'external economies in one business unit are internal economies in some other within the industry'. The first quotation is in Frank Knight, 'On Decreasing Cost and Comparative Cost. A Rejoinder', *Quarterly Journal of Economics*, vol. 39 (Feb. 1925) p. 332. The second is in Arrow and Scitovsky (eds), op. cit. p. 222. Knight's was not the only doubtful voice at the time of the 'Graham protection controversy'. Many economists (despite the pronouncements of Marshall and Pigou) were sceptical about the whole idea. See Chipman, 'A Survey of the Theory of International Trade, Part 2' (1965), op. cit. pp. 736–49, for a summary of views on this matter.
23. The first remark was made by K. L. Anderson, the second by Haberler and the third by Viner. The references are: K. L. Anderson, 'Tariff Protection and Increasing Returns', in *Explorations in Economics: Notes and Essays Contributed in Honor of F. W. Taussig* (New York: McGraw-Hill, 1936) p. 167; Haberler, *Theory of International Trade*, op. cit. p. 201; Viner, *Studies*, op. cit. p. 481.
24. This was suggested by Viner: A national firm derives cost savings from the expansion of world output of its product; in Viner's words, 'if the external economies are a function of the size of the world industry, and not of the national portion of it'. Viner, *Studies*, op. cit. p. 480.
25. Caves, op. cit. p. 169.
26. Ibid. p. 169. Caves lucidly summarises Tinbergen's explication on pp. 171–2 and fig. 7. See J. Tinbergen, *International Economic Cooperation* (Amsterdam: Elsevier, 1945) appendix 1.
27. M. C. Kemp, *Three Topics in the Theory of International Trade* (Amsterdam: North-Holland, 1976) p. 111. See Wilfred J. Ethier, 'Decreasing Costs in International Trade and Frank Graham's Argument for Protection', *Econometrica*, vol. 50, no. 5 (Sept. 1982) pp. 1243–68, especially sec. 6. Arvind Panagariya, 'Variable Returns to Scale in Production and Patterns of Specialization', *American Economic Review*, vol. 71, no. 1 (March 1981) pp. 221–30. Both Ethier and Panagariya provide lucid discussions of Graham's argument.

28. H. Herberg and M. C. Kemp, 'Some Implications of Variable Returns to Scale', *Canadian Journal of Economics*, vol. 2 (Aug. 1969) pp. 403–15; Panagariya, op. cit. p. 222. Apparently, Herberg and Kemp were the first to sort out and correct the common misunderstanding about the shape of the production-possibility frontier for the case under discussion.
29. Ethier points out that in the realistic small-country/large-country case, 'the small country would never, as a result of the tariff, export manufactures' – the increasing-returns commodities; hence it is not an infant-industry argument. W. J. Ethier, op. cit. p. 1262. Cf. Haberler's suggestion that if external economies could be ascertained, Graham's 'argument for a tariff is clearly an exact parallel to the infant-industry argument'. Haberler, *Theory of International Trade*, op. cit. p. 207.
30. Ethier, op. cit. p. 1262.
31. For an influential analysis of this approach, see W. Ethier, 'Internationally Decreasing Costs and World Trade', *Journal of International Economics*, vol. 9 (1979) pp. 1–24.
32. Paul Krugman, 'Strategic Sectors and International Competition', in Robert M. Stern (ed.), *US Trade Policies in a Changing World Economy* (1987), op. cit. p. 226.
33. Ethier, 'Decreasing Costs in International Trade and Frank Graham's Argument for Protection', loc. cit. p. 1263, note 27.

7 Trade and General Equilibrium

1. See 'The Theory of Comparative Costs and its Use in the Defense of Free Trade' (1930), reprinted (in English) in Anthony Y. C. Koo (ed.) (1985), op. cit. pp. 3–19. The original German article appeared in 1930 under the title 'Die Theorie der komparativen Kosten und ihre Auswertung für die Begründung des Freihandels', *Weltwirtschaftliches Archiv*, vol. 32, no. 2. (1930) pp. 349–70. This seminal paper was virtually reproduced in Haberler's classic treatise, *Der Internationale Handel* (Berlin: Verlag von Julius Springer, 1933) pp. 132–56. The English translation of the treatise appeared in 1936 – *The Theory of International Trade, with its application to Commercial Policy*, op. cit.
2. Early praise for Haberler's approach came from Marian Bowley (1937). Referring to attempts to dealing with the analytical problems mentioned in the text above, she said that Haberler's approach was 'undoubtedly the best, largely because it demonstrates and admits, instead of trying to evade, the impossibility of attaining precision along these lines'. Marian Bowley, *Nassau Senior and Classical Economics* (1937), op. cit. pp. 201–2. In 1959, Sir John Hicks in a comparison of the treatments of productive factors along Ohlin–Samuelson lines and in terms of Haberler's opportunity-cost approach, wrote: 'In this respect, the comparative cost theory, in terms of opportunity cost, is a much more *suitable* apparatus for the study of international trade.' J. R. Hicks, *Essays in World Economics* (Oxford: Clarendon, Press, 1959) p. 266.
3. About this burst of creative energy, Robert Mundell writes: 'In 1930 . . . the theory of foreign trade was in the doldrums. Then suddenly after

1930, a new generation brought the field to life.' Robert A. Mundell, 'Abba Lerner on the Theory of Foreign Trade', in H. I. Greenfield, A. M. Levenson, W. Hamovitch and E. Rotwein (eds), *Theory for Economic Efficiency: Essays in Honor of Abba P. Lerner* (Cambridge, Mass.: MIT Press, 1980) p. 144.

4. Viner later summarised his paper in Viner, *Studies*, op. cit. p. 521.
5. Abba P. Lerner, in *Economica*, vol. 12 (old series) (Aug. 1932) pp. 346–56. Reprinted in Lerner, *Essays in Economic Analysis* (London: Macmillan, 1953) pp. 85–100.
6. Lerner, *Essays*, op. cit. p. 87, note.
7. Abba P. Lerner, 'The Diagrammatical Representation of Demand Conditions in International Trade', *Economica* (new series) vol. 1 (Aug. 1934) pp. 319, 320. See the comments in John S. Chipman, 'A Survey of the Theory of International Trade', part 2, op. cit. pp. 696–7.
8. A theoretical relation he later fully analysed in his famous 1936 article on 'The Symmetry Between Import and Export Taxes'.
9. Mundell, 'Abba Lerner on the Theory of Foreign Trade', loc. cit. p. 145.
10. Lerner's elegant, clear and succinct proof of the factor-price equalisation theorem was read at one of Lord Robbins's seminars (LSE) fifteen years before Samuelson's first article on the topic. When the latter came out, Lord Robbins recalled Lerner's seminar paper and urged Lerner to publish it – a copy of which was still in Robbins's possession. In 1984, Tibor Scitovsky (one of Lerner's students in 1935) recounted a story he heard concerning the non-publication of the article in 1934. Apparently, one of Lerner's students who had offered to type the manuscript lost it on a London bus; and since 'that was Lerner's only corrected copy and because he was working on several other papers at the time, he could not be bothered to reproduce the lost manuscript'. See Tibor Scitovsky, 'Lerner's Contribution to Economics', *Journal of Economic Literature*, vol. 22 (Dec. 1984) p. 1554. Lerner's paper as originally written, was eventually published in 1952 – 'Factor Prices and International Trade', *Economica* (new series) vol. 19 (Feb. 1952) pp. 1–16. Reprinted in Lerner, *Essays* (1953), op. cit. pp. 67–84.
11. Mundell, 'Abba Lerner on the Theory of Foreign Trade', loc. cit. pp. 147–8.
12. Wassily W. Leontief, 'The Use of Indifference Curves in the Analysis of Foreign Trade', *Quarterly Journal of Economics*, vol. 47 (May 1933) pp. 493–503. Reprinted in Jagdish Bhagwati (ed.), *International Trade* (Harmondsworth: Penguin Books, 1969) pp. 21–9.
13. Lerner gives a good summary of the dispute between Edgeworth and Bastable in his article 'The Symmetry Between Import and Export Taxes', *Economica*, n.s. vol. 3 (Aug. 1936) pp. 306–13. Reprinted in Richard E. Caves and Harry G. Johnson (eds), *Readings in International Economics* (London: Allen & Unwin, 1968) pp. 197–203.
14. In the classical discussion of this question by Marshall (and Edgeworth also), two limiting examples were considered: the customs revenues were assumed to be spent either entirely upon export goods or entirely upon imports. Lerner's geometrical technique was able to handle the realistic intermediate cases as well, i.e. the case where preferences are not

aggregable and the government has preferences that differ from the public.

15. Mundell, op. cit. p. 146.
16. See, P. A. Samuelson, 'Jacob Viner, 1892–1970', *Journal of Political Economy*, vol. 80 (1972), reprinted in H. Nagatani and K. Crowley (eds), *The Collected Scientific Papers of Paul A. Samuelson*, vol. 4 (Cambridge, Mass.: MIT Press, 1977) p. 912. For other biographies and appreciations of Viner, see W. J. Baumol and Ellen Viner Seiler, 'Jacob Viner', in *International Encyclopaedia of the Social Sciences, Biographical Supplement*, vol. 18 (New York: Macmillan and The Free Press, 1979) pp. 783–7; Lionel Robbins, *Jacob Viner: A Tribute* (Princeton: Princeton Univ. Press, 1970); Donald Winch, 'Jacob Viner as Intellectual Historian', in W. J. Samuels (ed.), *Research in the History of Economic Thought and Methodology*, vol. 1 (New York: The Jai Press, 1983) pp. 1–17.

    Viner was born in Montreal (Canada). After graduate studies at Harvard under Frank Taussig, the rest of his career was spent in the United States, first in Chicago and later at Princeton. Viner's students at Chicago included Paul Samuelson and Martin Bronfenbrenner.
17. Viner, *International Economics* (1951), op. cit. p. 16.
18. Viner's uncompromising advocacy of free trade did not endear him to leading Latin American economists when he addressed them on the subject of trade and development in the University of Rio de Janeiro, 1950. He attributed to them (i.e. the economists associated with ECLA – Economic Commission for Latin America) the 'fantastic idea' that agriculture was a symbol of poverty, and rejected arguments for the industrialisation of Latin American countries based on policies of protection and import substitution. Recently, Raúl Prebisch recalled the debate he then had with Viner over the latter's challenge to ECLA's ideas. See Raúl Prebisch, 'Dependence, Development, and Interdependence', in G. Ranis and T. P. Schultz (eds), *The State of Development Economics: Progress and Perspectives* (Oxford: Blackwell, 1988) p. 35. Viner's Brazilian lectures were published as *International Trade and Economic Development* (Oxford: Clarendon Press, 1953). For an evaluation of ECLA's reception of Viner's talk, see Celso Furtado, *A Fantasia Organizada [An Organised Fantasy]* (Rio de Janeiro: Editore Paz et Terra S/A, 1985).

    Viner's dismissal of Manoilescu's earlier plea was another instance of his attitude. Among Manoilescu's critics, 'only Jacob Viner . . . threw Ricardo's book at the author', as N. Georgescu-Roegen recalls. Georgescu-Roegen, 'Mihail Manoilescu', loc. cit. p. 300.
19. Viner, *International Economics*, op. cit. p. 12.
20. Eugene Rotwein, 'Jacob Viner and the Chicago Tradition', *Journal of Political Economy*, vol. 15, no. 2 (1983) p. 276.
21. Ronald Findlay recently revealed that when studying economics at the University of Rangoon (Burma) in the early 1950s, two books (both by Haberler and already established classics for twenty years) were required reading for honours students. 'These were *Prosperity and Depression* and *The Theory of International Trade*.' Findlay, review of *Selected*

Essays of Gottfried Haberler, *Journal of Economic Literature*, vol. 25 (Sept. 1987) p. 1346.

22. Thomas D. Willett, 'Gottfried Haberler on Inflation, Unemployment, and International Monetary Economics: An Appreciation', *Quarterly Journal of Economics*, vol. 97, no. 1 (Feb. 1982) p. 165.
23. This idea provided the basis for 'specific-factors' models of trade (which focus on asymmetry in the degree of factor mobility between sectors) developed by Jones and Samuelson forty years later.
24. Ronald Findlay made an interesting remark recently concerning the affinity of Haberler's opportunity-cost approach with the new 'specific-factors' model of trade: 'Indeed, a case could be made that his [Haberler's] "opportunity cost" approach is more in conformity with the spirit of this [specific-factors or Ricardo-Viner] model than the "real cost" approach of Viner.' See Ronald Findlay, review of *Selected Essays of Gottfried Haberler* (1987), loc. cit. p. 1347.
25. Paul A. Samuelson, 'International Trade and the Equalisation of Factor Prices', *Economic Journal*, vol. 58 (June 1948) p. 182. Earlier, Samuelson declared: 'the doctrine of opportunity cost, properly stated, in no way contradicts the so-called pain cost theory of value. In fact, when stated with full qualifications, the doctrine of opportunity cost inevitably degenerates into the conditions of general equilibrium.' Samuelson, 'Welfare Economics and International Trade', *American Economic Review*, vol. 28 (1938) p. 263.
26. Murray C. Kemp, *The Pure Theory of International Trade*, op. cit. p. 97.
27. Haberler, 'Some Problems in the Pure Theory of International Trade', *Economic Journal*, vol. 60 (June 1950) p. 224, and 'Real Cost, Money Cost and Comparative Advantage', *International Social Science Bulletin*, UNESCO, vol. 3 (Sept. 1951) p. 55n. Both articles are reprinted in Koo (ed.), *Selected Essays of Gottfried Haberler*, op. cit. pp. 37–54 and pp. 21–36 respectively.
28. Robert E. Baldwin, 'Gottfried Haberler's Contributions to International Trade Theory and Policy', *Quarterly Journal of Economics*, vol. 97, no. 1 (Feb. 1982) p. 144.
29. Haberler, *Theory of International Trade*, op. cit. Preface to the German edition, p. viii.
30. Ibid. Preface to the English edition, p. v. Long ago Haberler called attention to the phenomenon of intra-industry trade and described some of its manifestations: product heterogeneity within aggregates, seasonal fluctuations, border trade (e.g. wheat imported into Western Germany and exported from East Germany). Ibid. p. 34, n. 2.
31. It was at that time that Ohlin presented his thesis to Gustav Cassel for the licentiate degree (*licentiatus philosophiae*) of the University of Stockholm. This was an early brief version of the theory of international trade that Ohlin developed into his doctoral dissertation, *Handelns teori [The Theory of Trade]* (Stockholm: Centraltryckeriet, May 1924), and his later book, *Interregional and International Trade* (1933), op. cit. Referring to what Ohlin said in his memoirs, Otto Steiger reported that Heckscher's approach inspired Ohlin 'while walking along Unter den

Linden in Berlin in 1920 . . . to formulate the theorem of differences in productive factor endowment as the cause of *trade in general*'. See Otto Steiger, 'Bertil Ohlin, 1899–1979', *History of Political Economy*, vol. 13, no. 2 (1981) p. 181. When in 1977 he was awarded the Alfred Nobel memorial prize jointly with James Meade, the citation referred to *Interregional and International Trade* as Ohlin's principal contribution.

32. Cassel's simplified general-equilibrium model of a closed economy is contained in his book, *Theoretische Sozialökonomie* (1918), translated (from the original fifth edition) as *The Theory of Social Economy*, new rev. edn (New York: Harcourt, 1932). Ohlin included in his book a nine-page algebraic appendix of a simple two-country Cassellian general-equilibrium system. Heckscher's work originally appeared in the David Davidson festschrift in *Ekonomisk Tidskrift* (1919), but was only published in English translation in 1949 as 'The Effect of Foreign Trade on the Distribution of Income', in *Readings in the Theory of International Trade*, edited by Ellis and Metzler (1949), op. cit. pp. 272–300. The ideas in Heckscher's 1919 article were stimulated as the result of a review by Wicksell of an earlier work by Heckscher, i.e. Knut Wicksell, 'Svenska produktionsproblem', *Forum*, vol. 6 (Jan. 1919) pp. 16–17, 29–31.
33. Ohlin, *Interregional and International Trade* (1933), op. cit. p. 589.
34. Caves, op. cit. p. 3.
35. Samuelson, 'Bertil Ohlin 1899–1979', loc. cit. p. 151.
36. Haberler, *Survey of International Trade Theory*, op. cit. p. 4. Some will say that Haberler's prediction is only wishful thinking. Geographers and economists hold different perspectives and theoretical traditions. Among economists, the Ricardian tradition dies hard: zero factor mobility between countries or regions and full commodity mobility between countries or regions. Geographers and location theorists, however, start with basic features determining the immobility of factors and goods (localisation factors) and then go on to describe the resultant patterns of trade. The geographer's starting-point is the economist's finishing-line. The former is partial equilibrium, the latter general equilibrium. Although Ohlin's treatise was an attempt to integrate trade and location theories, the effort was criticised by certain location theorists (e.g. Walter Isard) on the ground that it failed to bridge the gap between the concerns of the two disciplines. For a brief comment in connection with Isard's opinion, see Harald Dickson, 'Bertil Ohlin', in *International Encyclopedia of the Social Sciences*, op. cit. p. 606.
37. Ohlin, *Interregional and International Trade*, pp. 54–5, 146–7.
38. Samuelson, 'Bertil Ohlin 1899–1979', loc. cit. p. 152.
39. Ibid. p. 152.
40. Ohlin, op. cit. p. 30.
41. Ibid. p. 105.
42. Of course, the break with classical theory was less dramatic than Ohlin imagined. Nevertheless, it represented an important development – for at least two reasons. Ohlin's theory provided a sufficient or minimal condition for profitable international trade even if the latest technology is distributed evenly throughout the world. Secondly, by incorporating

the factor market into the model it allows a more explicit investigation into the effects of international trade on the domestic distribution of income.

43. Ohlin, op. cit. pp. 30–1. Elsewhere in his book, pp. 31–4, 568–70, Ohlin mentions the names of other economists (apart from Heckscher and Cassell) who had anticipated the Heckscher–Ohlin hypothesis – G. del. Vecchio, Taussig, Angell and Viner in the early twentieth century. Professor Blaug refers to 'Longfield's discovery of the modern factor proportions theory of international trade, for which Bertil Ohlin . . . gave Longfield full credit'. Mark Blaug, *Great Economists Before Keynes* (1986), op. cit. pp. 135–6. In addition to the passages in Longfield's *Lectures on Political Economy* (1834) cited by Ohlin, other relevant material appears in Longfield, *Three Lectures on Commerce* (1835), reprinted in R. D. C. Black, *The Economic Writings of Mountifort Longfield* (New York: 1971) pp. 56–8.
44. Viner, *Studies*, p. 504.
45. See George J. Stigler, *Essays in the History of Economics* (Chicago: Chicago Univ. Press, 1965) ch. 10; 'Stuart Wood and the Marginal Productivity Theory', pp. 287–301, esp. pp. 294–5. The essay was originally published in 1947. Robert Mundell, 'Abba Lerner on the Theory of Foreign Trade', loc. cit. p. 148.
46. See Simon Power, 'The Origins of the Heckscher–Ohlin Concept', *History of Political Economy*, vol. 19, no. 2 (1987) pp. 289–98. Power makes it clear that in tracing the origins of the H–O hypothesis he is concerned with the 'Heckscher–Ohlin concept', not the standard $2 \times 2 \times 2$ textbook model. The article is interesting, in that it extends and elaborates Viner's discussion of the concept's antecedents and suggests that some of the French writers (Sismondi, Turgot) derived their ideas from British sources.
47. Samuelson began his obituary appreciation of Ohlin (1981) with the sentence: 'Ohlin will live forever as one of the great innovators in the theory of international trade', p. 147. Ohlin's innovation might have reached a wider audience (i.e. the English-speaking world) a decade earlier but for an unfortunate incidence which Ohlin later recalled. At Cassel's suggestion, Ohlin sent to Edgeworth in the spring of 1922 a condensed version of his licentiate thesis for publication in the *Economic Journal.* This included chs 1–3 and the celebrated mathematical appendix of his 1933 book. Edgeworth referred the material to Keynes and asked for his opinion. At the end of August 1922 Keynes replied on a piece of notepaper: 'This amounts to nothing and should be refused, J.M.K.' By mistake the note came into Ohlin's possession – 'I still have the note, and regard it as a valuable document' (Ohlin, 1977). The ill-fated article was never published. Ohlin generously remarked afterwards: 'Even Jupiter may shut his eyes sometimes' (Ohlin, *Memoirs*, 1975). See Ohlin, 'Appendix III: Some Comments on Keynesianism and the Swedish Theory of Expansion Before 1935', in D. Patinkin and J. C. Leith (eds), *Keynes, Cambridge and the General Theory* (London: Macmillan, 1977) p. 161; vol. II of Ohlin's autobiography, *Bertil Ohlins memoarer, 1940–1951, Socialistisk skördetid kom bort* (Stockholm: 1975)

p. 107; also Otto Steiger, op. cit. pp. 181–2.

48. W. F. Stolper and P. A. Samuelson, 'Protection and Real Wages'. The article first appeared in *Review of Economic Studies*, vol. 9 (1941) pp. 58–73, and has been reproduced in several places, e.g. Jagdish Bhagwati (ed.), *International Trade* (1969), op. cit. pp. 245–68. The quotation is at p. 267.

49. Metzler's paradox occurs when foreign demand is extremely inelastic and all the tariff revenue is spent on exports. See L. A. Metzler, 'Tariffs, the Terms of Trade, and the Distribution of National Income', and 'Tariffs, International Demand, and Domestic Prices', both in *Journal of Political Economy*, vol. 57 (1949) pp. 1–29 and 345–52, respectively.

50. The Stolper–Samuelson theorem can be analysed in terms of Jones's 'magnification effect', which relates factor prices to commodity prices in the 2×2 setting on the assumption that there is no joint production: a given proportional change in commodity prices results in a greater proportional change in factor prices, such that one factor price increases unambiguously (in terms of both commodity prices) relative to the other factor price. Thus an increase in the price of the import good (through protection) leads, in a magnified fashion, to an increase in the return to the scarce factor and a reduction in the return to the abundant factor. This magnification result (in an open economy) depends, however, on the protective effect of the tariff: i.e. protection must, to begin with, raise the domestic relative price of the import good. Hence, Metzler's paradox is still a relevant consideration.

    On magnification effects (commodity prices on factor prices, and factor supplies on outputs), see R. W. Jones, 'The Structure of Simple General Equilibrium Models', *Journal of Political Economy*, vol. 73 (Dec. 1965) pp. 557–72.

51. Paul A. Samuelson, 'International Trade and the Equalisation of Factor Prices', *Economic Journal*, vol. 58 (June 1948) pp. 163–84, reprinted in *Collected Scientific Papers of Paul A. Samuelson*, vol. 2, ch. 67.

52. In the same year (1949), Lloyd Metzler remarked, 'the theory of international trade might have been advanced considerably, in the English-speaking world at any rate, by an earlier translation of Heckscher's pioneering article'. L. Metzler, 'Tariffs, the Terms of Trade, and the Distribution of National Income', loc. cit. p. 4. Caves writes that Wicksell 'anticipates the result reached forty years later by Stolper and Samuelson, but his proof is not sufficient'. Caves, op. cit. p. 64.

53. This concept was discussed earlier by McKenzie in the context of his activity analysis approach – Lionel W. McKenzie, 'Equality of Factor Prices in World Trade', *Econometrica*, vol. 23 (July 1955) pp. 239–57. Countries with endowments in the same cone of diversification produce both goods using the same technique and also have the same factor prices. Countries with endowments in different cones use different techniques and may have different factor prices. Countries specialise in the production of one of the goods if their endowments are in none of the cones. See Chipman, 'A Survey of the Theory of International Trade: Part 3', loc. cit. pp. 19–35.

54. Samuelson, 'International Factor-Price Equalisation Once Again', *Eco-*

nomic Journal, vol. 59 (June 1949) pp. 181–97, reprinted in his *Collected Scientific Papers*, vol. 2, ch. 68. Samuelson, 'Prices of Factors and Goods in General Equilibrium', *Review of Economic Studies*, vol. 21 (1953–4) pp. 1–20; reprinted in *Collected Scientific Papers*, vol. 2, ch. 70.

55. Mundell, 'Abba Lerner on the Theory of Foreign Trade', loc. cit. p. 149.
56. See T. M. Rybczynski, 'Factor Endowment and Relative Commodity Prices', *Economica*, vol. 22 (Nov. 1955) pp. 336–41. The Rybczynski theorem thus links outputs to factor supplies, given output prices. The H–O theorem, in the form which identifies the structure of trade as a function of factor supplies, is in fact a corollary of the Rybczynski theorem.
57. Robert E. Baldwin, 'Gottfried Haberler's Contribution to International Trade Theory and Policy', loc. cit. p. 144. Incidentally, before Rybczynski, this fact was pointed out by Samuelson: see Samuelson, 'International Trade and the Equalisation of Factor Prices', loc. cit. p. 171.
58. For reviews of this literature, see Chipman (1966) op. cit., and A. Takayama, *International Trade*, op. cit. ch. 18, pp. 543–75.
59. See Henry Y. Wan, Jr, 'Samuelson and Trade Theory: From the Methodological Perspective', in George R. Feiwel (ed.), *Samuelson and Neoclassical Economics* (New York: Kluwer Nijhoff Publishing, 1983) pp. 148–9.
60. See Samuelson, 'Prices of Factors and Goods in General Equilibrium', loc. cit. p. 10. The relationship is presented by Samuelson in the general context of n goods and r factors; but by specifying $i = K, L$, and $j = 1, 2$ in the above equation it can be related, of course, to the familiar 2-sector, 2-factor model. For Jones's contribution to duality relationships, see Ronald W. Jones, 'Duality in International Trade: A Geometrical Note', *Canadian Journal of Economics*, vol. 31 (Aug. 1965) pp. 390–3, and Jones, 'The Structure of Simple General Equilibrium Models', loc. cit. pp. 557–72. Although Samuelson's expression for the reciprocity relationship is elegantly presented, the proof is rather sketchy. For a more extended discussion, see R. W. Jones and José A. Scheinkman, 'The Relevance of the Two-Sector Production Model in Trade Theory', *Journal of Political Economy*, vol. 85 (Oct. 1977) pp. 909–35.
61. Jones, 'International Trade Theory', in E. Cary Brown and Robert M. Solow (eds), *Paul Samuelson and Modern Economic Theory* (New York: McGraw Hill, 1983) p. 91.
62. Wan, op. cit. p. 149.
63. Commenting on the enormous literature spawned by the Leontief paradox, Edward Leamer recently remarked: 'It is hard to identify another empirical finding in economics that has had such an enormous impact on how economists have spent their time.' Edward E. Leamer, *Sources of Comparative Advantage: Theory and Evidence* (Cambridge, Mass.: MIT Press, 1984) p. 51. For a summary of the empirical work on human capital and technology on trade patterns, see Leonard Gomes, *International Economic Problems* (London: Macmillan, 1978) ch. 7, pp. 143–59.
64. The exception referred to is Stephen Magee's well-known test of the

Stolper–Samuelson theorem. Stephen P. Magee, 'Three Simple Tests of the Stolper–Samuelson Theorem', in Peter Oppenheimer (ed.), *Issues in International Economics* (Stocksfield: Oriel Press, 1978) pp. 138–52. Magee (using evidence from US Congressional hearings) showed that contrary to the prediction of the Stolper–Samuelson theorem, labour and capital agree overwhelmingly on trade policy. Trade unions and manufacturers often take the same side on the trade question – not ranged one against the other, as theory suggests. The clash of class interests is noticeably absent. The phenomenon of pressure groups organised by industry rather than by factors of production was noticed long ago by J. E. Cairnes (1823–75).

65. See J. L. Ford, *The Ohlin-Heckscher Theory of the Basis and Effects of Commodity Trade* (London: Asia Publishing House, 1965) pp. 12–23.
66. Neil de Marchi, 'Anomaly and the Development of Economics: The Case of the Leontief Paradox', in S. J. Latsis (ed.) *Method and Appraisal in Economics* (Cambridge: Cambridge Univ. Press, 1976) pp. 109–127.
67. See Bert Hamminga, 'Neoclassical Theory Structure and Theory Development: The Ohlin–Samuelson Programme in the Theory of International Trade', in W. Stegmüller, W. Balzer and W. Spohn (eds), *Philosophy of Economics: Studies in Contemporary Economics*, vol. 2 (New York: Springer-Verlag (Berlin), 1982) pp. 1–15. Hamminga gives a couple of examples to illustrate his argument. One refers to the 1941 Stolper–Samuelson article where the authors arrive at their conclusion – 'We have shown that there is a grain of truth in the pauper labour type of argument for protection' – through a process of dropping various restrictive assumptions. Hamminga asks: 'Whence this grain of truth? No statistical or otherwise observational material is introduced, so the grain of truth must stem from the possibility, shown by Stolper and Samuelson, to remove "restrictive assumptions" . . . thereby allowing for more possible cases in which their theorem still is true.' Hamminga, loc. cit. p. 9.
68. Mark Blaug, *The Methodology of Economics: Or How Economists Explain* (Cambridge: Cambridge Univ. Press, 1980) p. 212.
69. Blaug, ibid. p. 213.
70. Frank Hahn quoted in Blaug, op. cit. p. 191. Donald F. Gordon, Review of Blaug's *Methodology of Economics* in *Journal of Political Economy*, vol. 91, no. 4 (1983) p. 712.
71. The Duhem–Quine thesis springs from the ideas of the French physicist Pierre Duhem and the American logician Willard van Orman Quine. John Passmore writes: 'Quine follows Duhem in arguing that the scientist brings to the test of experience a set of propositions, not an isolated assertion.' John Passmore, *A Hundred Years of Philosophy* (Harmondsworth: Penguin Books, 1968) p. 404. For an interesting application of the D–Q thesis to recent controversies in macroeconomics, see Rod Cross, 'The Duhem–Quine Thesis, Lakatos and the Appraisal of Theories in Macroeconomics', *Economic Journal*, vol. 92 (June 1982) pp. 320–40.
72. Edward E. Leamer, 'The Leontief Paradox Reconsidered', *Journal of Political Economy*, vol. 88, no. 3 (1980) p. 495.

73. Leamer, ibid. p. 496.
74. Richard A. Brecher and Ehsan U. Choudhri, 'The Leontief Paradox: Continued', *Journal of Political Economy*, vol. 90 (1982) pp. 820–23.
75. Robert M. Stern and Keith E. Maskus, 'Determinants of the Structure of US Foreign Trade, 1958–76', *Journal of International Economics*, vol. 11 (1981) pp. 207–24.
76. Alan V. Deardorff, 'Testing Trade Theories and Predicting Trade Flows', in Jones and Kenen (eds), *Handbook of International Economics*, vol. 1, op. cit. p. 485.
77. James R. Melvin, Review of *The Handbook of International Economics* in *Canadian Journal of Economics*, vol. 19 (1986) p. 586.
78. Leamer, *Sources of International Comparative Advantage*, op. cit. p. 48.
79. James E. Anderson, Review of Leamer's book cited above, in *Journal of Economic Literature*, vol. 25 (March 1987) p. 146.
80. Keith E. Maskus, 'A Test of the Heckscher–Ohlin–Vanek Theorem: The Leontief Commonplace', *Journal of International Economics*, vol. 19 (1985) p. 209.
81. Wilfred J. Ethier, 'Higher Dimensional Issues in Trade Theory', in Jones and Kenen (eds), *Handbook of International Economics*, vol. 1, op. cit. p. 161.
82. Ronald Jones and José A. Scheinkman, 'The Relevance of the Two-Sector Production Model in Trade theory', loc. cit. pp. 909–35.
83. See Ronald W. Jones, 'A Three-Factor Model in Theory, Trade and History', in J. N. Bhagwati, R. W. Jones, R. A. Mundell and J. Vanek (eds), *Trade, Balance of Payments and Growth: Essays in Honor of Charles P. Kindleberger* (Amsterdam: North-Holland, 1971); Paul A. Samuelson, 'Ohlin Was Right', in *Collected Scientific Papers*, vol. 4, part VI, no. 254.
84. See Wolfgang Mayer, 'Short-Run and Long-Run Equilibrium for a Small Open Economy', *Journal of Political Economy*, vol. 82 (1974) pp. 955–67.
85. For example, the Stolper–Samuelson approach suggests that economic interests organise across industries along factor lines. Some gain and others lose from trade liberalisation. In fact, such effects have not been detected in cases such as the formation of the EEC and theUS–Canada Autopact. As a result of rationalisation within firms, there have been gains to all factors of production.
86. James R. Markusen and James R. Melvin, 'Trade, Factor Prices and Gains from Trade with Increasing Returns to Scale', *Canadian Journal of Economics*, vol. 14 (1981) pp. 450–69.
87. James A. Brander and Barbara J. Spencer, 'Tariffs and the Extraction of Foreign Monopoly Rents under Potential Entry', *Canadian Journal of Economics*, vol. 14 (1981) pp. 371–89; also 'Export Subsidies and International Market Share Rivalry', *Journal of International Economics*, vol. 18 (1985) pp. 82–100.
88. See, e.g. James A. Brander, 'Rationales for Strategic Trade and Industrial Policy', in Paul R. Krugman (ed.), *Strategic Trade Policy and the New International Economics*, op. cit. pp. 23–46.
89. Alan V. Deardorff and Robert M. Stern, 'Current Issues in Trade

Policy: An Overview', in Robert M. Stern (ed.), op. cit. p. 34. For another critique, see Gene M. Grossman, 'Strategic Export Promotion: A Critique', in Krugman (ed.), op. cit. pp. 47–68.

90. Elhanan Helpman and Paul R. Krugman, *Market Structure and Foreign Trade: Increasing Returns, Imperfect Competition and the International Economy* (Cambridge, Mass.: MIT Press, 1985).
91. Wilfred J. Ethier, 'The Multinational Firm', *Quarterly Journal of Economics* (Nov. 1986) pp. 805–33.
92. Ronald Findlay and Stanislaw Wellisz, 'Endogenous Tariffs, the Political Economy of Trade Restrictions and Welfare', in J. N. Bhagwati (ed.), *Import Competition and Response* (Chicago: Chicago Univ. Press, 1982).
93. Stephen P. Magee and Leslie Young, 'Endogenous Protection in the United States, 1900–1984', in Robert M. Stern (ed.), *US Trade Policies in a Changing World Economy* (1987), op. cit. pp. 145–95.
94. See J. Peter Neary, 'Comment on "Endogenous Protection in the United States, 1900–1984"', in Stern (ed.), op. cit. p. 205.
95. Wolfgang Mayer and Raymond Riezman, 'Endogenous Choice of Trade Policy Instruments', Working Paper No. 85–8, Jan. 1985, University of Iowa.
96. Max W. Corden, 'The Normative Theory of International Trade', in Jones and Kenen (eds), *Handbook of International Economics*, vol. 1, op. cit. p. 112.
97. Charles P. Kindleberger, 'A Further Comment', in William N. Parker (ed.), *Economic History and the Modern Economist* (Oxford: Blackwell, 1986) p. 85. For the findings of Kindleberger's research, see idem. *Economic Response: Comparative Studies in Trade, Finance and Growth* (Cambridge, Mass.: Harvard Univ. Press, 1978) – 'Group Behaviour and International Trade', pp. 19–38, and 'The Rise of Free Trade in Western Europe, 1820–1875', pp. 39–65.

8 Balance of Payments Theory

1. Anne O. Krueger, 'Balance of Payments Theory', *Journal of Economic Literature*, vol. 7 (March 1969) p. 1.
2. J. S. Chipman, 'Balance of Payments Theory', in J. Creedy and D. P. O'Brien (eds), *Economic Analysis in Historical Perspective* (London: Butterworth, 1984) p. 186. Haberler, as well, notes: 'The theory of the adjustment mechanism of the balance of payments is as old as economic theory itself.' Gottfried Haberler, 'A Survey of International Trade Theory' (1961), op. cit., reprinted in *Selected Essays of Gottfried Haberler* (1985), op. cit. p. 77.
3. J. S. Mill, *Principles of Political Economy* (1865). Reprint (New York: Augustus M. Kelley, 1961) p. 618.
4. Mill, ibid. pp. 627–8.
5. J. S. Mill, *Principles*, 7th edn (London: Parker & Co., 1871) book iv, ch. viii, sec. 4.
6. J. Robinson, 'The Need for a Reconsideration of the Theory of

International Trade' (1973), reprinted in Robinson, *Collected Economic Essays*, vol. IV, op. cit. p. 20.

7. Alfred Marshall, in *Official Papers of Alfred Marshall* (ed.), J. M. Keynes (1926), op. cit. p. 170.
8. Marshall, *Money, Credit and Commerce*, op. cit. p. 145.
9. Marshall, *Official Papers*, p. 172. It is obvious Marshall adopts an eclectic approach to the equilibrating mechanism: the price-specie flow mechanism combined with what is now known as the monetary approach. But, as recent research shows, both types of adjustment mechanisms do not help to clarify the causes of gold movements – at least for the early period of the gold standard's operation. Marcuzzo and Rosselli (1987) suggests that it was gold-merchants' behaviour which maintained the purchasing-power parity of gold in terms of currencies. They found no evidence to support the view that 'gold flows realized the purchasing power parity of gold in terms of traded commodities'. See Maria Cristina Marcuzzo and Annalisa Rosselli, 'Profitability in the International Gold Market in the Early History of the Gold Standard', *Economica*, vol. 54 (Aug. 1987) pp. 367–80.
10. Marshall, ibid. pp. 127–8.
11. I. Fisher, *The Purchasing Power of Money* (1922). Reprint (New York: Augustus M. Kelley, 1965) p. 172.
12. Fisher, ibid. p. 93.
13. See, J. Laurence Laughlin, *The Principles of Money* (New York: Scribner, 1903) pp. 220–1, 268–9, 372, 614–15. See also Viner, *Studies* (1937), op. cit. pp. 316–18.
14. Haberler, *The Theory of International Trade*, op. cit. p. 29. Chi-Yuen Wu makes a similar point about Laughlin's reasoning, saying that it is not a sufficient argument against the possibility of a connection between price levels and gold flows. 'On the contrary,' he continues, 'it amounts to saying that differences in prices, if they do exist at all, will be adjusted quickly by the movement of goods. That was exactly what the classical theorists maintained.' Chi-Yuen Wu, *An Outline of International Price Theories* (London: George Routledge & Sons Ltd., 1939) p. 207.
15. Laughlin, *Principles of Money*, op. cit. pp. 380–2.
16. Paul A. Samuelson, 'A Corrected Version of Hume's Equilibrating Mechanisms for International Trade' (1980), reprinted in *The Collected Scientific Papers of Paul A. Samuelson*, Kate Crowley (ed.) (1986), op. cit. p. 401.
17. Laughlin, op. cit. p. 382. See also ibid. pp. 252–3, 371–2.
18. Knut Wicksell, *Interest and Prices* (1898). Reprint (New York: Augustus M. Kelley, 1965) pp. 157–8.
19. Knut Wicksell, *Lectures on Political Economy*, first published in Swedish, 1906. English trans. by E. Classen, edited by L. Robbins (London: Macmillan, 1934–5), vol. II, *Money*, pp. 97–8. On Wicksell's rejection of Say's law and other aspects of his monetary theory, see Bertil Ohlin, 'On the Slow Development of the "Total Demand" Idea in Economic Theory: Reflections in Connection with Dr Oppenheim-

er's Note', *Journal of Economic Literature*, vol. 12 (1974) pp. 888–9, 893–4.

20. Wicksell, 'International Freights and Prices', *Quarterly Journal of Economics*, vol. 32 (Feb. 1918) p. 405.
21. Frank W. Taussig, *International Trade* (New York: Macmillan, 1927) p. 37.
22. F. W. Taussig, *Principles of Economics* (New York: Macmillan, 1911) p. 458. Frank Taussig (1859–1940) was the Henry Lee Professor of Economics at Harvard and also editor of the *Quarterly Journal of Economics*.
23. Taussig's influence was widely felt in the United States – through his writings and his outstanding students. Frank Fetter writes: 'The familiarity of American economists with the specie-flow price-adjustment analysis and the belief that this was the accepted classical analysis . . . owes much to Taussig's influence.' See Frank W. Fetter, *The Development of British Monetary Orthodoxy, 1797–1875* (Cambridge, Mass.: Harvard Univ. Press, 1965) p. 228, note.
24. Taussig, *International Trade*, op. cit. p. 261.
25. For an excellent summary of the writings of members of the Harvard School, see Michael D. Bordo, 'The Gold Standard: The Traditional Approach', in M. D. Bordo and A. J. Schwartz, *A Retrospective on the Classical Gold Standard 1821–1931* (Chicago: Chicago Univ. Press, 1984) pp. 55–67. Apparently, it was Ohlin who first referred to them as the 'Harvard School'.
26. Jacob Viner, *Canada's Balance of International Indebtedness, 1900–1913: An Inductive Study in the Theory of International Trade* (Cambridge, Mass.: Harvard Univ. Press, 1924); reprinted by Porcupine, Philadelphia (1977). This was Viner's doctoral dissertation. Later in his *Studies* (1937) he said: 'I concluded that the Canadian mechanism corresponded in all of its important aspects to the mechanism as formulated in the classical doctrine', pp. 413–14. Taussig gave a summary of Viner's work in *International Trade*, op. cit. ch. 19.
27. Viner, ibid. p. 295. For the literature critical of Viner, see Gerald M. Meier, 'Economic Development and the Transfer Mechanism: Canada, 1895–1913', *Canadian Journal of Economics and Political Science*, vol. 19 (Feb. 1953) pp. 1–19; John A. Stovel, *Canada in the World Economy* (Cambridge, Mass.: Harvard Univ. Press, 1959). Commenting on Viner's study, Kindleberger recently observed that Viner's results did not satisfy 'the Dominion Statistician, R. H. Coats', and that Meier's results 'came out much closer to Coats, that is, maintaining that Canadian expansion in the West led simultaneously to an export surplus and borrowing in London, rather than borrowing to the expansion and then to the import surplus'. See Charles P. Kindleberger, *International Money: A Collection of Essays* (London: Allen & Unwin, 1981) pp. 285–6.
28. H. D. White, *The French International Accounts, 1880–1913* (Cambridge, Mass.: Harvard Univ. Press, 1933). The book was White's doctoral thesis for which he was awarded the David A. Wells Prize for 1931–2.

29. Harry G. Johnson, 'The Transfer Problem and Exchange Stability' (1956), reprinted in Johnson, *International Trade and Economic Growth* (London: Allen & Unwin, 1958) p. 169; John S. Chipman, 'The Transfer Problem Once Again', in G. Horwich and P. A. Samuelson (eds), *Trade, Stability and Macroeconomics: Essays in Honor of Lloyd Metzler* (New York: Academic Press, 1974) p. 19. Chipman's essay is an extensive reappraisal of the issues involved. Keynes (1929) introduced the phrase 'transfer problem' into the professional literature, but the term originated in the Report of the First Committee of Experts on Reparations (1924) – the committee under the chairmanship of General Charles G. Dawes (a Chicago banker, American ambassador to the UK and later Vice-President of the US) charged with responsibility for determining the magnitude of German reparations.
30. P. A. Samuelson, 'The Transfer Problem and Transport Costs: The Terms of Trade When Impediments are Absent', *Economic Journal*, vol. 62 (June 1952) pp. 278–304; *Collected Scientific Papers*, vol. 2, ch. 74. Idem. 'The Transfer Problem and Transport Costs, II: Analysis of Effects of Trade Impediments', loc. cit. vol. 64 (1954) pp. 264–89; *Collected Scientific Papers*, op. cit. ch. 75. Samuelson's first published comments on the problem were in his 1945 review of Jacob Mosak's *General Equilibrium Theory in International Trade* (1944). He agreed with Mosak's conclusion, stating: 'Absolutely no presumption in either direction seems indicated.' See Samuelson, *Collected Scientific Papers*, vol. 2, ch. 63. Samuelson's 'no presumption' case rests on the use of the exchange model – supply effects are impounded by the assumption that outputs do not respond to price changes. Hence, the effects of a transfer which disturb world markets for tradeables can be determined by examining the sign of world excess demand for either commodity at the initial terms of trade. In the 1954 paper, Samuelson does however find some support for the orthodox case when artificial impediments to trade (notably tariffs, but excluding monetary transport costs) are present.
31. See Samuelson, 'On the Trail of Conventional Beliefs About the Transfer Problem', in J. Bhagwati *et al.* (eds), *Trade, Balance of Payments and Growth* (1971), op. cit. pp. 327–51. Here, Samuelson seeks to redress the balance by explicitly incorporating supply responses, particularly in regard to a non-traded commodity (leisure). He had earlier indicated in his review of Mosak that 'there may be something after all in the orthodox position that terms of trade shift against the paying country', and referred to Mosak's consideration of production effects ('the relative substitutability and complementarity of domestic products and factors with the import and export goods of each country'). Op. cit. p. 944.
32. There was some uncertainty – perhaps there still is – as to what precisely was the classical position. Writing in 1931, Haberler referred to the 1917–18 debate between Taussig and J. H. Hollander, in which 'Taussig presented the Thornton–Mill version but was apparently of the opinion that he spoke in the vein of Ricardo', whilst Hollander 'took the orthodox Ricardian view, but believed that he was defending the generally recognized theory of the classics'. Haberler, 'Transfer and

Price Movements', in *Selected Essays of Gottfried Haberler*, op. cit. p. 134.

33. Adam Smith, *Wealth of Nations*, book IV, ch. 1. Quoted by J. S. Chipman in 'Balance of Payments Theory', loc. cit. pp. 194–5. Chipman points out that Smith does not actually state that the foreign expenditure will be equal to the export surplus, but it was an obvious inference that was subsequently drawn by King and Wheatley. Chipman, op. cit. p. 195.
34. P. King, *Thoughts on the Restriction of Payments in Specie at the Bank of England and Ireland* (London: T. Cadell and W. Davies, 1803). For Chipman's quote, see Chipman, op. cit. p. 202.
35. King, ibid. pp. 83–5. In the last sentence King obviously meant 'balance of payments' rather than 'balance of trade'; and furthermore, the argument implicitly assumes identical preferences and absence of transport costs. Without these assumptions, a change in the terms of trade might also have been required to restore equilibrium. See Chipman, op. cit. p. 203.
36. See, e.g. McCulloch's evidence in *Report from the Select Committee on the State of Ireland* (London, 1825) pp. 814–15.
37. Work cited. Reprinted, F. A. von Hayek (ed.) (London: Allen & Unwin, 1939) pp. 131, 139, 151, 156.
38. C. F. Bastable, 'On Some Applications of the Theory of International Trade', *Quarterly Journal of Economics*, vol. 4 (Oct. 1889) p. 15.
39. Bastable, ibid. p. 16.
40. J. Shield Nicholson, *Principles of Political Economy*, vol. II, op. cit. pp. 287–91.
41. Nicholson, ibid. p. 290.
42. A. C. Pigou, 'The Effect of Reparations on the Real Ratio of International Interchange', *Economic Journal*, vol. 42 (Dec. 1932) pp. 532–43.
43. Lloyd A. Metzler, 'The Theory of International Trade' (1948), loc. cit. p. 218. Metzler himself in a series of papers between 1942 and 1973 analysed the transfer problem in terms of endogenous income and expenditure effects (on the assumption of constant prices). See, e.g. idem. 'The Transfer Problem Reconsidered', *Journal of Political Economy*, vol. 50, no. 3 (June 1942) pp. 397–414.
44. See B. Ohlin, 'The Reparations Problem', in *Index*, no. 28 (April 1928) published by Svenska Handelsbanken, Stockholm, pp. 2–33; Ohlin, 'Transfer Difficulties, Real and Imagined', *Economic Journal*, vol. 39 (June 1929) pp. 172–8; idem. 'A Rejoinder', *Economic Journal* (Sept. 1929) pp. 400–4.
45. C.-Y. Wu wrote: 'The doctrine of adjustment of the balance of payments through changes in the demand schedules . . . found one of its best presentations in Wicksell's *Lectures* . . . Wicksell's statement is so excellent that we have associated the doctrine with his name.' Wu, op. cit. p. 279.
46. In 1925, Graham analysed the transfer problem along lines essentially similar to those adopted by Ohlin later – particularly the examination of the role of price changes of tradeable and non-tradeable commodities

and the consequent shift in output (resource reallocation) between these sectors without causing any movement of the terms of trade. See F. D. Graham, 'Germany's Capacity to Pay and the Reparation Plan', *American Economic Review*, vol. 15 (June 1925) pp. 209–27.

47. J. M. Keynes, 'The German Transfer Problem', *Economic Journal*, vol. 39 (March 1929) pp. 1–7; ibid. June 1929, pp. 179–82; ibid. Sept. 1929, pp. 404–8.

48. Keynes, in *Economic Journal*, March 1929, p. 6. Keynes's pessimism concerning the ability of the Germans to turn around their balance of payments from deficit to surplus was also challenged at the time by Fritz Machlup. Even as Keynes was writing, the deficit had disappeared under the pressure of capital flows and domestic monetary adjustments. In 1927 the German trade balance deficit was RM 2847m, which gave way to a small surplus of RM 36m in 1929. See Machlup's reminiscences in Fritz Machlup, 'My Early Work on International Monetary Problems' (1980), loc. cit. pp. 126–31. For an early commentary on the Keynes–Ohlin debate, see Haberler, 'Transfer and Price Movements' (1931), loc. cit. pp. 133–42. According to Samuelson: 'What led to Keynes's exaggerations [of the inability of Germany to pay reparations] was an undue reliance on the classical economists he was later to caricature: J. S. Mill and Alfred Marshall had not really mastered their basic foreign-trade theory.' Samuelson, 'The Keynes Centenary' (1983), in *Collected Scientific Papers*, vol. 5, op. cit. p. 275.

During the Second World War it was believed that Keynes's rhetorical bluster against reparations and his denunciation of the Versailles peace settlement (as in his bestseller, *The Economic Consequences of the Peace*) fuelled German resentment. The controversy he raised, it was alleged, was to some extent responsible for the rise of Hitler – an opinion some modern historians share. See D. E. Moggridge, *Keynes* (London: Macmillan, 1976) pp. 59–62, for some comments.

49. See Samuelson, 'Bertil Ohlin 1899–1979', loc. cit. p. 158. Many economists are inclined to believe Friedrich von Hayek, an early sparring partner of Keynes and one who knew him well. Hayek wrote: 'I have reason to doubt whether he [Keynes] ever fully mastered the theory of international trade.' F. A. Hayek, *New Studies in Philosophy, Politics, Economics and the History of Ideas* (London: Routledge & Kegan Paul, 1978) p. 285.

50. H. S. Ellis and L. A. Metzler, 'Introduction', in *Readings in the Theory of International Trade* (1950), op. cit. pp. x–xi. Earlier, Samuelson had the same impression: 'Here, for once, Keynes seemed to be in the uncharacteristic position of siding with the classical camp . . . with such orthodox stalwarts as Pigou and Taussig.' Samuelson's (1945) review of Mosak's *General Equilibrium Theory in International Trade*, loc. cit. p. 943. Samuelson went on to express his surprise 'that Keynes, who has recently placed so much emphasis on income effects, should have left their elucidation to Ohlin', ibid. p. 944. In his obituary tribute to Ohlin, Otto Steiger explained that the pioneering distinction between national income and aggregate spending was one 'which Keynes at that time quite failed to grasp'. Otto Steiger, 'Bertil Ohlin, 1899–1979', loc. cit. p.

182. In a recent exposition of the transfer problem (treated mathematically and considering general cases), Chipman concluded that the debate between Keynes and Ohlin was 'really a dispute . . . as to whether the production-possibility surface was or was not strictly concave to the origin'. John S. Chipman, 'International Trade', in *The New Palgrave: A Dictionary of Economics* (1987), op. cit. p. 945.

51. Whereas in 1914 Europe had 10 currencies all with fixed gold parities and fixed exchange rates, in 1920 there were 27 paper currencies, none with a gold parity, i.e. all floating.

52. The calling of the Conference was really a British initiative, fully supported by Lloyd George. The preliminary ideas and agenda stemmed from a speech (later published) before the British Association by Ralph Hawtrey, Director of Financial Enquiries at the Treasury, in September 1919, urging adoption of the gold-exchange standard. This scheme, together with certain proposals by Keynes on exchange stabilisation, were put to the Conference by the British delegation. By relieving the strain on Britain's slender gold reserves and increasing the demand for sterling, the gold-exchange scheme would have eased Britain's planned return to the gold standard at the pre-war parity. France, Belgium and Italy saw the British proposals as an attempt to force devaluation on their countries while Britain pursued a deflationary policy. The principle was, however, generally supported by the Conference – it adopted the twelve 'Currency Resolutions', several of which recommended the gold-exchange standard (e.g. legislation designed to allow central banks to create domestic liabilities against foreign-currency assets convertible into gold). The gold-exchange standard was not a new development. It functioned (even before 1914) in the Dutch East Indies, Holland, Japan, Austria-Hungary, India, the Philippines, Panama, and several South American countries. For Hawtrey's article, see R. G. Hawtrey, 'The Gold Standard', *Economic Journal*, vol. 29 (1919) pp. 428–42. For the British Treasury's proposals, see 'Draft Proposals for an International Gold Standard', Treasury Memorandum to Foreign Office, 10 April 1922, PRO 371/7427.

53. As a measure of the rapid development of the gold-exchange standard and success in economising on gold, consider that already in 1927 foreign exchange holdings accounted for 42 per cent of the total reserves of twenty-five European central banks, compared with 27 per cent in 1924. In 1928, foreign currency amounted to 45 per cent of France's official reserves. In 1932, Karl Blessing (late Governor of the Deutsche Bundesbank) calculated that the foreign exchange holdings of European central banks 'in the years 1928 to 1930 amounted to 8 to 10 times the volume of the years immediately preceding the war'. Karl Blessing, 'The Gold Exchange Standard', Bank for International Settlements (BIS), C.B. 60, 1932, p. 10. With such a large ratio of foreign exchange to total international reserves, the new system was extremely vulnerable to shifts in the composition of reserves brought about by the decisions of non-centre countries – the gold reserves of a 'key currency' country could be rapidly depleted by the conversion of a non-centre country's foreign-exchange balances into gold, as happened after 1928.

54. The stabilisation of the franc on 25 June 1928 at a value of 25.51 francs to the dollar or 3.92 cents per franc, instead of the prewar parity of 19.30 cents, undervalued the franc relative to its purcashing power and enabled France to draw gold away from the United States and Britain. Under the impact of a strong balance of payments through capital inflows, repatriation of French capital on a large scale and a favourable current-account balance, France was overwhelmed by a 'golden avalanche' in the late 1920s. French gold reserves went up from $0.7 billion in January 1927 to $2.3 billion in August 1931. The gold accumulation by the Banque de France led to monetary stringency in the United States and deflationary pressure in Great Britain. Britain's gold reserves were almost depleted. The panic that began with the collapse of the Kredit-Anstalt in May 1931 threatened to wipe out what remained of Britain's reserves.
55. Committee on Currency and Foreign Exchanges after the War, *First Interim Report* (London: HMSO, 1918). Reprint (New York: Arno Press, 1979). The Committee's chairman was Lord Cunliffe, then Governor of the Bank of England. The Committee recommended various steps which had to be taken on the road to Britain's eventual return to the gold standard at the prewar parity of £3. 17s 10½d per fine ounce of gold (or $4.86 per £). Much of the Report was drafted by Ralph Hawtrey.
56. The problems associated with the interwar gold-exchange standard were highlighted both before and after its collapse in 1931. When the system was again adopted after the Second World War the same misgivings were voiced in the 1960s about the unviability of a system based on the use of a national currency as an international reserve asset or 'parallel' world currency. The interwar critics included the Gold Delegation of the League of Nations, Gustav Cassel and Fritz Machlup. In the postwar period, the warnings were reiterated by Jacques Rueff and Robert Triffin, among others. Kindleberger, however, rejects these criticisms, arguing that the gold-exchange system is an evolutionary creation stemming from the natural impulse towards greater international financial intermediation. The instability of the gold-exchange standard, he says, 'is part of the instability of money in general, resting on Gresham's law . . . Do not blame the gold-exchange standard; blame money.' See Charles P. Kindleberger, *A Financial History of Western Europe* (London: Allen & Unwin, 1984) p. 360; see also Kindleberger, *International Money*, op. cit. pp. 287–9. Triffin has recently repeated his warnings in 'The IMS (International Monetary System . . . or Scandal) and the EMS (European Monetary System)', *Banca Nazionale del Lavoro Quarterly Review*, no. 162 (Sept. 1987) pp. 239–61.
57. The phrases 'rules of the game' or 'rules of the gold standard' were apparently first used by Keynes in the early 1920s. Following the rules, in Keynes's sense, meant reinforcing the money-supply changes resulting from reserve flows so as to maintain a stable ratio between the central bank's gold reserves and monetary liabilities. In modern literature, it is often used to refer to a situation where the central bank merely refrains from 'sterilisation', i.e. the bank does not offset the

impact of reserve flows through open-market operations. See Arthur Bloomfield, *Monetary Policy under the International Gold Standard, 1880–1914* (New York: Federal Reserve Bank of New York, 1959) p. 47. It was the 'discovery' of the technique of open-market operations by the Federal Reserve Board which allowed Benjamin Strong, Governor of the Federal Reserve Bank of New York, to initiate his policy of sterilisation in the early 1920s which resulted in a rise of the proportion of gold to notes and deposits to the abnormally high level of 70 to 80 per cent.

58. Gustav Cassel, *The Downfall of the Gold Standard* (Oxford: Clarendon Press, 1935) p. 3.

   Opinion on the issue concerning the extent to which central banks followed the 'rules of the game' under the pre-1914 gold standard, was much influenced by Bloomfield's 1959 evidence that central banks did not follow the 'rules' at all times and consequently the actions of such banks were discretionary, not automatic. This opinion has recently been challenged by Sommariva and Tullio in respect of the actions of the Reichsbank. On the basis of an econometric test in the spirit of the modern monetary approach to the balance of payments, the authors find that the negative correlation between changes in domestic assets and foreign assets of the Reichsbank (gold flows) observed by Bloomfield had 'not much to do with whether the Reichsbank was observing the rules of the game or not'. Causation was probably bi-directional, and indeed they find that the 'direction of causation was mostly from domestic assets to foreign assets as predicted by the monetary approach to the balance of payments . . . rather than the reverse as implied by Bloomfield'. See Andrea Sommariva and Giuseppe Tullio, *German Macroeconomic History 1880–1979 – A Study of the Effects of Economic Policy on Inflation, Currency Depreciation and Economic Growth* (London: Macmillan, 1987) p. 4 and ch. 2. See also idem. 'International Gold Flows in Gold Standard Germany: A Test of the Monetary Approach to the Balance of Payments, 1880–1911', *Journal of Money, Credit, and Banking*, vol. 20, no. 1 (Feb. 1988) pp. 132–40.

59. J. Robinson, 'The Need for a Reconsideration of the Theory of International Trade' (1973), loc. cit. p. 20.
60. Cassel, op. cit. p. 4.
61. J. Viner, 'International Aspects of the Gold Standard', in Q. Wright (ed.), *Gold and Monetary Stabilization* (Chicago: Chicago Univ. Press, 1932) p. 9. Referring to the gold discoveries in the 1850s and 1890s Viner remarked that the gold standard 'was able successfully to invoke miracles to keep the breath of life in it'. The discoveries and improved processes of extracting gold 'came to the rescue of the threatened gold standard at the exact melodramatic moments'. Viner, *International Economics* (1951), op. cit. p. 136.
62. J. M. Keynes, *A Tract on Monetary Reform* (1923), in vol. 4, *The Collected Writings of John Maynard Keynes* (London: Macmillan, 1971) p. 138.
63. Jacob Viner, 'Gold and Monetary Stabilization', Harris Foundation

Lecture, 1932. Reprinted in his *International Economics*, op. cit. p. 138.

64. P. Barrett Whale, 'The Working of the Pre-war Gold Standard', *Economica*, vol. 4 (Feb. 1937) pp. 28–9.
65. For a brief doctrinal history of PPP, see Jacob Frenkel, 'Purchasing Power Parity: Doctrinal Perspectives and Evidence from the 1920s', *Journal of International Economics*, vol. 8 (May 1978) pp. 169–91. A more extensive treatment is given in Thomas M. Humphrey and Robert E. Keleher, *The Monetary Approach to the Balance of Payments, Exchange Rates, and World Inflation* (New York: Praeger, 1982) ch. 11, pp. 310–41. An excellent survey of the PPP literature is provided by Lawrence Officer, in 'The Purchasing-Power Parity Theory of Exchange Rates; A Review Article', *IMF Staff Papers*, vol. 23, no. 1 (March 1976) pp. 1–60. The entire May 1978 issue of the *Journal of International Economics* was devoted to the controversy surrounding PPP. Student needs are well served by Rudiger Dornbusch's first-class critical exposition in *The New Palgrave: A Dictionary of Economics*, op. cit. pp. 1075–84.
66. Cassel's development of the PPP doctrine (the inflation theory of exchange rates) is contained in several books and papers starting as early as 1916. The main sources are: G. Cassel, 'The Present Situation of the Foreign Exchanges', *Economic Journal*, vol. 26 (March, Sept. 1916) pp. 62–5, 319–23; Cassel, 'Abnormal Deviations in the International Exchanges', *Economic Journal*, vol. 28 (Dec. 1918) pp. 413–15; Cassel, *The World's Monetary Problems: Two Memoranda* (London: Constable, 1921). A useful summary of Cassel's theory is to be found in James M. Holmes, 'The Purchasing-Power Parity Theory: In Defense of Gustav Cassel as a Modern Theorist', *Journal of Political Economy*, vol. 75 (Oct. 1967) pp. 686–95.
67. See L. B. Yeager, 'A Rehabilitation of Purchasing Power Parity', *Journal of Political Economy*, vol. 66 (1958) pp. 516–30; H. S. Houthakker, 'Exchange Rate Adjustment', in *Factors Affecting the United States Balance of Payments*, Joint Economic Committee, 87th Congress (Washington, D.C.: Government Printing Office, 1962) pp. 287–304; B. Balassa, 'The Purchasing Power Parity Doctrine: A Reappraisal', *Journal of Political Economy*, vol. 72, no. 6 (Dec. 1964) pp. 584–96; P. A. Samuelson, 'Theoretical Notes on Trade Problems', *Review of Economics and Statistics*, vol. 46, no. 2 (1964) pp. 145–54.

    Writing in 1958, Sir John Hicks referred to PPP as 'a theory which, in the view of many modern economists, is quite discredited'. J. R. Hicks, *Essays in World Economics* (Oxford: Clarendon Press, 1959) p. 127.
68. Denis O'Brien follows Viner in claiming that 'the classical economists showed good sense in not advancing Purchasing Power Parity as a theory, for it is only roughly true, due to the importance of non-traded goods and of capital movements'. D. P. O'Brien, 'A. Marshall, 1842–1924', in D. P. O'Brien and John R. Presley (eds), *Pioneers of Modern Economics in Britain* (London: Macmillan, 1981) p. 59. In classical (Ricardian) theory, non-traded or domestic goods and capital movements were ruled out by assumption, so these could hardly have given cause for rejecting PPP on theoretical grounds; but in any case the

adherence of the classical economists (Ricardo, Thornton, Wheatley, Blake) to the doctrine has been amply documented by a long list of experts in the field, notably Angell, Bresciani-Turroni, Einzig and Haberler. Keynes, indeed, credits Ricardo with invention of the doctrine and Cassel with the name-giving. Viner's explanation for the classical economists' lack of interest in PPP was that they had little understanding of the notion of a statistical average of prices (or general price level). Haberler finds this quite unconvincing: 'one can have a clear idea of a phenomenon before it has been measured, and one can vaguely refer to something before anyone has given a precise definition'. See *Selected Essays of Gottfried Haberler* (1985), op. cit. p. 90. Humphrey and Keleher, op. cit. pp. 317–27, document in detail classical interpretations of the doctrine, and Jürg Niehans writes that PPP's 'basic idea goes back at least to the Ricardian period'. Jürg Niehans, 'Purchasing-Power Parity under Flexible Rates', in P. Oppenheimer (ed.), *Issues in International Economics* (1980), op. cit. p. 255. Bernholz traces the idea back more than four centuries. See Peter Bernholz, *Flexible Exchange Rates in Historical Perspective*, Princeton Studies in International Finance, no. 49 (Princeton, N.J.: Princeton Univ. Press, 1982). See also Leonard Gomes, *Foreign Trade and the National Economy* (1987), op. cit. pp. 105–6.

Undoubtedly, some earlier writers confused PPP with the 'law of one price', but evidently this was not the case with Martin de Azpilcueta (Navarro) of the School of Salamanca, whose 1556 remarks, according to Bergstrand, 'capture the essence of the PPP doctrine'. Jeffrey H. Bergstrand, 'Selected Views of Exchange Rate Determination After a Decade of "Floating"', *New England Economic Review*, May/June 1983, Federal Reserve Bank of Boston, p. 17. Niehans, however, credits Pehr Niclas Christiernin, a Swedish economist at the University of Uppsala, with 'the first statement of the open-economy corollary of the quantity theory, namely, purchasing-power parity' in 1761. Jürg Niehans, 'Classical Monetary Theory, New and Old', *Journal of Money, Credit and Banking*, vol. 19, no. 4 (Nov. 1987) p. 414, n. 5.

69. R. Dornbusch and P. Krugman, 'Flexible Exchange Rates in the Short Run', *Brookings Papers on Economic Activity*, no. 3, 1976, p. 540. Leland B. Yeager, 'The Image of the Gold Standard', in M. D. Bordo and A. J. Schwartz, *A Retrospective on the Classical Gold Standard*, op. cit. p. 659.
70. This conclusion follows from the monetarist approach which claims that the exchange rate, being an essentially monetary phenomenon, can affect only 'money things' – the general price level – and cannot permanently change the underlying real phenomena such as the trade balance or the terms of trade. This claim is reinforced by the operation of international commodity arbitrage. However, this is not to deny that in the short run exchange rate changes do have significant effects on relative commodity prices or that relative price changes affect the balance of payments. See W. Robinson, T. R. Webb and M. A. Townsend, 'The Influence of Exchange Rate Changes on Prices: A Study of 18 Industrial Countries', *Economica* (Feb. 1979) pp. 27–50, for results

(relating to OECD countries during the 1960s and 1970s) which suggest that 'parity changes have a larger and quicker effect on the rate of inflation than they used to have, and a smaller effect on "real" variables such as the terms of trade, the balance of payments or the rate of growth', ibid. p. 48.

71. Formally, this law requires that for a given product, the elasticity of the domestic price with respect to both the exchange rate and foreign prices of the same product be unity. Put another way, it means that except for differences in transfer costs, the price – e.g. of a ton of steel rebars or a bushel of wheat – is about the same in New York, London, Tokyo or Amsterdam, using any currency as numéraire. Two conditions are necessary for the operation of the law: perfect commodity arbitrage, coupled with perfect substitutability. Several studies have revealed, however, that only few industries (and products) even at very fine levels of disaggregation – four-digit and above – have pricing behaviour that conforms to the law. The reasons for the departures from the law of one price, apart from transport costs and trade barriers, are: information costs, price discrimination in international trade, different commodity composition of the price indices, contract prices that differ from recorded prices, and product differentiation. As Frank Hahn recently observed: 'We ought to distinguish English tweed from tweed.' F. H. Hahn, 'Monetarism and Economic Theory', *Economica*, vol. 47 (Feb. 1980) p. 15.
72. The OPTICA (Optimum Currency Area) Report referred to is contained in Commission of the European Communities, *Inflation and Exchange Rates: Evidence and Policy Guidelines for the European Communities*, OPTICA Report II (Brussels: Feb. 1977). For theoretical analyses and discussion of the OPTICA proposals, see M. Fratianni and T. Peeters, *One Money for Europe* (London: Macmillan, 1978) especially ch. 7. The Report argued that changes in exchange rates among EEC countries during the early 1960s and mid-1970s predominantly reflected inflation differentials.
73. See I. B. Kravis, A. W. Heston and R. Summers, 'Real GDP Per Capita For More Than One Hundred Countries', *Economic Journal*, vol. 88 (1978) pp. 215–42.
74. Rudiger Dornbusch, *Dollars, Debts and Deficits* (Cambridge, Mass.: Leuven Univ. Press and MIT Press, 1986) p. 4.
75. G. Haberler, 'The International Monetary System in the World Recession' (1984), in *Selected Essays of Gottfried Haberler*, op. cit. p. 257.
76. Fritz Machlup, 'My Early Work on International Monetary Problems', loc. cit. p. 119. Adherents of the balance-of-payments theory included Karl Helfferich (German finance minister during the war), Othmar Spann (Machlup's dissertation supervisor), and the postwar president of the Reichsbank, Rudolf Havenstein. For a thorough modern study of the German inflation, see Carl-Ludwig Holtfrerich, *Die deutsche Inflation, 1914–1923* (Berlin: Walter de Gruyter, 1980).

    In his penetrating contemporary study of the German hyperinflation, Bresciani-Turroni maintained: 'During the months following the end of the war, the government budget deficit remained the primary cause of the increase in issues of paper money and the devaluation of the exchange rate.' See C. Bresciani-Turroni, *The Economics of Inflation: A Study of Currency Depreciation in Post-war Germany* (London: Allen & Unwin, 1937), quoted in Andrea Sommariva and Giuseppe Tullio, *German Macroeconomic History 1880–1979*, op. cit. p. 143. The latter book maintains Bresciani-Turroni's thesis using modern econometric techniques. The payment of reparations had nothing to do with the German hyperinflation: 'Between 1921 and 1923 hardly any reparations were paid by Germany. What is true *is* that the Germans made the depreciation of the Mark the excuse for not paying.' See Sefton Delmar, *Weimar Germany: Democracy on Trial* (London: Macdonald/American Heritage, 1972) p. 73. Inflation further accelerated when the Weimar government resorted to the printing press in order to finance the policy of passive resistance (the payment of strike money to German workers that were financed by discounting Treasury Bills with the Reichsbank) in the face of the Franco-Belgian military occupation of the Ruhr in January 1923. The objective of the Allied occupation was to force Germany to comply with the reparations settlement. It is generally believed that the hyperinflation was deliberately induced in order to discredit the reparations settlement.

77. G. Cassell, *Money and Foreign Exchange after 1914* (New York: Macmillan, 1922) p. 175.
78. Cassel, *The World's Monetary Problems* (London: Constable, 1921) p. 38.
79. Typically, PPP calculations were done after a particular mint parity had been decided upon by the authorities. The calculations often involved comparisons of wholesale price indices – an inappropriate choice since such indices are heavily weighted with internationally traded goods, the prices of which are constantly kept in line (through arbitrage) with the exchange rate. Thus at the time of Britain's 1925 return to gold at the prewar parity, relative wholesale prices indicated an overvaluation of only 3 per cent – one such calculation was made by Professor T. E. Gregory (later Sir Theodore Gregory). Keynes objected to this method of doing the sums, and claimed, on the basis of broader retail price indices (albeit his foreign index of retail prices was for the Commonwealth of Massachusetts not for the USA; his domestic index was the Ministry of Labour cost-of-living index), that sterling was overvalued by around 10 per cent. Commenting on this discrepancy in 1960, R. S. Sayers wrote: 'Keynes used the wrong index numbers and Gregory the right, yet Keynes got the right result and Gregory the wrong. So much for Purchasing Power Parity as an aid to policy!' Capie and Wood query this deduction: 'What that means is obscure – in what sense was Keynes's answer "right"?' They did not answer the question themselves, but suggested instead that Sayers's remark was inconsistent with his analysis which ascribed Britain's interwar economic difficulties to factors other than the choice of parity. Technically, Keynes's answer was right simply because he used the appropriate indices. Measures such as relative GDP deflators and consumer price indices indeed suggest that sterling overvaluation was about 11–14 per cent in 1925.

Forrest H. Capie and Geoffrey E. Wood, 'Policy Makers in Crisis: A Study of Two Devaluations', in Donald R. Hodgman and Geoffrey E. Wood (eds), *Monetary and Exchange Rate Policy* (London: Macmillan, 1987), p. 187; also for the reference to Sayers.

80. P. A. Samuelson, 'Disparity in Postwar Exchange Rates', in Seymour Harris (ed.), *Foreign Economic Policy for the United States* (Cambridge, Mass.: Harvard Univ. Press, 1948) p. 397.
81. Samuelson, Forewords to the Japanese Edition of *The Collected Scientific Papers of Paul A. Samuelson*, in *Collected Scientific Papers*, vol. 5, op. cit. p. 864.
82. Michel Chevalier, *Cours d'économie politique*, vol. 3, *La Monnaie* (1850) 2nd edn (Paris: Capelle, 1866) p. 653.
83. League of Nations, International Financial Conference, Brussels, *Verbatim Record of the Debates*, L. Delacroix's remarks, 1 October 1920, p. 112.
84. See Dan P. Silverman, *Reconstructing Europe After the Great War* (Cambridge, Mass.: Harvard Univ. Press, 1982) pp. 282–3.
85. See Silverman, op. cit. p. 283; Bertrand Nogaro, 'Une banque d'émission internationale: Le project Vanderlip', *Revue économique internationale* (1922 – I) pp. 147–56.
86. J. M. Keynes, *A Treatise on Money*, vol. II, *The Applied Theory of Money* (London: Macmillan, 1930). Keynes referred to the bank as 'the Supernational Bank', one 'to which the Central Banks of the world would stand in much the same relation as their own member banks stand to them'. Ibid. p. 399. The deposit liabilities of the Bank, called supernational bank money (S.B.M.), would be fully convertible into gold. Earlier, Keynes made proposals for reform of the international monetary system at the time of the Genoa Conference, 1922, and later on the occasion of the World Economic Conference, London 1933. His final effort was, of course, the International Clearing Union plan drawn up during the Second World War – stimulated initially by Hitler's 'New Order', in particular the need to counter the Nazi propaganda of Dr Walther Funk, banker and finance minister. On Keynes's proposals for Genoa, see 'The Genoa Conference', ch. 16 in *The Collected Writings of John Maynard Keynes*, op. cit. vol. XVII, pp. 354–69. For his 1933 proposals, see ibid. vol. IX, part vi, ch. 1. Keynes's Clearing Union plan, originally published as a British Government White Paper in 1943 (Cmd 6437, April 1943), is reprinted in A. P. Thirlwall (ed.), *Keynes and Economic Development* (London: Macmillan, 1987) pp. 147–78.
87. Keynes, *A Tract of Monetary Reform* (London: Macmillan, 1923) pp. 135, 154–8. Keynes was in fact one of the first to recommend official intervention in the forward exchange market as a means of controlling short-term capital movements without changing Bank rate or other short-term interest rates. This he did in connection with his pioneering exposition of the interest parity theorem. The proposal to manipulate the gold points, i.e. to create an artificial spread of about 2 per cent between the official buying and and selling price of gold, was designed to complement the technique of forward market intervention.

    In his 1922 Genoa proposals, whilst Keynes still recommended restoration of the gold standard (in its gold-bullion form) – 'I see no other solution of stabilisation practicable now, except this traditional solution – namely, a gold standard in as many countries as possible' – he guardedly pointed out that the way could best be approached through limited exchange-rate flexibility, a wider band (5 per cent) between the buying and selling prices of gold coupled with a crawling peg for currencies which had depreciated by less than 20 per cent.

88. Ragnar Nurkse compiled the classic record of the interwar experience in his *International Currency Experience – Lessons of the Interwar Period* (Geneva: League of Nations, 1944). In the 1930s there were 'dirty floats', and in the 1920s exchange rates were often moved under the influence of speculation in ways incompatible with fundamentals – thus aggravating the problem of domestic stabilisation. The basic trouble with the international monetary system during the Depression, according to Nurkse, was the complete lack of coordination of national policies of expansion. Nurkse came out in favour of fixed exchange rates, and his work is often cited as the source of the antipathy to exchange-rate flexibility amongst Bretton Woods planners; but the Nurkse report appeared too late for it to have had any influence on the discussions.
89. See Sir John Hicks, 'Keynes and the World Economy', in Fausto Vicarelli (ed.), *Keynes's Relevance Today* (London: Macmillan, 1985) pp. 21–7. There is still, of course, argument in the interpretative literature on Keynes as to whether he did in fact assume rigidity of nominal wages or even of downward inflexibility of money wage-rates. For instance, Kaldor said, 'Keynes never assumed wage rigidity – Chapter 19 of *General Theory* is devoted to changes in money wages.' Lord Kaldor, 'Keynesian Economics after Fifty Years', in D. Worswick and J. Trevithick (eds), *Keynes and the Modern World: Proceedings of the Keynes Centenary Conference* (Cambridge: Cambridge Univ. Press, 1983) p. 46. The wage-floor assumption is, however, widely attributed to Keynes (e.g. as a reason why labour markets are not always cleared by wages). He himself did present it as an empirical generalisation and attempted in the *General Theory* to give the assumption some behavioural (theoretical) justification. Nevertheless, Keynes's theory of unemployment does not depend on the assumption.
90. See Hicks's Presidential Address to the British Association (Sept. 1955), 'Economic Foundations of Wage Policy', reprinted in idem. *Essays in World Economics* (1959), op. cit. pp. 85–104.
91. Well-known explanations or suggestions about Keynes's conduct have been offered by Sir Roy Harrod, Lord Balogh, Lord Kahn, Sir George Bolton and John Williamson. See J. Williamson, 'Keynes and the International Economic Order', in Worswick and Trevithick (eds), op. cit. pp. 101–3, for a review of the various opinions; also James R. Crotty, 'On Keynes and Capital Flight', *Journal of Economic Literature*, vol. 21 (March 1983) pp. 63–5.
92. In *Economic Journal*, June 1946, p. 186.
93. Keynes, *Treatise on Money*, vol. II, op. cit. p. 402. Whatever it was that wrecked the Bretton Woods system – US deficits, disequilibrating

short-term capital flows, excessive exchange-rate rigidity – authoritative commentators believe Keynes has something to teach us. Sir John Hicks finds it in the warning to avoid 'excessive rigidity' in the design of a monetary constitution – 'it must not be too rigid as to be unworkable'. John Williamson declares, 'there is . . . a great deal that we can and should learn from Keynes about how to go about reconstructing a more ordered international system'. See Hicks (1985), op. cit. p. 27; and J. Williamson, 'Keynes and the Postwar International Economic Order', in H. L. Wattell (ed.), *The Policy Consequences of John Maynard Keynes* (London: Macmillan, 1985) p. 156.

94. Machlup's article 'The Theory of Foreign Exchange' appeared in *Economica*, New Series vol. 6 (1939) pp. 375–97, and in vol. 7 (1940) pp. 23–49. Reprinted in Fritz Machlup, *International Monetary Economics* (London: Allen & Unwin, 1966) ch. 1, pp. 7–50. Haberler developed the analysis in 1949 – see his article, 'The Market for Foreign Exchange and the Stability of the Balance of Payments: A Theoretical Analysis', *Kyklos*, vol. 3 (1949) pp. 193–218, reprinted in Koo (ed.), *Selected Essays of Gottfried Haberler*, op. cit. pp. 143–65.
95. Bickerdike's contribution to the theory of foreign exchange was first noticed by Lloyd Metzler in 1948 – see n. 96 p. 218 above. The reference was to Bickerdike's article 'The Instability of Foreign Exchange' (1920), loc. cit. pp. 118–22. The Foreign Exchanges', in *Essays in the Theory of Employment* (London: Macmillan, 1937) pp. 183–228; A. J. Brown, 'Trade Balances and Exchange Stability', *Oxford Economic Papers*, vol. 6 (April 1942) pp. 57–76; Lloyd Metzler, op. cit. pp. 225–8.
96. In Albert O. Hirschman, 'Devaluation and the Trade Balance: A Note', *Review of Economics and Statistics*, vol. 31 (Feb. 1949) p. 52.
97. Fritz Machlup, 'Elasticity Pessimism in International Trade' (1950), in Machlup, *International Monetary Economics* (1966), op. cit. p. 55.
98. Mundell, 'Abba Lerner on the Theory of Foreign Trade', loc. cit. p. 145.
99. John S. Chipman, 'A Reconsideration of the "Elasticity Approach" to Balance-of-Payments Adjustment Problems', in Jacob S. Dreyer (ed.), *Breadth and Depth in Economics: Fritz Machlup – The Man and His Ideas* (Lexington, Mass.: Heath & Co., 1978) pp. 49–85.
100. Haberler, in Koo (ed.), op. cit. p. 157. In a recent tribute to Haberler, Bhagwati and Chipman noted that Haberler was 'one of the earliest to perceive and stress the importance of monetary considerations in balance-of-payments adjustments . . . long before the "monetary approach" had become so fashionable'. See 'Salute to Gottfried Haberler on the Occasion of his 80th Birthday', *Journal of International Economics*, vol. 10 (1980) p. 316.
101. Fritz Machlup, 'My Early Work on International Monetary Problems' (1980), loc. cit. p. 137.
102. See Ronald I. McKinnon, 'The Exchange Rate and Macroeconomic Policy: Changing Postwar Perceptions', *Journal of Economic Literature*, vol. 19 (June 1981) p. 531.
103. Machlup, 'My Early Work', loc. cit. p. 137.

104. S. S. Alexander, 'Effects of a Devaluation on a Trade Balance', IMF *Staff Papers*, vol. 2 (April 1952) pp. 263–78. An earlier attempt to deal with endogenous changes in absorption and to show how absorption adjusts automatically to an exchange-rate change – the Laursen–Metzler effect – was the article by Svend Laursen and Lloyd A. Metzler, 'Flexible Exchange Rates and the Theory of Employment', *Review of Economics and Statistics*, vol. 32 (Nov. 1950) pp. 281–99. In addition, note that even Metzler with his strong Keynesian perspective gave an account of international adjustment (under conditions of full employment) which assigned an important role to the monetary sector, essentially similar to the Mundellian approach. See Metzler, 'The Process of International Adjustment under Conditions of Full Employment: A Keynesian View' (1960), reprinted in Caves and Johnson, *Readings in International Economics* (1968), op. cit. pp. 465–86.

105. See Harry G. Johnson, 'Towards a General Theory of the Balance of Payments', in Johnson, *International Trade and Economic Growth* (1958), op. cit. p. 165.

Tony Thirlwall, an early critic of the monetary approach, recently remarked: 'In the absorption approach to the balance of payments are clearly the seeds of the so-called monetary approach which sprang up in the 1960s as part of the monetarist anti-Keynesian revival, but which has since died a slow death.' See A. P. Thirlwall, 'What is Wrong with Balance of Payments Adjustment Theory?', *The Royal Bank of Scotland Review*, no. 157 (March 1988) p. 10.

106. James E. Meade, *The Balance of Payments* (London: Oxford Univ. Press, 1951) pts I–IV. Tinbergen's work is *On the Theory of Economic Policy* (Amsterdam: North-Holland, 1952). In his review of the development of trade theory between 1949 and 1965, Max Corden referred to Meade's work as 'the most important contribution to international trade theory published during the period under review'. See W. M. Corden, *Recent Developments in the Theory of International Trade* (Princeton: Princeton Univ. Press, 1965) p. 10. In the early 1960s several writers, mainly Australian, popularised Meade's synthesis in diagrams: e.g. T. W. Swan, 'Economic Growth in a Dependent Economy', *Economic Record* (Mar. 1960); Swan, 'Longer-Run Problems of the Balance of Payments', in H. W. Arndt and W. M. Corden (eds), *The Australian Economy* (Melbourne: Cheshire, 1963); W. M. Corden, 'The Geometric Representation of Policies to Atttain Internal and External Balance', *Review of Economic Studies*, vol. 28 (Oct. 1960) pp. 1–22.

107. See H. G. Johnson, 'Towards a General Theory of the Balance of Payments', loc. cit. pp. 153–68.

108. Nevertheless, as Kenen and Allen recognise, 'Meade was among the first to warn that a devaluation cannot improve the balance of payments of a fully employed economy if the government does not engineer a reduction in absorption or if labour will not countenance a cut in the real wage.' See Polly R. Allen and Peter B. Kenen, *Asset Markets and Exchange Rates: Modelling an Open Economy* (New York: Cambridge Univ. Press, 1983) p. 7.

109. Many years later (1978) Meade expressed dissatisfaction with his definition of 'internal balance'. When his book was written, the common assumption was that the money wage-rate was normally either constant or moved only very sluggishly, so it was generally taken for granted that if the government maintained a level of demand which preserved full employment, the money price level would be reasonably stable. He further declared that if he were to rewrite the book, 'I would do the underlying analysis not in terms of the reconciliation of the two objectives of external balance and internal balance, but in terms of the reconciliation of the three objectives of equilibrium in the balance of payments, full employment, and price stability'. See James Meade, 'The Meaning of "Internal Balance"', *Economic Journal*, vol. 88 (Sept. 1978) pp. 424–5.
110. The leading papers comprising the Mundell–Fleming model are: Robert A. Mundell, 'The Appropriate Use of Monetary and Fiscal Policy under Fixed Exchange Rates' (1962); Mundell, 'Capital Mobility and Stabilization Policy under Fixed and Flexible Exchange Rates' (1963); reprinted in R. A. Mundell, *International Economics* (New York: Macmillan, 1968) chs. 16 and 18; J. Marcus Fleming, 'Domestic Financial Policies under Fixed and under Floating Exchange Rates' (1962), reprinted in J. M. Fleming, *Essays in International Economics* (Cambridge, Mass.: Harvard Univ. Press, 1971) ch. 9.
111. See J. J. Polak, 'Monetary Analysis of Income Formation', IMF *Staff Papers* (Nov. 1957), reprinted in H. R. Heller and R. R. Rhomberg (eds), *The Monetary Approach to the Balance of Payments; A Collection of Research Papers by Members of the Staff of the IMF* (Washington, D.C.: International Monetary Fund, 1977). The book also contains other early papers dealing with the IMF version of the monetary approach. Polak was then Deputy Director of the Fund's Research Department. Williamson claims that Polak 'provided the first formal "monetary approach" model and established the basic conclusions of the monetary approach'. See Chris Milner (ed.), *Political Economy and International Money: Selected Essays of John Williamson* (Brighton: Wheatsheaf Books, 1987) p. 27.
112. Dietrich K. Fausten, 'The Humean Origin of the Contemporary Monetary Approach to the Balance of Payments', *Quarterly Journal of Economics*, vol. 93 (Nov. 1979) p. 658.
113. Domestic credit expansion (DCE) – not simply an expansion of the money supply – was the term apparently coined by Polak. During the 1960s its use was recommended by IMF officials as the proper target for monetary policy in open economies. It was succinctly defined by the Bank of England in 1969 when the British authorities were obliged to accept the IMF May 1969 Letter of Intent calling for precise targets for DCE: 'Put briefly, DCE may be viewed as the total arrived at after adjusting the increase in the money supply to take account of any change in money balances directly caused by an external surplus or deficit . . .' See Bank of England *Quarterly Bulletin* (Sept. 1969) pp. 363–4.
114. Chipman makes the point that this implies that country 2 sterilises its

surplus or offsets the money inflow by continued credit contraction. It is then a case of 'involuntary foreign lending' from country 2 to the deficit country 1. See Chipman, 'A Reconsideration of the Elasticity Approach', loc. cit. p. 75. An important implication of Polak's model is that under fixed exchange rates the nominal money supply becomes an endogenous variable, i.e. one not within the control of the authorities.

115. The principal papers of the Chicago version of the monetary approach are to be found in J. A. Frenkel and H. G. Johnson (eds), *The Monetary Approach to the Balance of Payments* (London: Allen & Unwin, 1976). See also H. G. Johnson, 'The Monetary Approach to Balance of Payments Theory: A Diagrammatic Analysis', *The Manchester School*, vol. 43 (Sept. 1975) pp. 220–74, and 'The Monetary Approach to the Balance of Payments; A Nontechnical Guide', *Journal of International Economics*, vol. 7 (Aug. 1977) pp. 251–68; M. Parkin and G. Zis (eds), *Inflation in Open Economies* (Manchester: Manchester Univ. Press, 1976).
116. See her critical review, Marina v. N. Whitman, 'Global Monetarism and the Monetary Approach to the Balance of Payments' (1975), in *Reflections of Interdependence* (Pittsburgh: Pittsburgh Univ. Press, 1979) ch. 4, p. 75.
117. Rudiger Dornbusch, 'Alternative Price Stabilization Rules and the Effects of Exchange Rate Changes', *The Manchester School*, vol. 43 (Sept. 1975) pp. 275–92.
118. J. Williamson, *The Open Economy and the World Economy* (New York: Basic Books, 1983) p. 201. For a critical review of monetary models, see Frank H. Hahn, 'The Monetary Approach to the Balance of Payments', *Journal of International Economics*, vol. 7 (1977) pp. 231–49. Kindleberger writes: 'It is hard for all but true believers to put much credence in the monetary theory of balance-of-payments adjustment'; and he gave two reasons for this opinion. See Charles P. Kindleberger, 'Assets and Liabilities of International Economics: The Postwar Bankruptcy of Theory and Policy', in Monte dei Paschi di Siena, *Economic Notes*, no. 2 (1982) p. 54.
119. Williamson, op. cit. p. 203.
120. On the monetary approach to exchange-rate theory, see Rudiger Dornbusch, 'The Theory of Flexible Exchange Rate Regimes and Macroeconomic Policy', and John F. O. Bilson, 'Rational Expectations and the Exchange Rate', in J. A. Frenkel and H. G. Johnson (eds), *The Economics of Exchange Rates* (Reading, Mass.: Addison-Wesley, 1978) chs. 2 and 5.
121. The reference here is to Ronald I. McKinnon and Wallace E. Oates, *The Implications of International Economic Integration for Monetary, Fiscal and Exchange-Rate Policy* (Princeton: Princeton Univ. Press, 1966). See also McKinnon, 'Portfolio Balance and International Payments Adjustment', in R. A. Mundell and A. K. Swoboda (eds), *Monetary Problems of the International Economy* (Chicago: Chicago Univ. Press, 1969); and J. Herin *et al.* (eds), *Flexible Exchange Rates and Stabilization Policy* (Boulder, Colorado: Westview Press, 1977).
122. Anne O. Krueger, *Exchange-Rate Determination* (Cambridge: Cam-

bridge Univ. Press, 1983) p. 90.

123. R. Dornbusch, *Dollars, Debts and Deficits* (1986), op. cit. p. 34.

124. Rudiger Dornbusch, 'Expectations and Exchange Rate Dynamics', *Journal of Political Economy*, vol. 84 (Dec. 1976) pp. 1161–76. Dornbusch's model accounts for the short-run volatility of the nominal exchange rate and also for the large swings in the real exchange rate. A similar analysis was put forward many years ago by Sir Dennis Robertson, and even earlier by Gustav Cassel in regard to the behaviour of the German mark and other currencies. Cassel noted the adverse consequences for output and employment of fluctuations in real exchange rates caused by overshooting and undershooting. See Cassel, *The World's Monetary Problems* (1921), op. cit. For some critical remarks on the Dornbusch 'overshooting' model, see Charles Goodhart, 'Exchange Rate Economics 1986: A Comment', *Economic Journal*, vol. 97 (March 1987) p. 21; also S. Brooks, K. Cuthbertson and D. G. Mayes, *The Exchange Rate Environment* (London: Croom Helm, 1986) pp. 73–6. J. A. Frenkel and C. A. Rodriguez, 'Exchange Rate Dynamics and the Overshooting Hypothesis', IMF *Staff Papers*, vol. 29 (March 1982) pp. 1–30, extend the Dornbusch model to account for finite speeds of adjustment in goods and asset markets, assuming 'the speeds of adjustment in various markets are less than infinite (which is obviously the case)', p. 28.

125. Krueger, *Exchange Rate Determination*, op. cit. p. 57.

126. Dornbusch, 'Exchange Rate Economics: Where Do We Stand?', *Brookings Papers on Economic Activity*, vol. 1 (1980) p. 152.

127. Allen and Kenen, op. cit. The authors explain that they sought to update Meade's analysis of price and expenditure effects by linking it with a broad approach to asset-market equilibrium that looks at money and bond markets – an approach they declare, 'much richer than the monetary approach and less doctrinaire in its implications', p. 4.

128. Dornbusch, *Dollars, Debts and Deficits*, op. cit. p. 54. One analyst at least believes that the failure of modern theories to account for exchange-rate behaviour springs from a reticence on the part of theorists to recognise fully the role of capital flows as principal determinants of exchange-rate movements. Referring to the implications of the continuous changes in world financial markets, Henry Kaufman writes, 'capital flows, as opposed to trade flows, will become fully established as the major determinant of foreign exchange values'. Henry Kaufman, *Interest Rates, The Markets, and the New Financial World* (London: I. B. Tauris & Co., 1986) p. 122.

129. Dornbusch, 'Exchange Rate Economics: Where Do We Stand?', loc. cit. p. 145. Kindleberger also deplores the tendency for economists' views to polarise around one or other of the three balance-of-payments theories, since in the long run the three theories converge – markets for goods, income and money all have to clear in equilibrium. 'In the short run, however, it is a mistake to lean exclusively on a single model, one or another can take the lead.' See Kindleberger, 'A Further Comment' (1986), loc. cit. p. 89.

130. In a recent article (1987), Frenkel and Razin wrote that the extended

Mundell–Fleming model 'is still the "workhouse" of traditional open-economy macroeconomics'. Jacob A. Frenkel and Asaf Razin, 'The Mundell–Fleming Model A Quarter Century Later', IMF *Staff Papers*, vol. 34, no. 4 (Dec. 1987) p. 568. The paper provides an exposition of the model and its extensions into a unified anlytical framework. For a thorough treatment of the model, see R. Dornbusch, *Open Economy Macroeconomics* (New York: Basic Books, 1980). The model has been critically evaluated by Douglas D. Purvis, 'Public Sector Deficits, International Capital Movements, and the Domestic Economy: The Medium Term is the Message', *Canadian Journal of Economics*, vol. 18 (Nov. 1985) pp. 723–42.

Bibliography

This short bibliography lists only those histories and surveys relevant to the theme of the book. The footnote references should be consulted by those requiring specific or more detailed bibliographical sources.

Angell, James W., *The Theory of International Prices: History, Criticism and Restatement*, Harvard Economic Studies, vol. 28 (Cambridge, Mass.: Harvard Univ. Press, 1926). Reprinted (New York: Augustus M. Kelley, 1965).

Bhagwati, J. N., 'The Pure Theory of International Trade: A Survey', *Economic Journal*, vol. 74 (March 1964) pp. 1–84; reprinted in idem. *Trade, Tariffs and Growth* (London: Weidenfeld & Nicolson, 1969).

Bloomfield, A. I. and Ethier, Wilfred, 'Developments in International Economics', in Sidney Weintraub (ed.), *Modern Economic Thought* (Oxford: Blackwell, 1977).

Bordo, Michael D., 'The Gold Standard: The Traditional Approach', in M. D. Bordo and A. J. Schwartz, *A Retrospective on the Classical Gold Standard 1821–1931* (Chicago: Chicago Univ. Press, 1984) pp. 23–113.

Caves, R., *Trade and Economic Structure: Models and Methods*, Harvard Economic Studies, vol. CXV (Cambridge, Mass.: Harvard Univ. Press, 1960).

Chipman, J. S., 'A Survey of the Theory of International Trade', *Econometrica*, vol. 33 (Oct. 1965) pp. 685–760, and vol. 34 (Jan. 1966) pp. 18–76.

Corden, W. M., *Recent Developments in the Theory of International Trade*, Special Papers in International Economics No. 7 (Princeton: Princeton Univ. Press, 1965).

Haberler, Gottfried, *A Survey of International Trade Theory*, Special Papers in International Economics No. 1 (Princeton: Princeton Univ. Press, 1961).

Humphrey, Thomas M. and Keleher, Robert E., *The Monetary Approach to the Balance of Payments, Exchange Rates, and World Inflation* (New York: Praeger, 1982).

Jha, N., *The Age of Marshall: Aspects of British Economic Thought 1890–1915*, 2nd edn (London: Frank Cass, 1973) pp. 31–79.

Jones, R. W. and Kenen, P. B., *Handbook of International Economics*, vols I and II (Amsterdam: North-Holland, 1984, 1985).

Metzler, Lloyd A., 'The Theory of International Trade', in H. S. Ellis (ed.), *A Survey of Contemporary Economics* (Philadelphia: Blakiston, 1948) pp. 210–54.

Shone, Ron, *The Pure Theory of International Trade*, Macmillan Studies in Economics (London: Macmillan, 1972).

Taussig, F. W. (ed.), *Selected Readings in International Trade and Tariff Problems* (Boston: Ginn & Co., 1921).
Viner, Jacob, *Studies in the Theory of International Trade* (1937) (London: Allen & Unwin, 1955).
Wu, Chi-Yuen, *An Outline of International Price Theories* (London: George Routledge & Sons Ltd, 1939).

Index